# **About** Island Press

Since 1984, the nonprofit organization Island Press has been stimulating, shaping, and communicating ideas that are essential for solving environmental problems worldwide. With more than 800 titles in print and some 40 new releases each year, we are the nation's leading publisher on environmental issues. We identify innovative thinkers and emerging trends in the environmental field. We work with world-renowned experts and authors to develop cross-disciplinary solutions to environmental challenges.

Island Press designs and executes educational campaigns in conjunction with our authors to communicate their critical messages in print, in person, and online using the latest technologies, innovative programs, and the media. Our goal is to reach targeted audiences—scientists, policymakers, environmental advocates, urban planners, the media, and concerned citizens—with information that can be used to create the framework for long-term ecological health and human well-being.

Island Press gratefully acknowledges major support of our work by The Agua Fund, The Andrew W. Mellon Foundation, Betsy & Jesse Fink Foundation, The Bobolink Foundation, The Curtis and Edith Munson Foundation, Forrest C. and Frances H. Lattner Foundation, G.O. Forward Fund of the Saint Paul Foundation, Gordon and Betty Moore Foundation, The JPB Foundation, The Kresge Foundation, The Margaret A. Cargill Foundation, New Mexico Water Initiative, a project of Hanuman Foundation, The Overbrook Foundation, The S.D. Bechtel, Jr. Foundation, The Summit Charitable Foundation, Inc., V. Kann Rasmussen Foundation, The Wallace Alexander Gerbode Foundation, and other generous supporters.

The opinions expressed in this book are those of the author(s) and do not necessarily reflect the views of our supporters.

# Ecodesign for Cities and Suburbs

# Ecodesign for Cities and Suburbs

Jonathan Barnett and Larry Beasley

ISLANDPRESS

*Washington | Covelo | London*

Island Press is a trademark of Island Press/Center for Resource Economics.

Library of Congress Control Number: 2014954410

Printed on recycled, acid-free paper

Manufactured in the United States of America
10 9 8 7 6 5 4 3 2 1

*Keywords:* alternative energy sources, balanced transportation, bicycle and pedestrian access, bicycle facilities, building massing and orientation, Bus Rapid Transit, climate change, edges, high speed rail, mixed-use development, multifamily site design, open-space and landscape design, parking, pedestrian network, solar access, street design, street network, suburban commercial development, suburban retrofits, sustainability, transportation, urban design, urban growth, urban parks, urban planning, urban policy, walkable communities, zoning

*To Nory*

*—Jonathan Barnett*


*To my partner, Sandy, first and foremost*

*To my mentor, Ray*

*To my friend, Bob*

*and*

*In memory of Miss Marion Campbell*

*—Larry Beasley*

# Contents

# 1. Ecodesign: Changing the Urban Growth Model

**A** great irony of modern times: As the majority of people in the world have shifted to living in cities, we have evolved a form of city that is not very hospitable to our everyday needs. As we blanket the world with these cities, we have evolved a form of urbanization that is not compatible with our environment. Our settlements and their settings are in a state of profound contradiction. The more people move to cities and suburbs, the less satisfactory they become, and they place increasing stress on the operating system of our whole planet. Ultimately, this is a dangerous situation.

Legislation and public awareness of sustainability have produced big improvements in air and water quality, but there are still massive problems, especially with carbon emissions. There is huge skepticism about whether it is possible to do anything about these problems without hurting the economy and making it difficult to accommodate necessary growth.

New kinds of urban design plans and guidelines that shape development, preserve and restore older areas, and construct well-liked public places have made many cities more livable; but most real-estate investment still produces routine structures that do little to create attractive places, and urban growth continues to destabilize the natural landscape and spread out cities far more than is necessary.

In developed countries, new construction almost always takes place after a complicated and often contentious official approval process. What then gets built frequently follows simplistic development templates that ignore the rich diversity of human needs and the complex forces of the natural environment. Too often, people assume that political gridlock and real-estate market forces make a more sustainable and livable growth model impossible.

We don't agree, for two reasons.

First of all, urban growth is produced by the interaction of many component parts, and each of these components has been significantly improved somewhere. If all these improvements could be put together, they would produce a far different and superior growth pattern. Some places have gone further and now have improved growth templates already in operation, at least at a district level. In this book, we have assembled the component parts of a superior growth model from innovations that have already become reality. The political and economic feasibility of the examples we describe has thus already been established.

Our second reason is that climate scientists, who once warned about changes by the end of this century, now tell us that significant change is under way right now, bringing more and bigger storm surges to coastal and river cities, more droughts endangering food supplies and causing drinking-water shortages, and more forest fires in inhabited areas. Adapting to climate changes already under way and preventing the worst future climate change scenarios make protecting natural systems and reshaping real-estate development an immediate, urgent problem, not just an issue for future generations.

## An Example of Improved Sustainability and City Design

In one place, at least, an improved growth model started with a very simple idea: to bring homes and workplaces closer together. Back in the 1980s in Vancouver, on Canada's west coast, in a delta crisscrossed by branches of its river and by many inlets from the sea, there was a big worry about huge costs for new roads and bridges. Civic leaders decided it would be cheaper and easier to cluster population growth into a few dense town centers than pay for the expensive infrastructure needed to support sprawl. They believed that this was especially relevant in the inner city where most jobs were located. This inner city sits on a large peninsula, and it had lots of room to grow by replacing obsolete rail yards and industrial areas. The idea took off and morphed into a rich and full vision of a fresh way to live in North America, adding progressive notions about livability, environmental compatibility, fiscal management, entrepreneurial governance, and inclusive public engagement as well as an emphasis on elegant urban design. Then, in the early 1990s, an influx of new investment turned these ideas into action, and the whole inner city was quickly and dramatically transformed, creating what has been popularly dubbed "Vancouverism."

The results are now there for all to see (figure 1-1). Today, more than 110,000 people live comfortably in the core city in a dense, mixed-use, walkable, and gracious arrangement. The population includes not just "singles" and "empty nesters" but also thousands of families with children, low-income households, and people with special needs. A constellation of neighborhoods—with varied housing types, local shops, some dispersed workplaces, and commercial and community services—clusters around a business center that offers just short of 300,000 jobs. These neighborhoods are all framed within a well-developed open-space system of parks, beaches, pedestrian walkways, and protected bikeways. Origins and destinations for jobs, housing, recreation, and day-to-day activities are close together. More than 60 percent of trips are made by nonmotorized means, mostly walking but also by bicycle and even rollerblades. Most other trips are on transit, including a local bus system and rail rapid transit for longer trips. Fewer commuters come into the core city in their cars every year, although the job base is growing. Instead, improved transit and better proximity are handling the growth. Walking trips are usually short, about fifteen or twenty minutes or less, and walking from one end of the core city to another need take no more than thirty-five minutes. Walking and cycling have become the natural way to move around, bringing exercise into everyday activity. Walking is comfortable, enjoyable, healthy, and much more convenient than auto or even transit travel. The car is definitely accommodated, but urban activity does not defer to the car or give it more than adequate space. There are no freeways coming into the core city, and there are almost no surface parking lots. Some of the old automobile infrastructure is being demolished and the land used for other diverse purposes. The street system supports all transportation modes, and the public realm is a complete network that ties everything together (figure 1-2).

**Figure 1-1** The transformation of downtown Vancouver is an example of ecodesign in action. This view of the Coal Harbour neighborhood shows slim residential towers on townhouse podiums, with open views along a waterfront park. The park and the housing sites were reclaimed from a redundant rail yard. This new neighborhood is typical of what has become known as Vancouverism: urban densities, but also great amenities.

In Vancouver's inner city, there is an emphasis on amenity: attractive architecture and landscape, protected views of mountains and water, shelter from the weather, cultural and community facilities, nightlife, a vivacious sidewalk culture, and a domestic feel in neighborhoods (figure 1-3). Almost all the cost of this commonwealth of amenities is secured from new projects as developer contributions, and almost no capital funds have had to be drawn from the tax base or public borrowing.

Shorelines in Vancouver have been reconstructed to regenerate marine life. The local landscape now hosts urban wildlife. Waste recycling is pervasive. Dis-

**Figure 1-2** In Vancouver's inner city, housing for all different types of households sits within a context of connected parks, with priority for walking and cycling and with good transit access. Here is the walkway/bikeway in North False Creek, which was developed from another obsolete rail yard.

**Figure 1-3** New development in Vancouver's core is arranged into coherent neighborhoods with a full range of public amenities, local shopping, and streetscapes hospitable to walking. In the center of Southeast False Creek Village we see a place where the community comes together on a day-to-day basis. This development is a strong example of public-private cooperation. Originally built as the 2010 Olympic Village, it has been repurposed by private investment.

trict energy plants are being expanded. One neighborhood, the former Athletes Village for the 2010 Olympics, has a LEED (Leadership in Energy and Environmental Design) Platinum Neighborhood certification because of advanced systems for managing waste, water, and energy. Prime agriculture land is protected throughout the region, and the overall prevailing density of the region is about twice that of Seattle, Washington, a similar-sized U.S. city nearby. Vancouver's core city is as close to carbon neutral as any place in North America.

Hundreds of thousands of people were involved in designing the overall plan and the area plans for Vancouver's inner city, but the city government has taken the leadership role and facilitated a widely supported vision. The whole place is carefully and comprehensively planned, and the entire structure of regulations has been reinvented. In this new kind of regulatory regime, there are few fixed rules for Vancouver's development management, although the urban design intentions for the core city are among the most articulated and codified in the world. Regulations are flexible and offer incentive opportunities. Development is seen as a privilege rather than a right, and decisions are negotiated. There is peer review and public review of all proposals, and all specific development approvals are made in public outside the political context of the city council. The politicians adopt the plans and policies and audit the processes, but day-to-day decisions on development applications are made by experienced professionals with careful input of citizens, peers, and proponents.

## Other Successes That Point Toward a New Growth Model

Many other downtowns, suburban centers, and neighborhoods have also seen great improvements, and despite all the inequities and deterioration that still afflict cities, urban centers are in a very good place compared with where they were in the 1970s. Cities like Boston, San Francisco, Toronto, and Charleston, South Carolina, are among the important success stories. Including examples beyond Canada and the United States, Helsinki is in the midst of transforming old industrial districts into attractive new neighborhoods designed to absorb development that would otherwise go to suburbs. Hammarby Sjöstad in Stockholm is a model of a sustainable urban district. Copenhagen, Melbourne, and New York City are among the places that have made their cities more walkable and friendlier for cyclists. In Boston, Madrid, and Seoul, the blighting influence of old elevated highways has been replaced with new urban landscapes. Transit-oriented development is beginning to give a new structure to suburbs; there are many examples of compact but comfortable residential areas that are beautiful to see, and new and old public places that are delightful to be in. There has been great progress in preserving old and historic buildings and districts, in encouraging the efficiencies and convenience of mixed-use business centers, and more recently in making individual buildings more sustainable.

Much of this success has come from partnerships created by government, the development community, and citizens. They have helped counteract misguided urban practices that were meant to be reforms but that distorted and diminished urban and suburban life, practices that started during the building boom after World War II and continue to this day.

## Turning the Exceptional into Everyday Practice

The best examples of livable and responsible development continue to be exceptions. We need to find a way to turn promising exceptions into everyday practice. We need to integrate the practice of planning and urban design with environmental conservation and change the design of our built environment to adapt to climate change and create more desirable places.

Despite its many successes, Vancouver still has big sustainability and livability issues. Housing affordability is an increasingly difficult problem, and finding solutions is now taking up a lot of civic time and resources in both public and private sectors. Homelessness has decreased from past years, but it is not yet eradicated. Although the core is progressive on all the fronts of sustainability, the larger region is not performing nearly as well. Auto dominance still prevails, traffic can be frustrating, pollution is still endemic, suburbs continue to expand into open lands, and newer neighborhoods are incomplete. These problems bring down the overall level of sustainable performance for the city region when compared with the lead cities elsewhere in the world. So, Vancouver is only a partial success, and partial successes are not going to be enough.

## Ecodesign: Integrating Environmental Preservation and Livability

Vancouver is part of a movement in many parts of the world that is rethinking how to manage the relationship between the built and the natural environments using innovation and experimentation. We like the term *ecodesign* to define this new perspective: a way of looking at cities and their hinterlands that integrates considerations of environmental soundness and resilience with human health and well-being. It is an attitude about how the city needs to be built or transformed, but also managed and operated, to find a harmony between urban systems and natural systems in a way that also contributes to human experience and social life. It embraces an ethical tenet that in our settlements, we hold responsibilities—not just for ourselves but also for our setting, with all the rich life and patterns that exist there, and for all the people around us.

Applying an understanding of natural ecosystems to the development of cities and regions goes back at least as far as the late 1960s to the pioneering work of Ian McHarg and Philip Lewis.[1] We have also learned from our own long experience as city designers how important it is to incorporate an understanding of natural systems into the design and development process. We are not the first to use the term *ecodesign*. It has been defined by Ken Yeang as the integration of the natural and constructed environments and applied by him primarily to architecture.[2] Others have used this term for product design. We believe that it can have a more general meaning for cities and suburbs. *Eco* reminds us that everything we build becomes part of both local and global natural systems and will influence them for good or ill. *Design* is a reminder that new development should always be part of a coherent, responsive structure that satisfies what people need and want.

If, as we do, you see ecodesign as a summation of diverse innovations now under way or being thought about around the world, you know that it cannot be doctrinaire. It has to embrace the complexity of city patterns and city life and the endless things that people want to do and to build. It has to aspire to reconcile the many functional aspects and mutual accords for communities to live together, as well as the experiential dimensions for personal and family fulfillment that, all together and in great variety, create a robust and satisfying place. It must also embrace the beautiful complexity of nature, the interplays within an ecosystem, and the way that human beings can be a part of that ecosystem without diminishing it or dominating it. It aspires to many different kinds of arrangements and circumstances between people and their setting whereby we respect, conserve, and even contribute to the balances that are essential for tranquil coexistence.

## A Pathway, Not a Prescription

We see ecodesign principles reflected in many separate examples of urban repair or new development. Sometimes these examples are small interventions, and sometimes they are specific innovative systems to be interwoven within an existing urban fabric. More often, ecodesign has involved arrangements for new or reclaimed urban districts. But nowhere yet do we see ecodesign describe the complete pattern of any city.

The forward-thinking ideas implemented in relatively few places could become the prevailing way to manage growth and development throughout the United States and Canada as well as elsewhere in the world. Such an outcome is feasible, both economically and politically. It is possible to improve the quality of life for the people who live in a city or suburb and at the same time offer new and different opportunities for investors and developers. The same principles can help governments cope with unprecedented levels of growth and change. In this book, we describe practical measures whose effectiveness has already been demonstrated and which, if used more widely and more pervasively, can produce significant benefits now and help secure the future for those who come after us.

There are four interrelated parts to creating an ecodesign framework that can inform the development of cities and suburbs. The chapters of this book are built around these themes:

- Adapting development to already inevitable climate changes while protecting the environment for the future: This is the focus of chapter 2.

- Balancing transportation modes to relieve traffic congestion while supporting more compact and better-organized places: Innovative ideas to this end are surveyed in chapter 3.

- Replacing outmoded development regulations and government incentives that continue to steer urban growth in the wrong directions: The history of this trend, the difficulties with the results produced, and the viable alternatives for government development management are discussed in chapter 4. The need to tap into and reshape consumer trends to drive change is also discussed in this chapter.

- Reshaping streets, public places, and public buildings to make a livable environment available to all, rather than just affluent people living in a few special areas: The potential of this public domain is explored in chapter 5 along with directions to shape the public realm for environmental, social, and economic benefits.

In this first chapter, we describe basic axioms of ecodesign that should inform every project that affects the built or natural environment, and we consider the philosophical and ethical basis of ecodesign. Our concluding commentary in chapter 6 concerns the ways in which ecodesign principles can be implemented: how to tap new financing resources, how to use new forms of regulations, how to decide about what measures are essential, and what needs to be done first.

Throughout this book, we will illustrate our points by reference to the innovative practices that are already under way or have already been accomplished in many cities and suburbs. We believe that the best case is made from successes already in place, those that have made it through tough processes of approval and are now evident for all to see. Of course, our book cannot be a compendium of every ecodesign action. Many extraordinary projects, policies, and initiatives have not been referenced, although they are nonetheless admired.

## Six Axioms of Ecodesign

Ecodesign means combining what have too often been considered opposing perspectives: what the environment needs to retain its integrity versus what people need from cities and suburbs. Following ecodesign principles requires special care and respect for both. Among the many innovations for improving cities and suburbs completed or under way around the world, we have come to see a shared set of axioms concerning both how to do things and how to achieve a common set of objectives. Frustration about past practices and attitudes has helped these new creative forces emerge. Consensus has formed around six axiomatic statements for how urban change can most responsibly take place. For some readers, these statements will seem obvious because you have been paying attention to them for as long as you have been engaged with these issues. If you look around at what is happening to the built and natural environment in general, however, you will see that these concepts are not as widely applied as they need to be. We firmly believe that the following axioms should underlie any urban or suburban development process, always to be evaluated for the particular circumstances, but generally dependable and desirable.

1. *Embrace and manage complexity.* In cities as in nature, diversity is both spontaneous and structured into logical systems and organic inter-relationships. Every city needs to embody a wide variation in human expression. People don't just build cities; they also want to readily adjust them as their ideas, needs, and resources shift. People have basic functional requirements, as individuals and to live together, but they also have less obvious needs, and expectations on spiritual and per-ceptual levels. They have social and commercial networks and patterns that confer meaningful associations to their physical setting. There is a dynamic tension between the desire to transform and uneasiness with change that reinforces a desire for conservation. Adding the impera-tive to preserve the natural environment brings in yet another set of complications; but working within the limitations and possibilities of nature can also help manage the options for designing cities. The natural landscape is very much like a design; over time, the conflicting forces within the environment reach equilibrium. Recognizing this con-text can provide a hospitable pattern for other city design decisions. Keeping development within the carrying capacity of the landscape, understanding and working with local climate effects, and using natu-ral systems as part of the infrastructure can make human beings more a part of the dynamic complexity of nature without overwhelming it.

Accepting and dealing with complexity is vital because it yields balances, benefits, and possibilities that create a robust and satisfying place. Building a successful city means embracing this complexity.

2. *Make population and economic growth sustainable.* Any responsible urban policy has to accept population and economic growth. This reality cannot be avoided or denied. We must, however, accommodate that growth without trading off the ability of people to meet their needs in the future, without unduly mortgaging the wealth of the future, and without dangerously destabilizing natural systems now and in the future. There needs to be an equitable process, based on development regulating powers already in force, which can both facilitate and manage growth where there is high market demand and can constrain or deny growth in other places that have reached their natural carrying capacity, are oversubscribed, or are perhaps unsuitable for development at all. We also have to look back at places that are already urbanized but have been left behind by changing market forces. These places already have an infrastructure of services and facilities to accommodate growth that should be reused rather than wasted. Implementing such policies will take intelligent compromises among all the factors of place, people, and setting that are necessary to maximize freedoms and flexibilities while preserving or creating resilient, complete, healthy, and wholesome places.

3. *Make all design processes interdisciplinary.* Because ecodesign means the integration of the artificial and natural environments, it usually needs to include not just the specifics of the immediate situation but also the totality of the context within which the design must be created. This concern with the whole situation makes every design process inherently multidisciplinary, acknowledging special expertise but also fostering joint design efforts among specialists. The resulting design, based on all the relevant factors, can often go in an unanticipated direction, finding opportunities to create valuable innovations.

4. *Always require public involvement.* From the first tentative conceptual thoughts to the completed project, the city design and development process should involve wide public engagement. A successful public process will secure genuine public contributions to shape designs and widespread public support to implement designs. This kind of process is already accepted for master plans by cities and suburbs. It can be hard work to obtain consensus for general concepts; it is even harder to make the consensus as specific as it needs to be to frame the day-to-day administration that implements or, all too often, replaces the plans. Inclusivity and participation are already understood to be

useful tactics, but—because they draw on the dynamic variety of human action, human culture and human transactions—they should always be valued for their own sake. It is, of course, difficult to facilitate public discussions, to enable rather than fetter free expression, and at the same time manage the inevitable conflicts. Our experience has been that it is possible to reach consensus while also protecting individual freedoms and rights, but the process will usually take time; it is a process of months, not days, and of many activities, not a singular event. The time commitment is worth it because public engagement can also discover opportunities, stimulate innovation, and foster experimentation. Public involvement is one way that the design process accommodates diversity and keeps it from channeling everything in a single direction. Instead, unique local knowledge is tapped, and hidden implications discovered. Technical evaluation and peer review can provide the kind of inquiry and critique that identifies weaknesses and unintended consequences.

5. *Respect both the natural and the built context.* Designers and government officials must begin with a clear conceptual and technical understanding of the environmental and social systems in which they will be working so they can both repair and improve them. There is integrity to the natural and built settings in which we design, and there are emotional values and embedded resources and energy in what already exists. Logical systems of use that have grown up over time and organic social relationships that should be understood and supported in design interventions can be found within what may seem to be broken-down remnants of earlier building programs. In all design situations, the first consideration should be to conserve, reuse, and recycle before destroying and disposing. Heritage is a resource. Waste is a resource. Everything in the existing situation is a potential resource. The widespread destruction of existing urban areas in the name of eliminating blight is now understood to have been far too sweeping. Cities are complicated places, and change should be incremental and made gently. Natural landscapes are also complicated places, and clearing them of natural vegetation and regrading them to meet preconceived engineering requirements should also be understood to be far too sweeping. Development within the natural landscape must always be designed for the specific situation. Careful stewardship of the built and natural assets can offer solutions using less energy and fewer resources and avoiding unexpected side effects. The designer, as the proposer of new development, needs to keep in mind the relations, networks, politics, and personal needs of society and should design with a commitment to civility, equity, fair treatment, and mutual help and respect. This need

extends beyond the obvious physical and organizational applications of social arrangements to the design's perceptual and psychological aspects.

At the same time, designers need to have a clear picture of the economy in which they make their proposals and understand how their designs will affect financial feasibility, how the design fits into the larger economic position of the region, and how their work can help create new opportunities for individuals and for society.

6. *Draw on many design methods.* Designers and planners should feel free to explore and use the many promising concepts of modern city building without feeling straight-jacketed by a commitment to any one of them. Modern technology gives us fascinating new structural, material, and technological possibilities to reshape buildings and places, but designers can also employ the principles of traditional city design to reestablish the human scale and coherence of our cities, especially as we learn how to tame the car. They should always integrate the fundamental principles of environmental protection. They can participate in the emerging movements of architectural expression and apply contemporary themes of fine art. They can explore the way that advances in systems thinking can help understand and manage complexity. There should not be one constraining ideology, but rather an approach that provides for the reconciliation and combination of design ideas.[3]

## The Scope of Ecodesign

Ecodesign concepts can inform the details of specific places, such as clusters of buildings, streets, and gathering areas. They can help mold the structure of neighborhoods, districts, and whole cities. They can guide the systems that handle the dynamics of full city regions. Ultimately, they can reconcile the human presence in broad ecological zones: the setting for the city, its suburbs, and its rural hinterlands. Ecodesign thinking is relevant to anyone who has a part in shaping or influencing the shape of cities and suburbs: designers, public officials, and politicians. It is a perspective that should assist students as they find their way into urban issues. It can also be a helpful perspective for consumers who are concerned about the effects of their consumption on the world and people around them. It should assist them within the market as they make their choices and at the polls when they select their governments and judge public policy.

We believe that ecodesign may have a special resonance for people who live in suburbs and for the public officials who are responsible for suburban form and management. There have been few innovative concepts to address issues that these people face; the common wisdom about design solutions has a distinctively urban bias that often does not seem relevant for suburbanites. In North America, however, the suburbs are where the great innovations for the twenty-first century will have to be made. These are the places where the majority of people will continue to live, and these are the places that many will continue to prefer over the alternatives. Ecodesign should open up thinking about respectful ways to reshape these suburbs for better environmental and social performance without losing the essential qualities that have drawn people to these communities in the first place. Using ecodesign principles can produce less intrusive and less destabilizing solutions, what Jaime Lerner, former mayor of Curitiba, Brazil, and one of the great urban innovators, calls "urban acupuncture" rather than major surgery.[4]

The overall purpose of what we are calling ecodesign is to transform the way urban regions develop, thereby making cities and suburbs more compatible with the environment and a more humane fulfillment of our individual and group needs. This agenda includes building on the progress already made in our core cities; tackling their remaining planning, design, and management problems; and addressing the deterioration of some of their older surrounding communities. For people who enjoy a suburban life exactly as it is today, there is a huge inventory of existing development that is not going to change. There is room for improvement, however, in many suburbs, particularly along commercial corridors. In the most recent suburbs, there is a need to find ways to connect isolated enclaves of development and make all these places less dependent on cars. When growth actually requires the creation of development at the metropolitan edge, the regulations governing how it happens need to be greatly improved. Any ecodesign agenda also has to go farther into the hinterlands of our metropolitan areas to secure and support agriculture, protect essential landscapes, and, where growth is needed, identify and prepare suitable areas for responsible city expansion. This agenda will also need to protect rural places and assets from random urban intrusions that could set off land speculation and destroy both ecological balance and rural character. At every scale, ecodesign needs to be about shaping and reshaping the city and its surrounding suburbs for better environmental and social performance.

We not only need to pay attention to the substance of urbanization and its natural setting, we also must understand the processes and institutions through which cities and suburbs are developed and managed, processes that have often perpetuated the same set of problems and outdated answers. We need to understand, critique, and work to improve the laws, policies, decision-making arrangements, and organizations that shape the places we now see and experience. We need to fix their problems, stop them from continuing to happen, and avoid piling more mistakes over past mistakes.

## Ecodesign: A Framework for Sustainable, Livable Cities and Suburbs

From a structural point of view, ecodesign can be a framework for the form of our communities: the walkable, park-once business center with transit access, coherent neighborhoods with different levels of density clustered together, a mix of uses, and all kinds of diversity in a context of protected open space. Such configurations build proximity of desirable activities back into a coherent pattern of urban development, rather than having everything randomly spread far apart. It is a framework for the built environment, with green values in new construction but also reuse of materials and respect for heritage. It is also about place-making: putting buildings and spaces together in a way that is not only usable but also attractive and memorable. Place-making requires good architecture, public art, and landscape design as well as an urban design system that creates a coherent built environment, respects fragile existing places and natural systems, and supports the dynamic relationships of people and activities that give places vitality.

From an infrastructural point of view, the framework is also about circulation within our communities, having transportation choices that emphasize walking and transit and that take the private car from its dominant role and place it within a logical array of movement alternatives. Balanced transportation builds on the advantages of structural proximity to create the walkable city, which means fewer and shorter car trips and more trips without the need for an automobile to move us around. The framework also includes social and community aspects, including cultural institutions and other neighborhood support. It is also a framework for managing water, waste, and energy in a conserving way, emphasizing local relationships, including local sources for food.

We are describing a framework that addresses many of the challenges we face in modern life, such as reaching goals of environmental compatibility, but it also addresses market resilience, and public health, and dynamic cultural expression and social engagement. All these factors foster individual and collective ingenuity and satisfaction.

## The Urgent Need for Ecodesign and Reason for Optimism

The difficult choices needed to achieve an ecodesign framework require innovative options that at this point are not part of the common wisdom of cities and suburbs; they exist in this special place or that, but they are not integral to the typical way we build and manage our urban areas. It may not even be known that new solutions exist and have been tested somewhere.

People experience the problems of modern urbanism and have become pessimistic about viable solutions. So, public expectations about the future of cities and suburbs have soured in a time when personal fulfillment is becoming a pervasive aspiration of millions of people. There can be a crisis of civic support when too many people move as far away from urban problems as they can, placing even more stress on the natural environment and making development even less sustainable. Or, people can simply tune out the issues: They assume that nothing can be done, and they don't want to hear about climate change, traffic congestion, or unequal opportunities; they just want to get on with their own lives.

Creative ideas and human ingenuity can address peoples' endemic pessimism about cities. Consider, for example, the inspirational success of the inner-city revitalization strategy of Portland, Oregon. We offer it, along with the story of Vancouver, as a positive preamble to all that we will be talking about in this book.

In the late 1960s, faced with an uncertain economic future and strong competition from suburban centers, the leaders of Portland decided to be proactive about the development of their downtown and its place in the region. They decided to make Portland more accessible, more attractive, and more diverse, with the intention of not only growing their jobs base but also their resident population.

Fortunately, early on, Portland understood the need for a metropolitan perspective. A regional transportation authority, TriMet was formed in 1969 and became very active in the following decade. A regional government was founded in 1978, and one of the earliest metropolitan growth boundary policies in North America was instituted by the State of Oregon in 1979. Government and citizens began to see Portland's historic center within the context of growing and diversifying suburbs, setting off four key moves that have transformed Portland.

Pivotal to everything was enhancement of transit (figure 1-4). Although the early years of TriMet saw continuing investment in automobile infrastructure, increasingly federal and other tax money was poured into a balanced transportation system. As early as 1977, a transit mall concept was put in place in the downtown for buses, and it was extended and upgraded in 2007–2009 for rail transit. From 1986 onward, the Metropolitan Area Express, called MAX, was expanded to become a four-line grid of light-rail transit connecting downtown to suburban centers. Denser mixed-use centers were encouraged around suburban transit stops. Streetcars in the central area were introduced in 2001. In 2009, commuter rail began, at that time one of only three such new systems in the United States. Cycling routes were also created, as well as enhancements for walking. Commuting using alternatives to the car is growing; in 2012, 12.1 percent of Portland commuters traveled by transit, 6.2 percent

**Figure 1-4** The inner city of Portland, Oregon, is a prime example of ecodesign thoughtfully applied to achieve urban revitalization. The Portland Streetcar, shown here in a typical downtown scene, offers balance to the transportation system so that people do not need to use cars as often as they usually would.

cycled to work, and 5.7 percent walked. Figures for the whole metro area are lower but are still above averages for other cities.[5]

Equally innovative has been smart and sustained investment in the public realm, not just at key locations but throughout the inner city. Portland has one of the most elegant and widespread streetscape programs in North America, focusing on landscaping the hard surfaces of sidewalks and leftover street rights-of-way, creating a comfortable, safe, and fascinating setting for walking and relaxing along the local streets. Some minor streets are closed to traffic, pedestrian pathways have been added with new development, and all public parks have been upgraded with landscape, public art, fountains, water-play features, and furnishings (figure 1-5). Street tree planting has been a priority for many years, and the result is a shaded, attractive perspective of trees along almost every walking street. To enhance this public realm investment, heritage buildings have been restored throughout the inner city, taking maximum advantage of federal tax credits and dramatically enhancing the overall ambience and hospitality of the streetscape.

Although many cities talk about removing unnecessary automobile infrastructure, Portland has taken decisive action that has opened up significant

**Figure 1-5** Portland has invested heavily in its public domain of parks, sidewalks, and other open spaces, which has helped draw many people back to the city, as illustrated by the crowd of families enjoying Jamison Square's waterscape. Portland's innovative housing design, particularly for midrise buildings, is also evident in this photo.

opportunities for the core city and removed negative impacts. In the 1970s, Harbor Drive was demolished and was replaced with what is now known as Tom McCall Waterfront Park, which extends dramatically along the Willamette River shoreline. In the 1990s, most of the Lovejoy Viaduct was removed, opening up the potential for a new residential area in the northwest sector of the inner city.

Today, there is talk of more such demolitions, not as an attack on the car culture, which is surely still strong in Portland, but simply to remove what are clearly excess dedications of land for auto movement that are an unnecessary blight on property nearby.

Portland's public initiatives have stimulated widespread private-sector activity to develop new workplaces and housing, accomplishing a primary objective of the local government, which was to repopulate the inner city, bringing back the vibrancy and energy that were traditionally there. Two strong efforts make the point.

Beginning in the early 1990s, a vast area called the Northwest Industrial Triangle was becoming increasingly obsolete, with major negative effects on the image of the city. The rail yard, warehousing, and industrial operations were no longer viable in this location. The removal of the Lovejoy Viaduct set off a major redesign and redevelopment of the area, renamed the Pearl District (figure 1-6), first repurposing solid, large-floor-plate historic buildings for housing, offices, and shops and then in-filling with stylish midrise buildings

**Figure 1-6** The Pearl District in Portland is an excellent example of a comprehensive new community created through repurposing of historic buildings, strategic in-fill of new buildings, addition of local services, and smart public-realm investment. This view of the local supermarket shows one of the ways the neighborhood is anchored and supported. The Pearl District shows how public-private collaboration can produce a neighborhood that works for residents, the city, and the property investors.

extending this mix of uses. This new construction represents some of the best architecture for midrise construction in North America. New park and walkway investments have rounded out the offerings for a complete, tight, and attractive community of more than 6,000 people in about 4,200 households, more than two-thirds of them rental units and therefore generally affordable.

Another area of redundant industrial and warehousing adjacent to the Willamette River has recently been totally redeveloped into what is now known as the South Waterfront Neighborhood. Since the early 2000s, this predominantly high-rise area has grown to accommodate more than 5,000 people in almost 3,000 households, 60 percent of them in rental units. It has its own waterfront walkway/bikeway and park as well as local shops, restaurants, and some offices. It calls itself an "ecodistrict" because of sustainability measures and green construction.

Through these and similar efforts, Portland is moving in a very positive direction, with more than 40,000 people now in residence in its central-city neighborhoods. This new growth and diversification continues. The core city is now competitive with its suburbs, and it is competitive with other cities. It is also more and more sustainable, with this factor becoming part of the vivid myth of what is popularly called "Portlandia."

Portland and Vancouver are strong examples of what we see in many places: smart and creative people taking up the challenge of the dysfunction, discomfort, and detrimental impacts of our cities and beginning to make a profound difference. They are inventing new urban templates and establishing new processes and institutions that can reconcile the contradictions between development and environmental preservation. They are raising the consciousness of people as both consumers and members of the body politic. These initiatives have to be more widely known, and they need to be better understood. They also should be brought together into a new way of building our cities and suburbs, the new growth model that we alluded to at the beginning of this chapter.

So, let's begin our detailed description of the ways that ecodesign concepts already in progress can add up to a better way of designing cities and conserving the natural environment. We turn first to adapting to climate change and limiting global warming, the subjects of chapter 2.

# 2. Adapting to Climate Change and Limiting Global Warming

**E**very year brings new discoveries that demonstrate that the world's climate is warming and the pace of change is accelerating. The urbanization of open land and the pollution caused by cities and suburbs are big contributors to global warming and to the climate and weather changes that we are beginning to experience. These changes, in turn, are placing stresses back on urban systems, particularly along the world's coastlines and in areas prone to drought. Severe weather events that used to happen only occasionally are becoming more frequent and more dangerous. Some essential actions to combat climate change must be taken by national governments and will also require international agreements to become fully effective, but much can be accomplished by the cumulative effect of smaller changes. Measures initiated by local governments and innovations made for individual projects can add up to widespread reform.

In this chapter, we explore local programs and policies that can be used by existing cities and suburbs to adapt to these new conditions and, at the same time, restructure urban growth to mitigate, if not eliminate, the ways that cities and urbanization contribute to climate change. We see three urgent challenges. The first, adapting city designs to cope with the predicted results of climate change, has not been receiving the immediate attention that is badly needed. The second, reducing the causes of global warming, is already recognized as a priority, but much more has to be done. Third, we need to redesign cities and suburbs so that they are in harmony with natural ecological forces, even contributing to those forces in positive ways, so that urban development becomes sustainable for the foreseeable future. We will not try to deal with the big intergovernmental issues—they are beyond the scope of a book about design—but we will describe promising efforts to deal with these three challenges. Some are currently in progress at smaller governmental levels; others are ideas that are yet to be widely implemented but have significant potential.

Climate scientist Paul Crutzen explains the reasons that weather changes can be attributed to worldwide population and economic growth in a well-known 2002 article. He begins by summarizing the basic numbers. During the past three centuries, world population has increased more than tenfold to seven billion and is expected to reach ten billion in this century, resulting in up to half the planet's land surface being modified by human activity. More than half of all accessible freshwater is used by people; remaining natural areas, such as tropical rain forests, are being developed at a fast pace, releasing carbon dioxide and strongly increasing species extinction. Rising numbers interact with rapid changes in technology. According to Crutzen, energy use multiplied by sixteen times during the twentieth century, causing 160 million tons of atmospheric sulfur dioxide emissions per year, more than twice the sum of natural emissions. Fossil-fuel burning and agriculture have caused substantial increases in the concentrations of greenhouse gases—carbon dioxide by 30 percent and methane by more than 100 percent—reaching their highest levels over the past 400,000 years, with more increases under way. All these factors contribute to rising world temperatures.[1]

As ocean temperatures rise, so do sea levels because water expands at higher temperatures. Polar ice caps and glaciers are also melting far more rapidly than scientists were predicting even a few years ago, bringing changes to air movements in the upper atmosphere, which in turn change the patterns of storms, plus adding water to sea levels when the ice was located over land. Rising sea levels, not long ago thought to be an issue at the end of this century, are now seen as an increasing threat to some coastal cities right now and for many others by 2050.

In addition, warmer oceans evaporate more water into the atmosphere. The result is that when rain or snowfalls occur, the volume of moisture in the storm is greater. Rising temperatures of ocean surfaces also transmit more energy into storms that form over water, resulting in larger and more powerful hurricanes and typhoons.

As land surface temperatures rise, more water is evaporated into the air. Crops need more water; more water is lost from reservoirs; and the snowpack on mountains decreases, which lessens river flows. When droughts occur as part of a normal climate cycle, the drought becomes more severe because of this moisture loss. If it turns out, as is likely, that climate change increases the frequency and severity of drought, these problems obviously intensify. Drying of vegetation also increases the risk of fire.

Warming temperatures also change the geographic ranges in which various kinds of vegetation can flourish. As a result, plant species are moving into higher latitudes in the northern hemisphere and more southern latitudes in the southern hemisphere. Changing temperature conditions affect the food supply, favoring some kinds of plants and making it more difficult to grow others. The ranges for insect species also change. In western forests in the United States, the populations of mountain pine beetles, which used to be held in check by cold winters, now have a much longer season and are killing large areas of trees, making forest fires more likely and more severe.

Unfortunately, learning to live with the climate changes already under way will not be enough. Worldwide temperatures have increased 0.8°C (1.4°F) above what used to be considered normal. Another degree of warming will be almost impossible to stop. Upper-range scientific projections of up to 5.8°C (10.4°F) of global warming in this century could be catastrophic. No one can be sure exactly what would happen, but humans have begun what is clearly a dangerous experiment. The conservative position is to limit change as much as possible.[2]

International efforts to reduce greenhouse gas emissions by making public commitments have not been encouraging so far. Improvements in the parts of the world that have mature economies have been offset by rapidly increasing emissions in developing nations. It is tempting for people to say, "I don't want to hear about climate change anymore; there is nothing that can be done to stop it anyway." But climate change cannot be ignored, because of the need to adapt to changes already taking place and because future changes are already inevitable. As the costs of adaptation become better understood, the case for limiting the future pace of climate change should become stronger and stronger. The world is already managing to survive—so far—under the threat of nuclear war, which would create consequences as catastrophic as the worst predictions about the effect of future climate change. The depletion of the ozone layer, a problem that Crutzen did much to define and bring to world attention, has been halted by international action. Long-term limitations to global warming will be difficult to achieve, but not impossible.

## Challenge 1: Adapting to Climate Change

Just about all climate scientists agree that rising sea levels, changing weather patterns, and more extreme storm events are the now inescapable effects of worldwide warming trends, which will continue for centuries, even if all the causes of global warming were to be stopped tomorrow. The four major concerns about living with climate change are as follows:

1. Adapting to sea-level rise and augmented risk from storms along coasts.
2. Adapting to more frequent "one-hundred-year" floods along inland rivers.
3. Adapting to increased duration and severity of drought from rising temperatures, including both safeguarding potable water resources and maintaining food supplies.
4. Adapting to increased risk of forest fires as a result of changes in the overall ecosystem.

Although adapting to these changes will not be easy, proven technology and design concepts to manage climate change already exist, as we show in this chapter, and innovative adaptive techniques continue to be developed.

### Adapting to Sea-Level Rise and Coastal Flooding

Rising sea levels, more intense storms, and changing weather patterns are already having an impact on the world's coastal areas. In the last few decades, an increasing number of dramatic and tragic weather events have been reported all over the world, but the recent experience of one of the world's largest metropolitan areas offers a sense of what many coastal cities can soon expect from climate change and what might be done to respond to this new reality.

In late 2012, the New York City region suffered a devastating blow. A very large tropical storm, which meteorologists named Sandy, hit the eastern seaboard of the United States. The storm came ashore along the coast of New Jersey south of New York City with winds just below hurricane force and massive waves accompanied by heavy rainfall. The storm covered an unusually large area, and meteorological conditions kept it from moving away for an unusually long time. It caused serious damage to cities and towns along the New Jersey coast; to New York City itself, especially lower Manhattan, where a power station and subway and vehicle tunnels were flooded, and the coastal areas of the boroughs of Staten Island, Brooklyn, and Queens; and to communities along the south coast of Long Island. Total damage in all the U.S. areas affected by Sandy has been estimated at $66 billion, with 159 deaths directly attributable to the storm or its aftermath.[3] Sandy made an unusual turn toward land because of changing air currents created by melting polar ice. It is possible that this condition could happen again or even become a settled pattern.

Until now, major storms have been treated as unpredictable events, with evacuation plans in place to protect people and insurance policies to cover damage. Generally, places are restored to the way they were; insurance policies don't pay for making things better than they were before a storm hit, and properties can be left as vulnerable as ever.

The U.S. government decided to use some of the money for rebuilding after Superstorm Sandy to make restored areas less likely to be damaged in the future. Along with the Rockefeller Foundation and other private organizations, the federal government funded Rebuild by Design, a research project to prepare innovative designs that could make areas at risk both more protected from future flood surges and more resilient from any flood damage. Henk Ovink, a high-level official at the Ministry of Infrastructure and the Environment in the Netherlands, was appointed a senior advisor to manage the process. Ten research teams were selected, including some of the most important figures in engineering, in climate science, and in urban design, planning, landscape architecture, and architecture.[4] Six proposals were ultimately funded for implementation or further study, although the money allocated for construction is not enough for the comprehensive solutions proposed by most teams. Ovink brought with him skepticism about pure engineering solutions because of experience with the flood barriers that have been deployed in the Netherlands since the 1980s. Under his guidance, the teams sought inventive design concepts that work with natural forces as well as against them. The Rebuild by Design program has been a valuable laboratory for looking intensively at how to redesign coastal regions to meet the threats created by climate change.

The team of New York's WXY Architects with West 8 Landscape Architects of the Netherlands proposed to protect New York Harbor and the nearby New Jersey and Long Island coasts by building new, artificial islands in the relatively shallow waters of the continental shelf, out in the Atlantic Ocean parallel to the land (figures 2-1 and 2-2). Using constructed environments as barriers is

**Figure 2-1** Proposal by WXY Architects and West 8 to build artificial islands on the continental shelf at the entrance to New York Harbor. The islands would become an armature for natural sand build-up, making them strong enough to deflect the powerful waves from tropical storms, prevent storm surges from entering the harbor, and also protect waterfronts on Long Island, to the north, and New Jersey to the south. The big question is, Would it work?

**Figure 2-2** Close-up view of the WXY/West 8 proposal to protect the estuary of the Hudson River, the entrance to New York Harbor.

a dramatically different strategy from the Eastern Scheldt River Barrier in the Netherlands (figure 2-3), where much of the estuary is closed by a dam and movable gates are lowered to stop storm surges coming in from the North Sea. This system is effective in preventing floods, but it has caused deterioration of the water quality in some rivers upstream from the barrier. The New York proposal preserves the natural tidal patterns and the flow of water from the Hudson River, and it allows ships to enter New York Harbor without going through gates. It is a bold concept, but the question remains: would it actually stop storm surges from pouring into the harbor and flooding low-lying areas again, as well as preventing waves from pounding up against the barrier beaches on either side? The new barrier islands were also likely to be the most expensive of the ten Rebuild by Design concepts and would need another set of artificial islands to the north, where the waters of Long Island Sound meet the East River, to give New York Harbor full protection. It is not surprising that this design concept was not selected for further funding, but it does show a way of dealing with storm surges using measures based on natural systems, as opposed to the engineering of the Delta Works in Holland such as the Scheldt Barrier. It was by far the most comprehensive of the Rebuild by Design proposals.

SCAPE Landscape Architects with Parsons Brinkerhoff Engineers also designed artificial islands as storm barriers, but at a much more modest scale. Government funding has been allocated to build their proposed "Living Breakwaters" within New York Harbor to protect the southern end of the Staten Island shoreline. These constructed environments are intended to evolve into part of the natural ecology, offering artificial habitats to permit introduction of various kinds of shellfish and other sea life (figure 2-4). Money is also allocated for a program to educate local school children about the new habitats. By breaking the force of surging tides before they hit the shore, the assumption is that current patterns of development along the shore can continue much as they were before Sandy. Presumably, if the breakwaters prove effective, the concept will be extended for more complete coverage.

The Copenhagen and New York–based Bjarke Ingalls Group (BIG) led a team of consultants to propose a U-shaped protective system around lower Manhattan covering 10 miles (16 kilometers) of waterfront that received some of the worst flooding after Sandy. This proposal has received the largest amount of the government implementation money. Rather than relying only on seawalls, much of the proposal consists of berms that can also be used as parks (figure 2-5). The portion selected to be built will create a "bridging berm" on the east side of lower Manhattan. The initial version of this proposal was to build a Dutch-style series of movable flood protection gates into the structure of an existing elevated highway. Questions about whether the highway structure could sustain the impact of a storm surge may have led to making the flood-resistant structure a berm instead. The decision to implement only

**Figure 2-3** The accepted engineering method of protecting a river estuary: the Scheldt River Barrier in the Netherlands, which has been in service since the early 1980s. Water can be seen flowing through the movable gates, which can be closed against a storm surge. Note that other portions of the shoreline are protected by a permanent dam.

**Figure 2-4** A more modest proposal than protecting all of New York Harbor, by the landscape architecture firm SCAPE, is intended to shield part of the shoreline of Staten Island, within the southern part of the harbor, with an artificial reef that can also become a habitat for marine life.

part of the berm also raises concerns about phasing: the berm could deflect, and possibly intensify, the force of the storm surge around the ends of the structure, making it worse than useless.

A team including the Brooklyn-based Interboro Partnership Urban Design and Architecture, New Jersey Institute of Technology, Technical University

Delft, and other consultants studied the south shore of Long Island east of New York City. People choose to live in this area because of its beaches, opportunities for sailing and boating, and other attractions of being near water, but the region's barrier islands and wetlands are vulnerable to storm damage. One answer is to say that such places should no longer enjoy government protections; people should either move inland or continue to live near the water at their own risk. Another answer is an expensive storm-surge barrier, but that does not protect against flooding from rivers that flow into the sea in this area. The team looked at a variety of ways to mitigate flooding, including berms and swales (figure 2-6). The government has chosen to fund this team's proposal for making the Mill River into a "slow stream" where stormwater can flow into adjacent wetlands. In this situation, partial implementation of the overall plan will not have negative impacts on other areas, but it also does nothing to help these other places.

**Figure 2-6** Proposal by a team led by Interboro Partners to add landscaped swales to roadways, renovate parks so that they can flood, and create wetlands to slow down flooding so that water can percolate into the ground or evaporate.

The University of Pennsylvania School of Design and Olin Partnership Landscape Architects chose to study how to protect the vulnerable Hunts Point region of New York City, located close to where Long Island Sound meets the East River. This area has a predominantly low-income population and is also the location for the food markets that serve the entire New York metropolitan region. There will be funding for further, more detailed studies of this complex area.

All the submitted proposals demonstrate that design thinking will be an essential part of climate change adaptation, an issue that will be of increasing importance to urban designers, landscape architects, architects, and engineers as the temperature of the air and oceans continues to rise and as storm surges, flooding, and the paths of big storms become an increasing threat. These proposals show the necessity for some big changes, but they also show the possibilities for more integrated adjustments of how we build and use our cities and suburbs. Even if all the nations of the world agree tomorrow to bring down carbon emissions sufficiently to stabilize the climate, the major climate changes already under way will continue to present difficult design and political problems for years to come.

## Adapting to Changing Coastlines and More Storm Surges

Figure 2-7, a montage of photographs taken from space at night, is a dramatic way of showing where people live because most of the light in the photos comes from cities. Many of the world's cities are located around coastal harbors, and most others are located along rivers, and, if you know the underlying

**Figure 2-7** Part of a composite photograph of Earth from space at night created by NASA. Most of the lights are cities, and many are located close to a coast or along a river.

geography, you can see the relationship in these photographs. This arrangement of the world's population is the legacy of the time when most bulk trading was done along water routes, still an important way of moving goods.

If Superstorm Sandy is an example of new weather patterns induced by climate change, with future flood surges amplified by rising sea levels, people, businesses, and governments face some difficult decisions. Continuing with the New York example, figure 2-8, a map by the U.S. National Oceanographic and Atmospheric Administration shows potential flood risk in the New York City region by 2050. Yellow is the limit of the flood surge after Sandy, which has established a new one-hundred-year floodplain. This floodplain is an official U.S. government map that shows the area where there is already a 1 percent chance of flooding each year. A panel of experts convened by New York City identified the potential for even greater floods caused by the higher sea levels expected by 2050. Substantial areas of the city will be at risk. The first set of issues is the ability of flooded areas, and particularly the subway and auto tunnels, to come back after a storm surge. Making these areas more resilient includes locating electrical and other mechanical systems in parts of buildings where they won't flood, redesigning the city's subway system to close air vents when a flood threatens, and installing pumping systems in tunnels that are capable of keeping up with rising waters. Protecting the Lower East Side and Battery Park City, both highly vulnerable, will require area-wide measures, such as the berm proposal by BIG. Because of rising sea levels, it

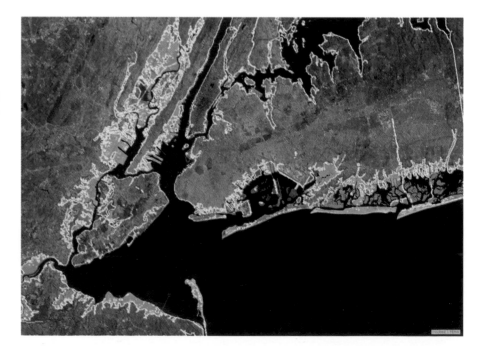

**Figure 2-8** A map prepared by the National Oceanographic and Atmospheric Administration showing potential flood risk in the New York City region by 2050. Yellow is the limit of the flood surge after Hurricane Sandy, which has established a new 100-year floodplain.

may make sense in the long term to let some other parts of the New York City waterfront return to shoreline or wetlands.

The Environmental Simulation Laboratory of the Department of Geosciences at the University of Arizona has created a way to gauge the risks of climate change for cities. These maps are not predictions; they match levels of potential sea-level rise to existing land contours on a Geographic Information System (GIS) map at 30 meters (about 100 feet) horizontal resolution, leaving open the question of when the flooding could occur. The first projection shows the potential effect of 1 meter (about 3.3 feet) of sea-level rise—the dark red—and 2 meters (about 6.6 feet) of sea-level rise—the brighter red—on downtown Norfolk and Portsmouth, Virginia (figure 2-9). If sea levels do rise to such heights, these areas will need to be protected by some kind of comprehensive system of levees, or they could be completely under water. Some places in Norfolk have already developed a new susceptibility to flooding after severe storms. Flooding related to sea-level rise could possibly be widespread in the whole area by the middle of this century.

Figure 2-10 uses the same color code to map 1 meter and 2 meters of sea-level rise on downtown Miami and Miami Beach. At 1 meter (3.3 feet), almost all Miami Beach and the Port of Miami are severely affected, and by the time sea-level rise reaches 2 meters (6.6 feet), the area of impact extends along the Miami River up to and beyond the airport. Unfortunately, the porous local geology may make levees and seawalls ineffective in south Florida. In addition to flooding, saltwater intrusion from rising sea levels in south Florida poses a threat to freshwater aquifers. Figure 2-11 shows the potential effect of only 1 meter of sea-level rise on the San Francisco Bay area. The city of San Francisco is at the lower left corner. The biggest issue shown on the map is not the effect on urbanized areas, but the potential for saltwater intrusion into the San Joaquin River valley, the main source of drinking water for much of central California.

Comparable maps for New Orleans show that city almost completely inundated at 1 meter of sea-level rise, although New Orleans is the only city in the United States that now, post Hurricane Katrina, may have an effective flood-surge protection system because the U.S. Army Corps of Engineers has rebuilt the levees that failed during the hurricane. The Gulf Coast of the United States and all of south Florida can expect major geographic changes as sea levels rise, and the entire East Coast shoreline, particularly barrier islands like those along the New Jersey Shore and Long Island, will be reshaped. Most shoreline cities and towns have been built on higher elevations, keeping their central areas above sea level for a long time, but the disappearance of nearby barrier islands and wetlands may make such places more vulnerable to flood surges. Tens of thousands of waterfront houses will certainly be at risk.

Figure 2-9 A projection by the Environmental Simulation Laboratory at the University of Arizona showing the effect of 1 meter of sea-level rise (about 3.3 feet), in dark red, and 2 meters (about 6.6 feet) of sea-level rise, in brighter red, on downtown Norfolk and Portsmouth, Virginia.

Figure 2-10 A projection by the Environmental Simulation Laboratory at the University of Arizona showing the effect of 1 meter of sea-level rise, in dark red, and 2 meters of sea-level rise, in brighter red, on downtown Miami and Miami Beach. At 1 meter (or 3.3 feet), almost all of Miami Beach and the Port of Miami are severely affected; at 2 meters (or 6.6 feet), the area of impact extends along the Miami River up to and beyond the airport. Porous local geology may make seawalls ineffective.

**Figure 2-11** A projection by the Environmental Simulation Laboratory at the University of Arizona showing the San Francisco Bay Area at only 1 meter (3.3 feet) of sea-level rise. The city of San Francisco is at the lower left corner. The principal area where saltwater is shown as intruding is the San Joaquin River Valley, the main source of drinking water for much of central California.

The University of Arizona Environmental Simulation Laboratory has used the same methods, at a less refined scale, 1-kilometer (0.6-mile) horizontal resolution, to assess the risk of rising sea levels globally. According to this simulation, important world cities at serious risk from a 1-meter rise in sea level include Tokyo, Singapore, Jakarta, Sydney, Rio de Janeiro, and Manila. Bangkok would be relatively unscathed at 1 meter, but at 2 meters, the whole metropolitan region could be under water. In Europe, almost all the Netherlands shows up as inundated at 1 meter of sea-level rise. For the Netherlands, where more than half of the land is susceptible to flooding and about an eighth of this land is actually below the current sea level, the government policy is to use whatever means are necessary to ensure that devastating floods will not occur.

During a major storm in the North Sea in 1953, surging waters broke through the flood protections in the Netherlands, killing more than 1,800 people and causing a huge amount of damage. Afterward, there was a national consensus that such a disaster should not be permitted to happen again, whatever the costs of prevention would be. By the 1980s, a series of flood barriers were in place, supplementing the dikes that have protected the low-lying Dutch countryside and cities for centuries.

The most extensive protective complex, known as the Delta Works, was built in the deltas of the Rhine, Meuse, and Scheldt Rivers. The largest is the Eastern Scheldt River Barrier, mentioned earlier as occupying a somewhat comparable situation to the mouth of New York Harbor, although without being the gateway to a major port. This barrier is equipped with a series of gates that can be lowered when a storm is approaching. Usually, they are raised to permit the river waters to flow out to sea. Another look at figure 2-3 shows an additional protective mechanism on the left, where delta waters are dammed up and permanently separated from the sea and the main flows are diverted to controlled channels.

A different type of movable barrier protects the entrance to the harbor at Rotterdam. Here, the gates can swing shut when a storm is approaching (figure 2-12). Although the Delta Works have been successful so far in preventing damage from storm surges, the reengineering of a river delta does slow down the overall movement of water in tributary streams, causing algae to bloom behind the dams and in rivers and canals that used to be clear.

The same 1953 storm also caused extensive damage along the east coast of England, with a storm surge going up the Thames River as far as central London. The authorities decided to build a movable storm-surge barrier across the Thames, and it began operation in 1982. The Thames barrier operates on a different principle from the gates in the Eastern Scheldt. Usually, the Thames gates rest on the bottom of the river and are raised when a storm surge is

**Figure 2-12** A ship sailing through the storm gates that defend the harbor at Rotterdam.

approaching; they are also sometimes raised to contain and moderate floods coming down the river. The gates are shown raised for routine maintenance in figure 2-13, seen from the downstream side. There are four navigable channels and six non-navigable channels. Ships too large for the barrier must dock farther downstream. The shorelines downstream also had to be reinforced to protect against surging waters deflected by the barrier. The latest figures available from the Environment Agency, which operates the barrier, are that it has been raised seventy-six times to prevent flooding from tidal surges and forty-three times to alleviate flooding from waters flowing downstream. The frequency of use has increased, with most of the closings taking place since 2000. During the winter of 2014, the barrier had to be closed an additional twenty-eight times. To manage rising sea levels and the need for more frequent closings, the barrier will need to be enlarged and improved by the 2030s.

Movable storm-surge barriers are being constructed to protect Venice, and barriers have recently gone into operation to protect St. Petersburg. The geography of many harbors would be suitable for an Eastern Scheldt–type of barrier. Boston's harbor, for example, could be protected by a similar installation combined with gates that would permit ships to enter when there is no storm.

All these flood and storm management solutions require massive engineering works, but they could be justified by the number of people they would protect and the property values they would safeguard. At the present time,

**Figure 2-13** The Thames River Barrier in London with the movable shields raised. These elements usually rest on the bottom of the river.

however, there is no political consensus in the United States or in most other countries to support this kind of expenditure, leaving individual cities and property owners to consider site-specific protection measures like elevating streets and buildings.

## Adapting to More Inland Floods

Freshwater flooding along rivers puts many noncoastal cities at risk. The Netherlands has also been in the forefront of dealing with this problem, because, as alpine glaciers melt, more and more water pours down the Rhine River and through the delta system that makes up a large part of the country. The Dutch have a new policy—called Make Room for the River—which permits selected areas to flood seasonally. River water, unlike seawater, causes much less permanent damage, if it can be kept away from vulnerable structures. The government is anticipating floods that could be greater than those in 1993 and 1995, which came close to overtopping existing dikes. A secondary objective, but an important one, is to improve the character of the landscape whenever possible. Measures completed by 2015 include moving dikes back from their current location to increase the width of the river, creating flood bypass channels, reducing obstructions by rebuilding bridge abutments, creating water-retention reservoirs, and "depoldering." A polder is an area that has been reclaimed as dry land by surrounding it with dikes and pumping out the water. In the first depoldering phase, residents of one polder have been relocated to higher ground around the perimeter so that the fields in the polder can be permitted to flood. This scenario may be a prototype for depoldering other vulnerable areas. Longer-range plans, which anticipate climate changes up to the end of this century, set aside land for more dike setbacks, more bypass channels, and a detention reservoir. Figure 2-14 maps the extent of the full program. Figure 2-15 shows the widening of the Waal River, part of the Rhine delta system, between Nijmegen and Lent to remove a bottleneck in the river that caused floods. A rebuilt bridge is shown in the rendering, making it less obstructive of flood-waters. The new engineering also provides an opportunity to add parkland and improve the relationships between the built-up areas and the river. The Delta Works that protect from North Sea storm surges and the reengineering of the rivers throughout the country offer a preview of what other nations—that up to now have been less vulnerable—may have to do to adapt to climate change.

Hamburg on the Elbe River in Germany is another place where climate change is predicted to bring rising floodwaters, which will change the historic relationships between the city and its waterfront. The Green Plan, to be implemented by 2040, will link 27 square miles (70 square kilometers) of new and existing green space within the city. Some of these areas will be designed to flood when necessary. At other times of the year, the whole system will make it far easier to walk and bicycle around the city, which should reduce automobile use and emissions, a marginal but useful benefit. The plan for developing a former harbor in the Hamburg city center puts new buildings and streets on base structures that are 26 to 30 feet (8 to 9 meters) above sea level. Public areas along the river are down at an elevation of 15 feet (about 4.5 meters), which makes for a pleasant design that mediates between the raised buildings and the river most of the year. These public areas can flood, however. Figure 2-16 shows Hamburg's Marco Polo Terraces under water during a storm in 2013, where life in the buildings, up at the higher level, goes on uninterrupted. Waterfront areas in other major cities may have to adopt comparable raised-building and street designs to deal with future floods or flood surges.

## Adapting to Drought and Securing Potable Water

Many places already have too much water at certain times of the year, and other places have too little. Climate change is accentuating both problems. In the United States, most of the area east of the Mississippi River can sometimes have too much water and much of the land to the west too little; the exception is the coastal areas of the Pacific Northwest. In places that already suffer from droughts, like Australia and California, changing climate and increasing population are putting more and more strain on water resources needed for both food production and urban and suburban living. Adapting to drought can involve both major engineering projects like desalinating seawater and damming estuaries to retain freshwater, as well as a multitude of water-saving devices that can be installed by individual households or businesses.

**Figure 2-14** This map shows the places along the Rhine River delta within the Netherlands where the riverbanks need to be moved to make more space for flooding and for more water storage near the river mouths.

**Figure 2-15** Rendering shows the widening of the Waal River in the Netherlands between Nijmegen and Lent to remove a bottleneck.

**Figure 2-16** Flooding in 2013, Marco Polo Terraces, Hafen City, Hamburg, Germany. The buildings are constructed on bases about 27 to 30 feet (8 to 9 meters) above sea level and are currently safe from floods, but the public spaces are at 15 feet (4.5 meters) and below.

## Desalinating Seawater

There is plenty of water in the world's oceans, and it can be made drinkable by running it through a desalination plant, although the process is expensive and energy intensive and the concentrated salt must be disposed of in a way that doesn't damage the environment. The Australian provinces have been pursuing a long-term policy of supplementing freshwater resources with desalination plants as a way of dealing with recurring droughts. The Victorian Desalination Plant, which has the capacity to supply a third of Melbourne's water needs, solves two of the problems connected with desalination. The electricity is supplied from a wind farm built for the purpose, and the plant can also draw on other renewable power resources. To protect the environment, the salt and other by-products of the process are reduced to solids and buried in a landfill rather than being returned as concentrated brine to the seawater, which has been done in some other desalination projects and which can have adverse effects on marine life. As a further protection, to minimize disturbance of coastal waters, the mouth of the intake pipe is more than half a mile (1 kilometer) out in the sea. The third problem is expense, but conventional reservoirs are expensive also, and any cost is better than a city running out of water. The project was begun during a prolonged drought. By the time it was finished in 2012, Melbourne's reservoirs, which had been dangerously low, had filled up again. Today, the plant, now proved to be in working order, is on standby: ready when needed, but not operating. The plant has a green roof, and its surroundings have been restored as an ecological park (figure 2-17). Sydney, Perth, Gold Coast, and Adelaide are other Australian cities with access to desalinated water. Desalination is heavily used in Israel, Saudi Arabia, the United Arab Emirates, and other Middle East countries.

There are many other examples of desalination coming into use around the world, but few of them have been subject to such a serious effort to be environmentally responsible as the plant near Melbourne. Desalination plants are insurance against running out of water in coastal regions, and many more are likely to be built. These new plants, however, need to be designed so that they don't make environmental problems worse by altering the salt level in adjacent waters or by their power needs adding more emissions to the atmosphere. The Melbourne plant demonstrates that these problems can be solved.

### Impounding Estuaries

Millions of gallons of freshwater flow out to sea every day from the mouths of rivers. If this water can be retained, it offers a viable resource for human use. The government of Singapore has turned Marina Bay, a saltwater estuary, into a freshwater reservoir by building a dam, almost 1,150 feet (350 meters) long, called a barrage, across the mouth of the bay (figure 2-18). This construction supplements Singapore's more conventional reservoir system, with the new freshwater bay supplying up to 10 percent of the country's needs. The water levels in the reservoir are managed by discharge pipes that let water run out into the sea at low tide and a pump system to move water over the barrage at high tide; and, of course, some of the water is drawn down by being pumped into Singapore's water supply system. The Marina Bay barrier is similar to the much longer Afsluitdijk, which was completed in the early 1930s in the Netherlands. This barrier turned a large saltwater estuary, the Zuiderzee, into the freshwater Ijsselmeer. The purpose of damming the Zuiderzee was to create more land that could be pumped dry, and it also created a source

**Figure 2-17** The Victorian Desalination Plant can provide for up to a third of the water needs of the city of Melbourne, Australia. Design architects, peckvonhartel.

**Figure 2-18** The dam across the mouth of Marina Bay in Singapore turns the water behind it into a freshwater reservoir. The saltwater Singapore Straits are in the foreground.

of freshwater. It was an early demonstration that such barriers are feasible. Singapore's Marina Bay barrage also functions as a flood-surge barrier; there had been flooding problems along the estuary before the barrier was built. As mentioned earlier, the freshwater San Joaquin River estuary in central California is at risk from rising sea levels. A barrier like the Singapore barrage might be a solution there.

### Recirculating Water

No one likes the idea of drinking water that has gone through a sewage treatment plant, but many cities draw their water from rivers that have sewage system outfalls upstream. If more used water could be recirculated and used again, the need to augment water supplies could be much reduced, even as populations increase. In Singapore, some sewage treatment plants now have an added purification process that produces what is cleverly branded as "NEWater." At present, this water is used primarily for industry. Israel is among the other countries that make extensive use of treated water from sewer systems, in this case mostly for crop irrigation. A 2012 report by the Water Science and Technology Board of the U.S. National Academy of Sciences describes many different ways in which purified wastewater can be recycled for different uses.[5] Clearly, these options may become necessary, and the technology for implementing them is likely to improve by the time it is needed.

*Conserving Water*

Many ways of conserving water, such as water reducers for showers and more efficient toilets, or just being careful how much water we use, are already well accepted and are even beginning to have some measurable effects as they become more widely adopted. Water barrels and cisterns that can be used to manage excess water are also useful for storing rainwater in drought areas. In the future, people are likely to look back in astonishment at the days when purified drinking water was used for washing cars and watering the lawn, instead of "gray water" collected from roofs, sinks, showers, and bathtubs and stored in cisterns. People seldom think about it, but having a lawn around an individual house as an emblem of social respectability derives much of its prestige from English country houses, where beautifully maintained lawns were an essential part of the setting. England has a much wetter climate than most of the suburbs in other English-speaking countries where maintaining a lawn continues to be a homeowner's responsibility, often enforced by local ordinances. *Xeriscaping*, a term invented by Denver's water department, defines an alternative wherein the landscaping around a house is composed of vegetation that will maintain itself without irrigation. In dry regions like Arizona and southern California, that means desert plants and an entirely different image.

In some places, it may become necessary to recirculate gray water to flush toilets, although doing so requires a separate plumbing system inside each house, and health departments are wary because they fear that people will start drinking gray water to save money on their water bills. Toilets and urinals that don't need to be flushed with water are an alternative technology. Flushless urinals can already be found in some new buildings. Composting toilets are available now, but they require some maintenance by the owners. Composting toilets are currently most acceptable in locations where the water supply is limited, and they have an important future in bringing better sanitation to the informal settlements that have grown up around cities in many parts of the world.

## Adapting to Threats to Global Food Supplies

The world population is projected to increase rapidly from 7 billion now to 9.6 billion by 2050, according to a United Nations report issued in 2012.[6] If widespread famine is to be prevented in the future, food resources, already strained, will require extraordinary management techniques. Droughts and floods make preventing food shortages even more difficult. Valuable agricultural land, which is often situated close to cities, continues to be lost to development. Often, local governments have had to implement expensive air-rights transfer or land acquisition programs to safeguard farm areas or environmental resources that should not have been opened up to development in the first place. In Canada's province of British Columbia, a more comprehensive solution, the Agricultural Land Reserve, has been in place since 1973. This provincial zoning program has comprehensively set aside from urban development the best agriculture land in the province and only allows it to be used for farming and ranching purposes. After initial challenges when it was set up, the system has proved to be both popular and resilient, and people now tend to see it as increasingly important, especially as food security and nearby food production have emerged as significant sustainability concerns.

Agriculture is always a major user of water, and irrigation is often used to take crops through dry spells even in places where there is reliable annual rainfall. In dry areas or in areas subject to drought, a large proportion of water use may go to agriculture. Food clearly needs to have a priority for water use, but it is important to make sure the water is used appropriately. A critical question for irrigating in dry areas is how much of the water will be lost to evaporation. Commonly used spray irrigation systems, the ones that produce those green circles you can see from an airplane, cover a large area efficiently but have a high evaporation rate. Drip irrigation from pipes that run beside the rows of plants can send most of the water down to the roots, although it is more trouble to organize and maintain than spraying. Metering the water supplied to farmers and charging for it at realistic rates would encourage conservation measures like drip irrigation. Eventually, it may become necessary in some areas to decide what crops to plant based on how much water they use.

### Urban and Suburban Agriculture

Can modern agribusiness and an international food distribution system feed the rapidly growing population of the world, or should there be a parallel system of smaller, more decentralized food production? As adverse environmental effects of mass-produced food and animals become more evident, how best can we prevent famine and the long-term deterioration of the soil? Traditional agriculture is still the basis for human survival in many parts of the world. These small farms and garden plots can be made more productive as their owners learn more about modern agricultural techniques and are equipped with affordable aids to cultivation. In developed countries, there has been a revival of local farms, with a rapidly emerging system of farmers markets and specialty grocers to distribute their products, although this trend is primarily about providing high-quality food to people who are willing to pay more money for it. It is nonetheless a strong indication that there is still value to be found in traditional agriculture, and these advantages ought to be preserved. Realizing the potential of small agricultural plots within existing suburban and urban areas is thus part of the ongoing evolution of the world food supply. More local food would save on transportation costs and the carbon emissions associated with moving food long distances, and the produce can be fresher and more varied.

If part of the labor in producing the food is provided by the consumer, food can also be more affordable. The options range from growing herbs in window boxes, to community gardens, to backyard plots, to converting lawns to gardens, to repurposing failed local golf courses as farms, perhaps as an agricultural cooperative, if the golf course belongs to a property association or a local community. A small movement toward urban farming is showing interesting possibilities in many cities.

In Vancouver, for example, there is at least one farmer who has made a go of it with market gardens on the roofs of a cluster of downtown buildings that had originally been designed as landscaped decorative roofs. A nonprofit organization called Soul Farms teaches out-of-work, sometimes homeless people to tend crops and now has more than 6 acres (2.4 hectares) of inner-city parking lots and vacant sites in production, using portable planting boxes. Such profitable market gardens can be made operational in forty-eight hours and provide multiple harvests in a year. Both of these efforts are supported by local restaurants and households who subscribe to a quota of vegetables each week. These efforts are tiny, but they offer big potential.

### Urban Greenhouses

Recently, a few entrepreneurs have built urban greenhouses on top of warehouses and parking garages to supply high-quality local food to restaurants and consumers. Roofs of industrial buildings represent a lot of acreage in a metropolitan region. There is clearly room for a big increase in the scale of urban greenhouse operations if they prove successful. Lufa Farms is based in a rooftop greenhouse over a warehouse in Montreal. The produce is distributed on a direct-to-consumer subscription model. Rainwater provides irrigation, and there is a system to recycle the water so that Lufa Farms does not depend on the city's water supply. Gotham Greens in New York City is another example of a rooftop food-growing system. Its first greenhouse was built on top of a warehouse in Greenpoint, Brooklyn (figure 2-19). There are now two more Gotham Greens rooftop farms in operation, and more are planned. Their distribution model includes selling packaged fresh food to grocery stores. These greenhouses are controlled environments that are productive all year, and heating, cooling, irrigation, and plant nutrition can be managed by a computer-aided system. Sky Greens, a greenhouse in Singapore, has attracted international attention because it has a water-powered rotation system that permits trays of growing vegetables to be stacked. This device permits more growing surfaces than the floor area of the building, a useful way of making a small urban plot more productive. Each tray receives less sunlight than it would from direct exposure all day, which makes such a system most suitable

**Figure 2-19** Inside the rooftop farm of Gotham Greens in Greenpoint, Brooklyn. The Greenpoint greenhouse was the first of three, and more are planned.

for tropical climates like Singapore's, where sunlight is intense. Movable trays also add an operating cost. The Alterrus system of movable planting trays, which operated a greenhouse on top of a parking garage in downtown Vancouver, went into bankruptcy and stopped operations, saying that its growing system lost money and the company ran out of options before they could make it profitable.

Although Alterrus is a cautionary example, rooftop greenhouses in cities are a less radical alternative to devoting entire buildings to urban agriculture in what are called vertical farms, an idea with many advocates, including Dickson Despommier of Columbia University in his book *The Vertical Farm*.[7] Building greenhouses on the roofs of existing warehouses or garages, which normally have structures that can support the additional weight, should be a much simpler and more scalable way of adding agricultural areas to cities than entire buildings devoted to vertical farming.

These examples show that there are many opportunities in cities and suburbs to add ways of growing food, which can help the world manage the food needs of a rapidly increasing population. Food costs and food distribution that minimizes spoilage remain big issues, however.

## Adapting to Forest Fire Risks

Fire is part of the natural life cycle of forests, but forest fires are becoming more frequent and more severe as climate change moves warmer weather closer to the polar regions. A warming climate means that winters are shorter, snows melt earlier, and the potential fire season becomes longer. As trees become less adapted to local climate, they can dry out and become more susceptible to insects and disease and are ultimately more likely to catch fire. Forest fires have increased fourfold in the United States since the 1970s. Climate change can bring trees in a forest to a tipping point, and an entire region can die off, as shown in photos of pinyon pines near Los Alamos, New Mexico (figure 2-20). In 2002, some of the trees are stressed and dying; by 2004, a photo from the same vantage point shows that all the trees have died. Dry timber in forests can be ignited by lightning or by careless, and occasionally malevolent, behavior by people. More frequent lightning storms can be expected in a warming climate, and more people are visiting or living close to forests today.

Forests can be managed to reduce fire risks by the clearing away of dried brush and dead trees. Only a small portion of the national forests in the United States are treated in this way every year, and the budgets for doing so have been reduced. Thomas Tidwell, chief of the U.S. Department of Agriculture's Fire Service, testified before Congress in 2013 that 42 percent of the national forests are in need of fire prevention treatment.[8] Tidwell also stated in the same testimony that the number of housing units within a half mile

**Figure 2-20** Die-off of pinyon pines. These photos are taken from the same vantage point near Los Alamos, New Mexico, in 2002 (left) and in 2004 (right).

of a national forest increased from 484,000 in 1940 to 1.8 million in 2000. The number of housing units within the boundaries of a national forest had grown from 335,000 to 1.2 million during the same period. He added that more than 400 million acres (more than 160 million hectares) of vegetated lands are at moderate to high risk from "uncharacteristically large forest fires," with more than 70,000 communities at risk.

In the United States, more than three million housing units are within national forests or within a half mile of the forest perimeter and are obviously on the front line of fire danger. There are ways to make a house less susceptible to fire—by clearing vegetation around it and by rebuilding using less flammable materials—just as houses can be protected from rising seas by raising them above previous flood surges. Over time, adapting to increasing forest fire danger is comparable to adapting to sea-level rise, but at some point the cost of maintaining houses in some locations will become untenable. Some areas will need to be rezoned as too dangerous for permanent habitation.

## Challenge 2: Reducing Causes of Global Warming

As we have seen in this chapter, there are many ways of adapting to the inevitable early phases of climate change that should make the transition manageable, although not easy. Hard choices will have to be made about living in vulnerable areas, and there will need to be expensive engineering works to protect major coastal cities. More extreme climate change, particularly sea levels rising to heights that require moving people away from coastal areas, should be avoided if at all possible by stabilizing and then reducing greenhouse gas emissions. Almost everyone agrees about the desirability of this objective, except those people who continue to deny the existence of climate change or refuse to accept that people have anything to do with it. How to accomplish greenhouse gas reduction is obviously a huge problem that will require unprecedented international cooperation. However, some ecodesign measures can help mitigate warming trends, notably by using distributed forms of renewable energy to power individual structures and reducing energy use in cities by innovative utility installations for entire urban districts. Making individual buildings as energy efficient as possible will also be important. There are also ways of managing urban development and growth that can prevent damage to the natural ecosystems, some of which we have already outlined as ways to adapt to climate change, and that will also help reduce causes of global warming.

## Using Distributed Renewable Energy

Only about a third of the energy used by power plants is converted into electricity for transmission along the power grid. In developed countries, about 5 percent of the energy in the grid is then lost in transmission, and in some less developed nations, as much as 20 percent can be lost. Photovoltaic panels, which convert sunlight into electricity right where the electricity is needed, are proving to be a more economically sound choice in some situations. Solar panels generate not only renewable energy, but the energy can then be used immediately in a building equipped with the panels. The obvious problem is, What happens at night or on cloudy days? The best answer right now is to keep the building connected to the power grid, transferring surplus electricity from the solar collectors to the grid when the sun is shining and drawing down power at night or on dark days. Batteries being developed today to enable more effective electric automobiles can also be used in buildings to store electric power. As technology and economics improve, many more buildings could be retrofitted with solar panels.

Groups of buildings can be designed to optimize the use of solar panels, as in the residential project in Freiburg, Germany, designed by Rolf Ditsch Solar Architektur, shown in figure 2-21. The site plan is organized according to a strict, south-facing orientation to achieve the best solar exposure. The angle of the roofs is also determined to be the best for solar exposure at Freiburg's latitude. The mixed-use building on the west side of the project is built at right angles to the other buildings, but the solar collectors still have the optimal orientation (figure 2-22). A project such as this one is still the exception even in Freiburg, internationally known for its encouragement of green

**Figure 2 -21** Aerial view of housing in Freiburg, Germany, shows the disposition of solar panels. The orientation is due south, and the angle is optimized for the location.

**Figure 2 -22** The Sun Ship, an apartment building in the Freiburg, Germany, housing development shown from the air in figure 2-21, with ground-floor retail along the street edge of the project. The building has its long sides to the east and west, but the solar panels still have their optimal south orientation. The design of the complex is by Rolf Ditsch Solar Architektur.

technology, where you can see in figure 2-21 that the neighboring buildings do not have solar panels. Comparable designs are feasible in many moderate-density locations.

Geothermal energy for heating and cooling individual buildings is another form of distributable energy generation. It boosts the efficiency of a forced-air heating system. About 10 feet (3 meters) below ground, the earth has a constant temperature somewhere in the low-50°F range (about 10°C). A closed loop of pipes filled with water can be constructed at this level, and the water in the pipes can be circulated continuously through the soil and then up into the building. If the air temperature is warmer than the ground temperature, the circulating water transfers the colder ground temperature to the geothermal unit, making the cooling process more efficient. In cold weather, the effect is the reverse, and the heating system is boosted. The geothermal system thus uses much less energy than a conventional heating and air-conditioning installation, but, at current energy prices, it takes more than ten years in most places for the savings to pay off. As with solar collectors, the effect on energy usage at a regional or national level requires that a large number of these geothermal units be in use, so some type of incentive for installing them would need to be found, comparable to the incentives for solar collectors.

Wind energy is already being used to generate power from gangs of turbines set up as wind farms connected to the power grid. Using wind power for individual buildings is not usual now, but could become significant in the future if small turbines become more efficient and can be damped to prevent vibration being transmitted to the buildings.

## Reducing Regional Emissions from Factories and Power Plants

Fossil fuels are still the cheapest energy, and there is always inertia that works against change. James Hansen, formerly at NASA and now at Columbia University, has been one of the strongest voices warning that burning fossil fuels is a leading cause of climate change. He suggests that there are many subsidies for fossil fuels that should not be given, that the price of using and emitting carbon should be raised by a tax, and that existing regulations for "scrubbing" emissions should apply to all and be enforced. He believes that making fossil fuels more expensive with a carbon tax is the best enforcement mechanism, and will lead to technical innovations that reduce carbon emissions.[9] To be effective, his prescriptions must be adopted throughout the world, especially in countries with huge populations such as China and India. Adoption of a carbon tax by nine states in the northeastern United States, by California, and by British Columbia in Canada, as well as by Scandinavian countries, is a sign of progress, but not yet at the scale that can address the worldwide problem.

Geothermal energy from places where sources of natural hot water, like a geyser, are readily accessible from the land surface already operate in several places in the world, including Iceland, Japan, and Sonoma County, California. Using enhanced geothermal energy for power generation, in which holes are bored several kilometers into the ground to reach natural sources of heat, is a feasible technology, according to a panel chaired by Jefferson Tester, a professor at the Massachusetts Institute of Technology. The panel concluded that energy from enhanced geothermal systems can draw on subsurface heat in many places within the United States to provide both electric power and heat in amounts that can have major effect on national energy use in the United States by 2050, with only minimal negative environmental consequences. This same conclusion obviously applies throughout the world. According to the panel, the research that would need to be done before large-scale adoption of enhanced geothermal energy would cost less than building a single new fossil-fuel power plant.[10]

## Reducing Energy Use in Transportation

According to the U.S. Environmental Protection Agency (EPA), emissions from transportation were 28 percent of total U.S. greenhouse gas emissions in 2012. According to Environment Canada, the figure in that country for the same year was 24 percent. Many people are at work on reducing transportation emissions, and the most likely outcome is that this aspect of the emissions problem can be solved by improving the way self-propelled vehicles operate (although reducing the need for individual car trips is also important, a subject we will return to in chapter 3). The ideal way of charging electric automobiles would be from photovoltaic or other renewable energy sources. Otherwise, although the car engines don't emit pollution, there will still be emissions at the power plants; in addition, transferring the energy source for automobiles to the power grid may well make the overall greenhouse gas problem worse because of inefficiencies in the grid. There are also serious concerns about the capacity of the power grid if this transition takes off too quickly. Technological improvements in the efficiency of both photovoltaic panels and batteries could combine to reduce the need for central power generation plants.

Another technology, hydrogen fuel cells, is a potentially attractive option for motor vehicles because the combustion product from hydrogen is water. Right now, hydrogen fuel cells are expensive, but the cost can come down with mass production. The more difficult problem is finding an environmentally responsible way to manufacture the hydrogen. The process of making hydrogen from natural gas, for example, is not efficient and produces little net benefit to the environment. Because many people are trying to solve this problem, hydrogen fuel cells could one day be as effective as electric cars in eliminating pollution along streets and highways.

**Figure 2-23** GIS composite ranking process for environmental factors in Florida. From top to bottom: habitat, water, wetlands, agriculture, contiguity.

**Figure 2-24** Resulting composite GIS map of Florida showing the land that emerged as most significant according to the five criteria of habitat, water, wetlands, agriculture, and contiguity. The darkest areas are the highest priority for preservation.

## Keeping New Development Away from Unsuitable Locations

Ian McHarg's book *Design with Nature,* first published in 1969, made a powerful case that architects, planners, and engineers should work with natural systems and not try to construct against them, just as the crew of a sailboat needs to understand wind patterns and ocean currents to travel safely and efficiently. McHarg wrote about the importance of dunes in protecting coastlines from erosion and how engineers often removed dunes so that people could live closer to the water, perhaps replacing them with seawalls, which are far less stable and permanent. He also wrote about the natural organization of the watersheds along rivers and how buildings that destabilize hillsides and wetlands along river basins produced unnecessary erosion and floods.

All the points that McHarg made are still relevant today, except that in McHarg's experience, the evolution of natural systems was so slow that for practical purposes nature could be considered to have a stable structure. Today, we are discovering that nature under the influence of global warming can change relatively rapidly, making the issues he identified even more urgent.

McHarg's recommendation in *Design with Nature* was to make an environmental inventory in advance of all construction so that development could be kept away from unsuitable locations. He invented a mapping system in which areas that were the most sensitive to damage from building construction were overlaid; the places not delineated on the overlays, or appearing on the fewest overlays, were the best places to build. McHarg made his overlay maps on tracing paper. His method is one of the bases of today's GIS programs, which still organize information in layers; these computer-based layers permit many kinds of complex calculations at a much finer level of accuracy than his paper-based approach.

Today, government agencies in the United States, Canada, and many other countries have excellent GIS maps that can help calculate in advance the risks of changing climate and identify the critical places where natural systems need to be sustained or repaired for environmental stability. A research studio at the University of Pennsylvania used McHargian methods in GIS to demonstrate conservation priorities for the state of Florida. The five layers in figure 2-23 show, from top to bottom, the areas that scored highest as places needed to preserve natural habitats; the places where land should be left open to preserve subsurface aquifers; the most important wetlands; prime agricultural land; and a fifth criterion, contiguity, or the need to preserve connections to and from land identified as critical. Figure 2-24 shows the map that emerges as a composite of the five criteria; the calculations included climate change estimates. Joining this map to the land in national and state parks plus land already acquired for preservation (figure 2-25) produces the Ideal Conservation Network, the places that need to be maintained as natural or agricultural land for Florida to be sustainable in the future, all brought together in figure 2-26. Making regional studies of the preservation of natural systems and the threats from climate change part of the process of urbanizing new areas could ensure that new roads and infrastructure would not open up areas for development that will have negative effects on agriculture or the water supply. Such a process would help avoid major future problems, such as potential flooding. An example of such policies is the Green Zone map (figure 2-27) prepared by Metro Vancouver after consultation with the local municipalities and the public. It shows agricultural land and environmentally sensitive land that should be preserved from development. Some of the preserved land can then be made available for recreation.

## Incorporating Environmental Mapping into Development Regulations

Maps like Metro Vancouver's Green Zone leave enforcement up to local government through development regulations. The ability of GIS to describe and predict complex outcomes can also be put to work establishing policy conclusions that, in turn, can lead to improved prescriptions for new development embodied in local development regulations.

GIS makes it possible to define environmental zones such as erodible slopes, riparian areas, water quality protection zones, wetlands, and flood and flood-surge zones, which can be added to the regulatory text and the official map. In areas that have not yet become urban or are in the process of being annexed, environmental zones can be established, much like land use zones, with a list of permitted uses in the code plus instructions for how such land should be developed if there is a separate development ordinance like a subdivision ordinance. In areas where development has already taken place and conventional zones are already established, these environmental restrictions can be mapped as overlays that recognize the underlying land use and density regulations but still protect natural features. A rudimentary version of such mapping was completed in a plan for the city of Abu Dhabi in the United Arab Emirates, where a concept called the green gradient was established to designate types and intensity of land development potential based on the varying overall level of environmental sensitivity across the city's footprint (figure 2-28). Translating such allocations from policy to practice in Abu Dhabi can demonstrate the fragility of such a system, but at least a consciousness of the environment has been built directly into the land use allocation planning process.

Coastal areas subject to flood surges from hurricanes or other big storms, mapped in the United States by the Federal Emergency Management Agency (FEMA), could be incorporated into the local GIS-based regulatory maps. Doing this would facilitate mapping of flood-surge zones, which include the FEMA

**Figure 2-25** GIS map of Florida showing land already under conservation.

**Figure 2-26** Combining land preservation priorities with existing conserved lands in GIS produces an Ideal Conservation Network for the state of Florida.

**Figure 2-27** Metropolitan Vancouver's Green Zone, a land preservation policy drawn up after consultation with the public and the municipalities in the region. With the British Columbia Agricultural Land Reserve, it secures key green lands from urban development.

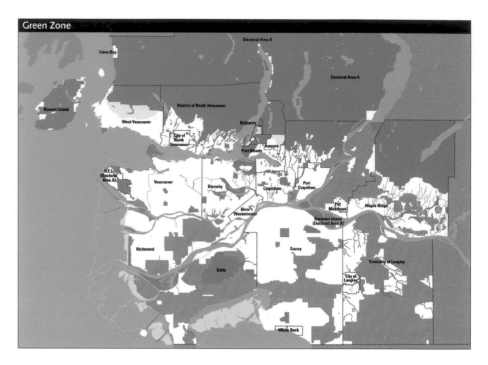

**Figure 2-28** In the United Arab Emirates, the Abu Dhabi Plan 2030, adopted in 2008, includes as a primary framework an environmental overlay called the "green gradient." This map shows the sensitive areas for which special development considerations come into play. Although at a broad scale, it makes the point about the need to be respectful of the natural setting, to be followed up with detailed regulations.

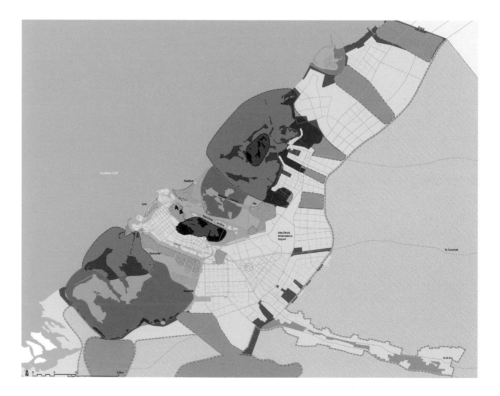

requirements for elevation of habitable floors and other structural requirements intended to minimize storm damage. These provisions are enforced
today by making development ineligible for insurance if it doesn't com-
ply. Enacting flood-surge zones would allow local governments to consider
whether they wish to permit new development in these zones and whether
they wish to enact more comprehensive requirements for new developments,
such as elevating the entire grade in such areas rather than raising the height
of individual buildings.

The maps used in making development regulation decisions need to be
changed to include GIS information about land contours, streams, and existing vegetation, and the regulations should be rewritten to reduce the amount
of regrading to preserve existing vegetation and contours as much as possible. In a natural setting, the land has evolved over time to deal with floods,
and the more conservatively such land is developed, the more future flood
problems can be minimized.

Environmental mapping can provide a more specific way of preserving
natural systems than using statutory growth boundaries that restrict the
development of roads, utilities, and buildings outside the boundary. Oregon's
growth boundaries are well-known examples. The advantage of an official
growth boundary is that it preserves land from urbanization until it is clear it
will be needed. The disadvantage, as seen in figure 2-29, is there is compara-
tively little land preservation within the boundary because urban services are
available everywhere. Such boundaries are also vulnerable to political pressures that have nothing to do with environmental determinants. Having both
growth boundaries and development regulations based on environmental
mapping would be an effective combination.

## Managing Development within Watersheds to Reduce Flooding and Erosion

In London and Hamburg, or other big cities, the cost of major engineering
investments like flood barriers and raised waterfront districts can be justified by the large numbers of people and properties protected. Rural areas protected from development can continue to function naturally. Many rivers and
streams around the world flow through areas that are already developed, but
not at the densities of London or Hamburg. For such places, the best course
of action will be to try to head off floods by retaining rainwater in the watersheds where it first falls. If the first inch of rain can be retained in the landscape and gradually absorbed, the rapid flows of water that cause flooding
and erosion can be greatly reduced. In cities that have stormwater systems
combined with the sewers, runoff from a storm can overwhelm the treatment plants, causing discharges of raw sewage into rivers or harbors. U.S.

**Figure 2-29** Housing development comes
right up to the edge of the official growth
boundary in metropolitan Portland, Oregon,
with farmland in the foreground.

**Figure 2-30** Map of watersheds, with boundaries shown as dark lines, in Lancaster County, Pennsylvania. Most of the watersheds drain westward into the Susquehanna River.

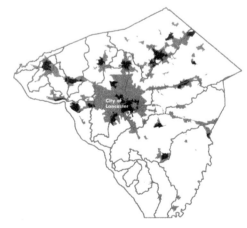

**Figure 2-31** The gray areas are the urban growth boundaries for Lancaster County, Pennsylvania, overlaid on the boundaries of the watersheds, shown in green. The darker areas are incorporated boroughs.

cities that are under orders from the EPA to correct this problem are finding that it is much less expensive, and should be equally effective, to apply many small devices to retain stormwater rather than the very expensive engineering solutions, like completely separating stormwater and sanitary sewer systems or building holding tanks at the treatment plant, that would otherwise be necessary.

All land areas are part of watersheds or drainage basins. The watershed for a large stream is composed of a hierarchy of smaller watersheds. For example, figure 2-30, a map of Lancaster County, Pennsylvania, shows the streams and the boundaries of the areas drained by each stream. Most of them drain into the Susquehanna River on the left side of the map, which flows into the Atlantic Ocean via Chesapeake Bay, a long way south. A second map (figure 2-31) shows the relationship of the built-up areas in Lancaster County to the watersheds. Early settlers tended to establish their buildings along the ridges that divide each watershed from the next, a canny choice as these are the areas least likely to flood. They established a pattern that persists today. A third map (figure 2-32) shows how drainage patterns, developed areas, and farmland interact.

Watersheds in places that have never been urbanized and are not farmed develop a natural equilibrium. Over time, hillsides stabilize, with the land held in place by vegetation. Stream banks also stabilize, floodplains and wetlands absorb seasonal variations in rain or snowfall, and much of the precipitation filters down to underground aquifers, while some of the water evaporates into the atmosphere.

As watersheds are turned into farmland and then developed with roads and buildings, the natural equilibrium is disturbed. Bulldozing hillsides to create farm fields or to make way for houses, constructing roads and parking lots that do not absorb water, stripping away trees and other vegetation all make water flow off the land much faster. The watershed can adjust to some of these changes, but as urbanization covers more and more of the land, the reengineered environment produces erosion and flooding. In many suburban areas in the United States, the government maps showing areas prone to flooding are so out of date that what was mapped as flooding every one hundred years is now under water frequently, and the floodplains have become much larger. Bigger storm events in a changing climate make this flooding even worse. The answer to the problem is a program to restore the capacity of watersheds to hold rainwater so that the amount of water flowing through them is slowed down while much of it is absorbed. The standard for measuring success is that streams should go back to being as close as possible to the way they were before any interventions by people.

Retaining water within drainage areas requires the antithesis of the big engineering projects initiated by the government in the Netherlands. Instead

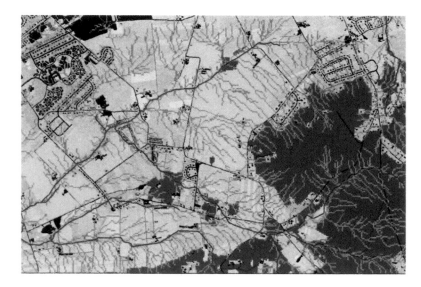

**Figure 2-32** Streets, buildings, and streams in a part of Lancaster County, Pennsylvania. Yellow indicates the properties officially preserved as farmland as part of a program that is based on individual ownership, not natural boundaries. The dark green areas are woodlands.

of one central government-sponsored work program, managing watersheds requires the actions of many individual landowners and local governments. Big objectives can be attained by a multitude of small actions, if communities enact regulations that are comparable to those already in use to keep buildings safe from fire or collapse and if local governments pay for relatively small adjustments to streets and parking lots.

Take, for example, the humble water barrel, at one time a mainstay of rural life. A drainpipe from the roof can easily be arranged to empty into a 55-gallon barrel (figure 2-33) or, of course, a larger container. The container should be equipped with a faucet. A drip irrigation hose can be attached to the faucet and the water used for plants in the yard. Or, a day or two after a storm has subsided, the barrel can simply be allowed to drain. When the weather is below freezing, the rain barrel can be disconnected. The Philadelphia Water Department reports that it has given away almost three thousand 55-gallon barrels, according to a count in 2012. Any household in Philadelphia can receive a free barrel, but someone from the house must attend a workshop to learn how to install it. Because the roof drains for typical Philadelphia row houses are usually attached directly to storm sewers or flow almost immediately into the streets, the city's water department estimates that equipping even this small fraction of city houses with rain barrels is intercepting ten million gallons of water a year. In any city, making rain barrels a requirement for all houses where the lots are below a certain size would be a simple regulatory action. The costs for individual homeowners could be subsidized, or could be paid for by a small monthly addition to the water bill.

**Figure 2-33** Downspouts on individual houses can easily be redirected into a rain barrel instead of the yard or, in cities, instead of straight into the stormwater system. This rain barrel is distributed free by PUSH Buffalo, a Buffalo, New York, nonprofit organization whose initials stand for People United for Sustainable Housing.

Water from roof drains that empty into large suburban yards can be absorbed into the landscape, but the water can also flow back into basements. A more upscale version of the rain barrel, suitable for larger suburban houses, is an underground cistern fed by multiple roof drains and possibly also by gray water from sinks and bathtubs. Such a cistern is equipped with an electric pump so that water can be used to wash cars, decks, and other outside areas as well as water lawns and plants; and, in a more sophisticated installation requiring a separate pipe system within the house, water from the cistern can even be used to flush toilets.

Rain barrels and cisterns are as effective a means of water retention as a landscaped roof garden. Green roofs are appropriate for new, large buildings like schools or offices, when the weight of soil, water, and plants can be taken into account when the building is designed. Green roofs also enhance views and offer recreation opportunities in dense cities. Toronto passed a green roof bylaw in 2010 that requires green roofs on all buildings with more than a gross floor area of just over 21,000 square feet (2,000 square meters), sets construction standards, and is administered with guidelines for biodiversity.

Green roofs don't work for buildings with pitched roofs, and most existing flat-roofed buildings were not designed for the weight that a working landscape imposes on the structure. If the rainwater from every building were retained in barrels or cisterns or was absorbed by green roofs, a major source of flooding would be contained and made much more manageable.

## Shaping Green Streets

Streets are another major source of rapid stormwater runoff that causes erosion and prevents replenishing aquifers. Streets are designed so that rain or melting snow will run from the center to gutters along each side. In heavy rainstorms, roads and highways can become rivers, although seldom deep enough to stop traffic. In built-up areas, the water runs into a storm sewer. Because streets can occupy as much as 25 or 30 percent of the land area in a central city, a high percentage of rainwater flows swiftly and directly into the stormwater system. Stormwater on suburban streets may also run into a drain, or it may be caught in a swale alongside the road. Major highways often have detention basins to catch rainwater runoff. A good way to slow stormwater runoff would be for water to be able to seep through the street into the soil underneath using permeable paving. Some paving products can be laid with spaces between them, and some have holes that permit drainage. These pavers can break under the weight of cars and trucks, however, and, if there is snow, plow blades can catch on the pavers and dig them up. Smooth, unitary paving materials are now available that will let water through and can withstand some traffic. Small streets can be repaved with this kind of pervious material, laid atop a bed of crushed stone, thus retaining the water for a time and letting it seep gradually into the soil. Pervious street-paving programs are being implemented in several cities, including Philadelphia as part of the Philadelphia Green Plan, Chicago as part of the Adding Green to Urban Design Plan, and Seattle, which has a long record of following green policies. Many smaller city streets can be repaved in this way, and the overall effect could greatly reduce the load on stormwater systems. Rebuilding with permeable materials can be scheduled whenever a street needs to be repaved. Back lanes in older residential areas can also help manage runoff. In Vancouver, a program, nostalgically called Country Lanes, avoids overall paving of these rights-of-way and fosters permeable surfaces and augmented vegetation to hold and absorb water (figure 2-34).

An alternative method for managing stormwater, when the right-of-way is wide enough, is to let water flow from the paved roadway into planting beds, as on the street in Portland, Oregon, shown in figure 2-35. The planting beds are trenches cut into the ground so that water will seep directly into the subsoil and down to the aquifer. The trees and other plantings help purify the water and are much more attractive and much safer for pedestrians than a ditch would be. The planting bed needs to be designed to fit the space allowed for it. The minimum would be 5 feet (1.5 meters) between the street and the sidewalk. At that width, it may make sense to use pavers on the sidewalk that are pervious to water; the paving for the parking lane can also be pervious even if the street is not.

Parking lots, in which acres of land are covered with an impervious surface, can also be fitted with planting beds between each aisle of parked cars so that water drains into the plantings, is filtered, and then seeps into the ground (figure 2-36). In areas where there is snow, the owners may prefer to keep the plantings around the perimeter of the lot so that the lot can be plowed more efficiently, but the area of the plantings should be equivalent to what would be needed if the planted trenches are between the parking aisles. Most development regulations require a percentage of the land be left as open space. If the planters are counted as open space, the owners should not ordinarily need more land to park the necessary number of cars.

Finally, large drainage ditches often built along major roads can be rebuilt as constructed wetlands. The plantings are not only more attractive than an open ditch, but much less of a hazard for people and animals.

Again, each of these individual actions will not have much effect on a watershed by itself, but if all streets are either pervious or green, all parking lots are designed to drain into planters, and constructed wetlands are built to manage drainage for larger areas, a watershed can be made to function much more as it would have when it was in its original natural state. In places

**Figure 2-34** Vancouver decided to make back alleys more attractive for walkers and more environmentally sensitive through a program called Country Lanes. This mature example emphasizes permeability and landscape. It is mostly a process of reducing impervious paving as much as possible, at the request of residents, or when lanes are scheduled for normal capital spending.

**Figure 2-35** Green streets, like this one in Portland, Oregon, use a variety of planting beds to retain water.

**Figure 2-36** Bioswale in a parking lot at the Museum of Science and Industry in Portland, Oregon. Stormwater is retained and filtered by the planting beds.

where flooding is a frequent problem, golf courses and public parks can be designed to flood, thus diverting water from built-up areas. The combination of environmentally based development regulations and careful design of stormwater runoff can make a huge difference in preventing flooding in cities and suburbs.

### Challenge 3: Creating Prototypes for Urban and Environmental Harmony

No one measure will solve the environmental contradictions that now exist in our cities, suburbs, and their hinterlands, which will need a comprehensive suite of actions, well integrated and coordinated with land use and development reforms. No city has yet achieved such a holistic strategy, so no city can be said to be even moderately sustainable. One reason is that we only add about 1 percent to most urban regions each year, so existing conditions overwhelmingly determine performance. Performance rating systems are starting to clarify a sense of direction for future building, and some cities are adding a green agenda for public properties and services, but we are a long way away from comprehensive reform and retrofit. Still, real breakthroughs are starting to show up at the scale of a city district or neighborhood. There are beginning to be places where some of the ecodesign methods described in this chapter are put together in the design of whole urban districts. Here are three examples, from Europe, the Middle East, and North America.

### Stockholm: Hammarby Sjöstad

Stockholm's Hammarby Sjöstad community occupies the site of an old port and industrial district. It was a contaminated brownfield site that has been cleaned and redeveloped, using the best currently available technology for sustainable energy, stormwater and sewage treatment, and solid waste disposal. The aim is to cut the negative environmental impacts in half compared with conventional development as practiced in Sweden in the 1990s. The plan (figure 2-37) was originally made as part of Stockholm's bid for the 2004 Summer Olympics, the games that ended up being held in Athens. When completed, the district will include 11,500 apartments housing about 26,000 people, and another 10,000 people are expected to work there.

The district has its own heating and wastewater treatment plants. The heating plant is powered partly by combustible waste collected within Hammarby Sjöstad, partly by biogas, some of which is produced by the district's sewage treatment plant, and also by heat converted from treated wastewater. This wastewater contains heated water from dish and clothes washers and from showers, sinks, and bathtubs. Some buildings are also fitted with solar panels.

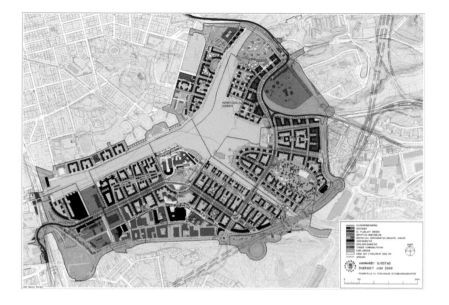

**Figure 2-37** Plan of Hammarby Sjöstad, a new district in Stockholm that replaces old industrial and harbor areas and is intended as a showcase of sustainable design techniques.

Water consumption is reduced by using efficient toilets and air-mixer water taps. Stormwater from the streets goes into a separate piping system where it is routed to holding tanks and a sedimentation pond to purify it before it runs into the sea. Rainwater from yards and roofs runs into a canal system (figure 2-38), which filters it before it runs into the sea.

There is an automated waste disposal system fed by chutes in the apartment buildings. Combustible waste goes into the power plant, and organic waste is converted for use as fertilizer. There are also recycling rooms throughout the district. So what appears to be a pleasant, but quite conventional, neighborhood is actually an advanced prototype (figure 2-39).

## Abu Dhabi: Masdar City

The new district of Masdar City, a planned development designed by Foster and Partners, is situated within the larger urban region of Abu Dhabi City adjacent to the large area designated and designed as the nation's new national capital district. Solar energy is an important part of the design of Masdar City, which is intended to become a zero-carbon, zero-waste community. There are to be solar collectors along the walls that will screen the city from wind, solar collectors on the roofs of buildings, and another land area devoted entirely to solar collectors. There is also a wind farm that will provide some of the energy for the project. The desalination plant that supplies water for the area is to be powered by solar energy. The Arabian Gulf location provides abundant sunlight, although the solar panels require continuing maintenance to keep them clean of windblown dust and sand.

**Figure 2-38** Along a canal in Hammarby Sjöstad, a landscape amenity that is also part of the stormwater management system.

The design is intended to apply lessons from traditional architecture in the region: buildings kept close together across narrow streets to provide shade and shelter outdoors, wind towers to capture and draw down cooling air currents, and windows protected by lattice shades. The district will cover 1,500 acres (607 hectares), will house 45,000 people when finished, and will have about 60,000 jobs. The first stage houses a university campus that is a center for research on sustainable development and the headquarters of the development company. The first group of apartments has been completed. They are equipped with the latest smart technology to monitor and conserve energy and resource use. The showers automatically turn off after a set interval, air conditioners are preset to 75°F (24°C), and lights are controlled by sensors.

Internal combustion automobiles are required to be garaged as soon as they reach the district boundaries. To some degree, auto access contradicts the aspiration to be carbon neutral because area workers will come by car from all over greater Abu Dhabi. There has also been criticism that the worker population is significantly out of proportion to the resident population, which makes commuting in for many workers an unavoidable necessity. There will be a rapid transit connection to the key destinations in the Abu Dhabi region

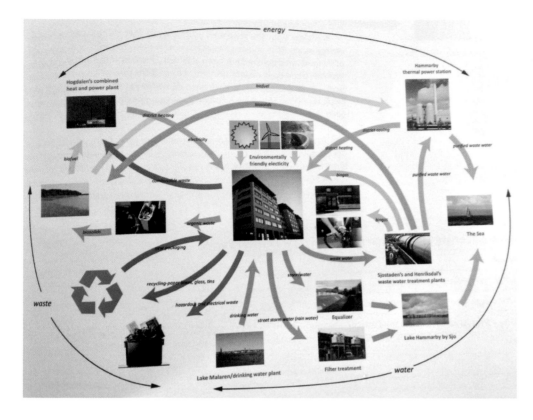

**Figure 2-39** Diagram of the energy, power generation, and waste management systems at Hammarby Sjöstad.

in the future, which will reduce commuting by car. Within Masdar City, the original plan called for an electric-powered personal movement system, sometimes called a horizontal elevator, in which you can step into the equivalent of an elevator cab at one location and program your ride to another via a network under the primary grade of the buildings and open spaces. This concept has now been abandoned for various kinds of electric vehicles, operating on the streets. Because Masdar City is intended to be a center for research in attaining sustainability, its design and technology are expected to evolve as the city is developed.

## Vancouver: Southeast False Creek

Southeast False Creek is a new neighborhood in a formerly industrial area just south of downtown Vancouver on the south shore of the city's major inner-city water body. The master plan (figure 2-40) was completed in 2004. The central portion was implemented as the Athletes Village for the 2010 Winter Olympic Games (figure 2-41) and converted to apartments (figure 2-42) after the games were over. The rest of the plan is in the process of being completed. The Olympic Athletes Village portion of the plan has received a Leadership in Energy and Environmental Design (LEED) Neighborhood Development plati-

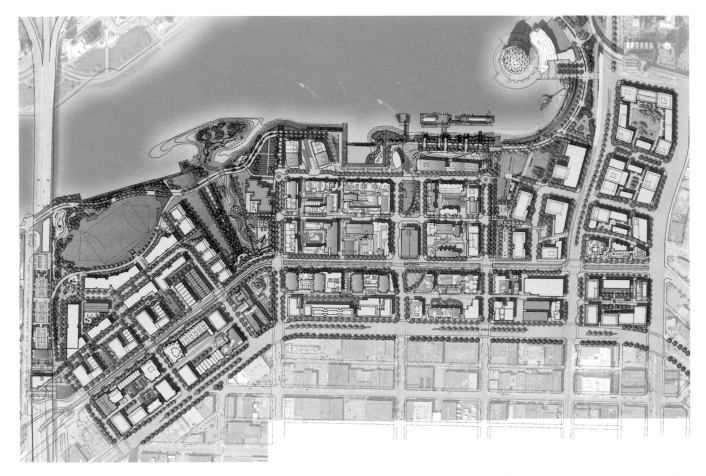

**Figure 2-40** The 2004 master plan for Southeast False Creek in Vancouver. The Athletes Village for the 2010 Winter Olympics is the central portion of the plan.

num rating, the highest LEED rating possible. One reason for the rating is a neighborhood energy utility plant that uses waste thermal energy captured from a city sewage pumping station to provide space heating and hot water to new buildings in all Southeast False Creek. Summer air conditioning is seldom needed in Vancouver residential buildings, so the plant is only for heating. The city says that this process eliminates more than 60 percent of the polluting emissions that would come from heating the buildings by conventional methods. Figure 2-43 shows how the system works.

This project also follows the well-known LEED approach to reducing overall energy and resources used by individual buildings, including collecting rainwater to flush toilets, using energy efficient exterior materials, and providing rain screens to protect exterior walls. It also meets other LEED requirements. Streets are narrow and lined with midrise buildings that allow light and sun to come down to grade level. Stormwater is channeled to an artificial stream

**Figure 2-41** View of the Athletes Village in Vancouver's Southeast False Creek area during the 2010 Winter Olympics.

**Figure 2-42** A recent view of Vancouver's Southeast False Creek neighborhood, with the former Olympic Village now converted to a mixed-use development.

**Figure 2-43** How the energy system works at Vancouver's Southeast False Creek (SEFC). Heat from the sewer system, which contains warm water from plumbing and appliances, is recycled to heat the buildings.

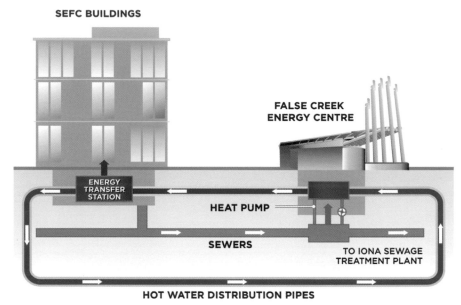

within the adjacent local park that scrubs the runoff before it goes into False Creek. Waste is recycled. Plots are assigned for residents' gardens. Rooftops are greened. There is a careful balance of housing with local shopping as well as civic standards for public amenities and services.

These three new districts perform well according to any contemporary measure and show that sustainable development can be implemented today for substantial parts of cities using current technology and typical economics. Because the innovations essentially replace more conventional components, they do not significantly change affordability or financial feasibility (although Southeast False Creek also has explicit requirements for low-income and affordable housing and Hammarby Sjöstad has a subsidized housing component). They also show what begins to happen as all the dimensions of sustainability are brought together through a careful management of both public and private responsibilities. In the next chapters, we will discuss how ecodesign can be brought up to city, regional, and even national levels and how it can start to address not only the 1 percent of new development that we constantly are adding to our cities but also to a retrofit of the other 99 percent that is already built.

Although the comprehensive measures that we have been discussing in this chapter promise big improvements in sustainability, the big question continues to be whether the world's nations can create the national and international agreements and programs needed to stave off the worst effects of climate change.

# 3. Balancing Cars and Other Transportation

The world has become footloose. From local trips within a neighborhood or city to national and international travel, modern technology has liberated most people in developed countries to move how they want, when they want, as often as they want, and whatever distance they want. This change has become one of the most profound characteristics of modern life. It has opened up dramatic opportunities for social, cultural, and economic development. It has transformed human relations and the experiences of where we live, and work, and visit.

The dramatic changes in transportation and movement options, and the benefits that come with them, have been driven by fossil fuels; and even where trains and transit run on electricity, most of the electrical energy in the world is generated by fossil fuel. Our new-found freedom of movement has had two fundamental consequences that were not understood when modern transportation came into common use. It significantly reinforced the explosion of pollution from fossil fuels that has led to the global climate crisis that we now face. It has also allowed the seemingly endless spread of cities, breaking down the intimate pattern of buildings and spaces that determined the scale of human experience in the past and that we admire so much in historic places and has set off the process of globalization that is reshaping human culture at every level.

Of all the transportation inventions that have shaped the modern world, the most pervasive and personal, in both use and consequences, is the private automobile. Daily life has completely changed because of the car and has been significantly enhanced for most people. In contemporary cities with few available transit alternatives, and especially in the new suburbs shaped by the automobile, being without a car can be a serious disadvantage. The car is embedded deep in our lives, deep in our culture, and deep in our psyche. The car also causes some serious problems. It takes more and more space for roads and parking away from other uses, and bulldozing the landscape for wider highways and bigger parking lots destabilizes natural systems. Traffic noise is a health hazard. Exhaust pollution endangers health as well as the climate. Thousands of people are killed or seriously injured in auto accidents every year. The amount of space and accommodation that we make for this essential device has to be managed to find a balance between its extraordinary utility and all the other activities that are needed in cities and suburbs.

Those concerned about balancing transportation are sometimes accused of wanting people to give up their cars. We don't think that this description is fair, and it is certainly not our position. The numbers of cars and trucks in the world will continue to increase, even in developed countries, but places that are now overly dependent on cars should have a much wider array of attractive ways to move around, especially a wider set of transit choices in a finer network. They should also have the choice of fewer trips and shorter trips by having day-to-day origins and destinations closer together or integrated. Where these choices are already available, the growth in the numbers of cars and trucks is projected to be far smaller than in other places. In this chapter, we discuss how more intense development is attracted to areas around transit stations so that transit systems can be a way of reshaping urban growth patterns. Bus rapid transit (BRT), a major improvement over conventional bus service, is a more affordable alternative than rail transit and can be economic along suburban commercial corridors. In compact centers and neighborhoods near transit, more daily trips can take place by walking or on bicycles, and changes to the design of streets can make walking and biking safer and can cut down on other kinds of traffic accidents. All these changes make cities and suburbs more sustainable and improve people's daily lives. Expanding railway service between urban regions that are within a few hundred miles of each other can cut down on the number of short airline trips as well as take some cars off highways because door-to-door trips on rail can be shorter than the amount of time needed to negotiate airports or highways. Our conclusion is that a more balanced transportation system that makes full use of trains and transit not only has great potential to reduce stress on the natural environment and make daily life more pleasant, but it can be paid for by public investment no longer needed for expanding highways and airports. In addition, when urban activities are planned to be close together, walking and bicycles can replace cars and transit.

Balanced transportation is a fundamental ecodesign principle, essential to dealing with both the environmental and livability problems of modern cities and suburbs. Technological improvements will continue to reduce pollution from different types of transportation, but the biggest reducer of pollution will be the more compact cities and neighborhoods that can be created when transit, bicycles, and walking are a stronger part of the transportation mix and a revived rail transportation sector delivers people to regional centers.

In chapter 4, we discuss ways to create compact, walkable places to live and work. In chapter 5, we discuss a more intimate level of place-making where the role of the car and the space dedicated to it are managed in relation to other kinds of transportation and other ways to use land.

## The Car Is Here to Stay

At one time, it looked as if oil supplies would reach a peak and begin to decline, and that would solve a lot of urban design and development problems. As shrinking supplies pushed up gasoline costs, people would not drive their cars as much. Emissions would go down. More people would want to live closer to city centers, supporting in-fill development and less growth at the urban fringe; transit ridership would increase and new transit lines would become feasible. We agree that such outcomes are desirable and necessary if we are going to moderate future climate change by urbanizing less land and reducing emissions. However, more and more ways to tap oil and gas are becoming feasible at prices people are willing to pay, although these new means of extraction can come with increased environmental costs. All over the world, as soon as people are wealthy enough, the personal mobility of the car is one of the first of the luxuries that they secure. They are prepared to pay a very high proportion of their income to maintain its benefits and to ignore the impacts of pollution and congestion. As long as cars are so popular, how can any government stop building new roads and highways?

Finding ways to reduce vehicle use is already difficult, and the trends are for more vehicles, not fewer. In the United States, with almost 320 million people, some 250 million cars and trucks are on the road. This is a ratio of vehicles to people of 0.78, close to one vehicle for every person, including all the children and all the people who chose not to, or can't afford to, own and drive a car. The ratio for Canada is noticeably smaller at 0.62, closer to figures for the rest of the world. For Australia, the number of vehicles per person is 0.65; for Japan, it is 0.59; and for the European Union, it is 0.55. The number of cars and trucks worldwide is about 1 billion, plus another 0.4 billion motorcycles, relating to a current world population of just more than 7 billion. By 2030, the estimates are for 1.7 billion cars and trucks and 0.9 billion motorcycles relating to an estimated global population of 8.3 billion.[1] The highest predicted increase in vehicle numbers will be in the Middle East, Brazil, India, and China where conventional gasoline or diesel engines, with all their emission problems, will probably be the norm for a long time.

Even where there are more balanced transportation systems, private vehicle numbers are predicted to grow, although at a lower rate than in other areas. For example, most of the countries in the European Union have diversified transportation systems that permit people in urban regions to reach many destinations by trains, rail transit, buses, or a combination of means. Usually, the bus stop or train station is within a short walk, service is frequent, and connections work smoothly. Sometimes, part of the journey can be by bicycle, and trains in countries like the Netherlands and Denmark are designed to let passengers bring their bicycles on board. Although the overall population of the European Union is expected to grow by only 5 percent by 2030, the trends in vehicle ownership predict a 31 percent increase in cars and a 17 percent increase in heavy vehicles. Such an increase would raise the number of vehicles per person in the European Union from 0.55 to 0.67. Predictions for Canada would bring the ratio of vehicles to population in 2030 up to 0.78, the current U.S. level. The U.S. ratio is predicted to reach 0.84 by 2030, when the overall population is expected to be 368 million.

The European Union includes countries at various stages of development. Will vehicle ownership grow in the Netherlands and Denmark, which have excellent, well-balanced transportation systems, including high levels of bicycle use? Right now, the answer seems to be yes, although not at the rates predicted for Poland, Hungary, or the Czech Republic. If current trends continue, the number of vehicles in Denmark would rise from 2.3 million in 2002 to 3.9

million in 2030, while the population increases only from 5.6 million to 5.9 million. In the Netherlands, the number of vehicles is predicted to rise from 7.7 to 10.2 million in the same period, while the population increases from 16.8 million to an estimated 17.3 million.[2]

The need to curb emissions may also become less of a restraint on vehicle use. Automobile technology is moving quickly toward alternative ways of using energy, including electric cars recharged by solar power or fuel cells using hydrogen. It is even possible that congestion on highways can diminish by using a computer-controlled driving mode that manages more cars safely at greater speeds, sometimes called the driverless car. It is likely that we will reinvent the car long before we run out of fossil fuel. That is good news in terms of cutting environmental impacts, but we still need to solve the problems that traffic and parking create for the humane shape of our cities and deal with the unsustainable expansion of our cities and suburbs, with its destabilizing effect on the natural environment, that is facilitated by the car.

Any change in car use requires making other means of transportation as appealing as driving. Most people will not give up their cars, but they might drive them less if driving is just one of an attractive array of options for moving around in future cities and suburbs, and especially if walking becomes the faster and easier alternative because of the short length of common trips.

## Effective Transit Systems Do Reduce Car Use

Having a balanced transportation system does make a difference in how many vehicles are in use. In 2030—if the predictions are correct—the number of vehicles per person in the Netherlands will be 0.58 while in the United States it will be 0.84. Even densely populated countries like the Netherlands and Denmark have rural areas without much effective local transit. They also have places that are not well served by freight railway lines, and trucks will always be the most flexible means of shipping goods.

Paying for the convenience of owning a vehicle need not translate into driving for large numbers of vehicle miles, which is the real issue and much more difficult to measure. Car owners can use transit much of the week and drive the car for longer trips on weekends. Transit is also a way to encourage walking and extending bicycle use with bike-share programs. Pedestrians can step on and off trains, and cyclists can return one bicycle, take a ride on transit, and borrow another cycle. Transit systems can also carry bicycles.

Effective transit is a missing piece of the transportation system in many places. Conventional buses and traditional streetcars, which share their right-of-way with other traffic, are useful for short distances, but they are often too slow and too infrequent for long routes and thus do not supply the need for effective transit.

Some big cities, like Paris, Tokyo, Moscow, London, and Mexico City, have mature underground transit systems. The original capital investment in these systems was large, but they are heavily used because it is possible to go to many destinations in different parts of the city by changing from one line to another. Tokyo's comprehensive transit system allows passengers to go almost anywhere within the metropolitan region. Mexico City's rail transit achieves a comparable flexibility, and the cost of travel, currently five pesos, makes it a very egalitarian way to get around. New York City's transit system is extensive and heavily used, but the metropolitan region is divided by the East and Hudson Rivers, limiting the opportunities to make cross connections. Montreal has a comprehensive transit system with the ability to make many connections and is the third most heavily used system in North America after New York and Mexico City. The Chinese government plans to have a comprehensive rail transit system in place in all its major cities. Nanjing's rail transit system, to give one example, started with a north-south line and an east-west line, but by 2050, there will be a comprehensive system that serves most destinations in the city.

Rail transit systems in the United States and Canada are usually limited to radial corridors, with lines converging at the traditional business centers. Critics of transit point out that in a modern metropolitan area there are now many important destinations reachable by highways that are outside rapid transit service areas. The Bay Area Regional Transit (BART) system is radial, although the system delivers almost equal access to downtown San Francisco and to downtown Oakland across the bay. Boston's system provides some flexibility of destinations within the central area. Chicago and Washington have good radial transit systems that also allow changing to different lines in the central area. Philadelphia has an old but still functional rail and transit system that covers a wide region, but it focuses primarily on the central city. Other North American transit systems are radial and serve the central business district, but many connections to important destinations are not along the rail corridors and are only made by local buses. Toronto is an important exception.

## Toronto's Big Move

Toronto, Canada's biggest city, currently has a four-line radial transit system and commuter rail lines east and west. Its plan, already in implementation, called The Big Move, will create a comprehensive transit system to connect most important destinations. Originally planned in 2008, with plans revised in 2013, the whole system is scheduled for completion by 2030. It will include

| | Today | By 2033 | |
|---|---|---|---|
| | **Our region** | **Current trends** | **With *The Big Move*** |
| Annual transit customers | 630 million | 800 million | 1.3 billion |
| Rapid transit route network | 500 km | 525 km | 1,725 km |
| % of people commuting to work by transit, walking or cycling | 26% | 25.4% | 39% |
| % of people who live within 2 km of rapid transit | 42% | 47% | 81% |
| Annual greenhouse gas emissions from transportation, per person | 2.4 tonnes | 2.2 tonnes | 1.7 tonnes |
| **Average daily commute time** | **82 minutes** | **109 minutes** | **77 minutes** |

**Figure 3-1** Figures in this table, prepared by Metrolinx to explain Toronto's Big Move transit expansion strategy, show what can be accomplished by transforming radial transit lines into a comprehensive transit system.

5.6 miles (9 kilometers) of extensions to the current rail transit system and a new rail line linking the airport to downtown Toronto, and it will also include 32.9 miles (53 kilometers) of new light rail and 37.3 miles (60 kilometers) of bus rapid transit, or BRT.

As set forth in figure 3-1, The Big Move plans to more than double transit users, as opposed to a much more modest increase to be expected based on population growth and current development trends. The number of people who live within a walkable distance of a transit station (defined as 1.2 miles, or 2 kilometers) would also double. The percentage of people commuting to work by transit, including walking or cycling, which is already high by North American standards, is predicted to rise substantially. This statistic recognizes that transit is needed to make walking, and to some extent cycling, part of a commute to work for many people. When this plan is fully implemented, there is predicted to be a decline in the greenhouse gases generated per person by transportation, reflecting the substitution of trains or BRT for less efficient

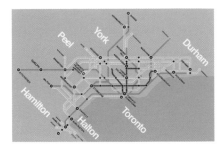

**Figure 3-2** Map of the comprehensive Metrolinx system in Toronto after completion of The Big Move in 2030. The yellow lines are new light rail and bus rapid transit (BRT) connections.

individual buses when making connections. The average commute time is expected to go down modestly, as opposed to increasing by almost half in the trend model.

Toronto's plans show how transit can become effective in a modern multicentered city, where jobs, shopping, and entertainment are dispersed among many locations. The yellow lines in figure 3-2 represent extensions to the existing radial system shown in red and green, which on completion will create a comprehensive system in which many different trips are possible. What is especially interesting is that most of the new elements are light-rail trains and BRT. Light rail is a familiar technology, somewhere between a train and a traditional streetcar. Light-rail trains generally have their own right-of-way or exclusive traffic lane and stop much less frequently than traditional street railways. Most of the new transit systems in the United States and Canada are radial systems using light rail; examples are in Dallas, San Diego, and Portland, Oregon, which also has a local streetcar as a downtown distributor. BRT is as different from the familiar city bus as light rail is from old-fashioned streetcars. It is a far less capital-intensive alternative that can provide many of the advantages of rail transit; thus, it puts transit within range of many cities and suburban areas that cannot support the costs of building a rail system.

## Bus Rapid Transit, a More Affordable Alternative

Typically, buses are slow. They can't move faster than the rest of the traffic on the road, they stop too often, and they take a long time to load and unload passengers. Most of the day, it is a long wait for the next bus. Many of the people who depend on buses use them because they have no other choice. Bus use is an important inequality issue because having to take a bus for a substantial distance usually means a long, slow trip. BRT is a way of using buses to move people at speeds and in numbers that are comparable to light-rail transit, at a far lower capital cost. With BRT systems, the people who have to depend on buses for transit can have an upgraded experience, and others who currently drive can find BRT an attractive option.

BRT requires an exclusive bus lane, one not shared with cars. The stops are spaced in a similar way to a rail transit system. At the stops, passengers board from a special platform where people buy tickets from machines before anyone boards the bus. When the bus arrives, it is longer than an ordinary bus and has special wide doors so that many people can get off or board at once. When the bus lanes cross intersections with other streets, a special technology—activated either by the driver or by sensors in the road—changes the traffic light at the intersection, giving the bus transit vehicle the right-of-way.

BRT began in Curitiba, Brazil, in the mid-1970s under the direction of Mayor Jamie Lerner, who was also an innovative leader in many other areas, such as job creation, floodplain management, and rubbish and garbage collection. The rapidly growing city clearly needed a transit system, and the only affordable option was to use buses. Rails for transit on streets or on separate rights-of-way need to be supported by strong foundations, which require digging up the street and often relocating utilities. Trains can only go up and down hills at maximum gradient of 1 or 2 percent, and not for long periods, so a rail transit route is likely to need bridges and tunnels to keep the system relatively level. Underground rail systems can be kept level and they cause the least disruption to traffic and real estate, but they are at least five times more expensive to build than surface rail systems. In Curitiba, an essentially radial main-line BRT system is connected to a variety of other bus transit corridors to create a comprehensive system without the construction costs associated with building rails (figure 3-3). As the system developed, Curitiba introduced a series of improvements, including three-part articulated buses so that the number of passengers per driver comes close to those found on light-rail trains and a method of collecting fares before passengers board, using raised platforms and multiple entry and exit doors on the buses. Today, BRT systems inspired by Curitiba can be found in many major cities, and acceptance of bus transit technology continues to increase.

Figure 3-4 shows a BRT trunk-line system in Istanbul where the bus transit has its own right-of-way in the middle of a major traffic artery and operates with stations that are similar to those used by conventional rail transit. An

**Figure 3-3** This photo offers a glimpse of Curitiba's BRT system, which operates on streets and highways and has become the prototype for BRT lines in many places. Note the articulated buses, which have a capacity similar to light-rail vehicles.

**Figure 3-4** This BRT system in Istanbul works like a rail line. There is room for tracks to be introduced later, but such a conversion might well not improve service unless four- or five-car trains were needed.

example from Bangkok (figure 3-5) shows a BRT vehicle stopped at a station. Having wide doors and a platform level with the vehicle speeds up getting off and boarding and avoids having individual passengers negotiate steps through narrow doors one at a time. The rendering in figure 3-6 shows part of Toronto's Big Move, a BRT line currently under construction along Highway 7 East near Valleymeade in an already densely developed suburban area just north of the Toronto city boundary.

## Leveraging the Transit and Real-Estate Connection

The connection between transit and real-estate investment is demonstrated in most cities that developed before World War II. These cities have corridors of more intense development along what used to be streetcar routes, even when the streetcars have been replaced by buses. Where rail rapid transit operates, there is usually more intense development immediately around the stations. Research related to more recent transit lines shows significant increases in residential and commercial property values within walking distances of transit stations.[3]

It is axiomatic in transit planning that people are much more likely to use transit if a station is within a ten-minute walk of where they live or where they are going. At an average walking speed of 3 miles an hour (about 5 kilometers

**Figure 3-5** A BRT vehicle that runs on city streets in Bangkok, Thailand. The central doors and raised platform speed up exits and entrances. In this kind of system, passengers buy tickets before boarding.

**Figure 3-6** Rendering of a BRT system under construction in the greater Toronto region as part of *The Big Move*. Stops will have ticket machines, vehicles will be articulated double buses running on a dedicated right-of-way, and stations for each direction are offset to save width needed for the right-of-way.

an hour), a ten-minute walk takes you about half a mile (a little less than a kilometer). People are even more likely to use transit if the station is within a five-minute walk. Spacing transit stations about 1 mile (1.6 kilometers) apart means that all along the line anyone who lives or works within half a mile from a station is no more than a ten-minute walk from transit. This concept is often illustrated by showing a transit corridor as a chain of ten-minute walking circles around each station.

There is a well-known argument against new transit systems—"No one will ride them"—but it is difficult to measure demand for a service that is not yet offered. The number of people using completed transit systems almost always exceeds official predictions. A vivid example is the Canada Line in Vancouver's Skytrain system, which opened in 2009 for the 2010 Olympics. By 2011, it had almost reached its 2021 ridership target, well before development around stations has consolidated, when ridership can be expected to increase even more.

The potential for transit-oriented development can be enhanced by selecting routes that run through areas that have development potential. The route for the light-rail line connecting Minneapolis and St. Paul was planned to create as much transit-oriented development as possible while connecting a series of locations with different established purposes. In densely populated areas, it can make sense to space stations only half a mile (just under a kilometer) apart, as in the downtown Minneapolis portion and the St. Paul suburban portion of this transit line, so that the walk to transit is five minutes or less, but improved transit access has to be balanced against creating too many local stations, which will slow down a transit trip. One reason that balancing regional transportation with transit is an important principle of ecodesign is that transit systems encourage more compact land-use patterns around stations, because some people will be attracted by the opportunity to make their trips on transit instead of driving their own cars. It takes time for this relationship to develop, and real-estate investors will often not make long-term commitments until they see the transit system in place.

## Transit Begins to Balance Car Use

When BART was being planned for the San Francisco area in the late 1960s and early 1970s, there was a controversy about whether to plan for development that would be attracted to the areas around the stations outside of downtown San Francisco. At the time, the prevailing opinion was that new development around stations in urban neighborhoods or suburbs was unlikely. Times have changed. A recent BART report listed eight completed developments around outlying BART stations, seven more approved, and seven in negotiations.[4] BART officials estimate the value of these developments at more than $3 billion. Looking at them from BART's point of view, the station-area developments represent an estimated 2.5 million new annual trips and almost $9 million in new annual revenue. From a regional development perspective, the almost 7,000 housing units and 500,000 square feet (a little less than 50,000

**Figure 3-7** Development around the Fruitvale Village station in Oakland, California, as seen from beneath the Bay Area Rapid Transit platform.

square meters) of office space at these stations removes some of the development pressure on unbuilt areas at the fringe of the metropolitan region. Among the completed projects are Fruitvale Village in Oakland (figure 3-7), the Pleasant Hill Center in Contra Costa County, and downtown Hayward on the East Bay.

The first line of the Vancouver Skytrain was completed in time for the opening of Vancouver's Expo '86, but it took some time for its development potential to begin to be realized. The 33-acre (13.4-hectare) Collingwood Village at a suburban stop along this line, was begun in 1990 by Concert Properties, but not completed until 2006. Today, it includes 2,500 condominium and rental apartments. The Skytrain stop is just visible at the far left of the aerial view shown in figure 3-8.

Since 1990, Los Angeles has opened two subway lines, four light-rail surface lines, and two BRT lines. The Gold Line, a light-rail connection from East Los Angeles through downtown and out to Pasadena, opened in 2003. The development around the Del Mar Station near Old Town Pasadena was actually begun in 2001 in anticipation of the new line, which, in that area, followed an old railway right-of-way. This development includes 347 apartments and 20,000 square feet (around 2,000 square meters) of retail. There is also a 1,200-car parking garage to accommodate commuters as well as residents. Pasadena's old Santa Fe Railway depot, which was on the site, was

**Figure 3-8** Collingwood Village, a high-density development at a stop on the Skytrain in Vancouver. This line was completed in time for Expo '86. Construction by Concert Properties of the 33-acre (13.4-hectare) development took from 1990 to 2006. The station is just visible in the far left of this photograph.

dismantled and rebuilt over the parking garage as part of the central courtyard (figure 3-9).

The Pearl District in Portland, Oregon, was rezoned from industry to a mixed-use neighborhood in the mid-1980s. The Portland Streetcar, which started operating in 2001, is the downtown distributor for the regional light-rail system, which had begun operating in 1986. Portland now has four lines that link the eastern and western sides of the metro region, with an extension to the airport. The streetcar ties the Pearl District to the light-rail system, which, as we described in chapter 1, helped create a major transformation of

an old industrial area into a vibrant location for both residents and businesses, all carefully planned and managed by the local government (figure 3-10).

Charlotte, North Carolina's Blue Line, a light-rail system operating in an existing rail right-of-way, opened in 2007 and is the first segment of what will be a larger regional transit system proposed in various forms since the 1980s. The line runs through an industrial corridor originally created by a freight railroad, although it is close to desirable residential districts. At the New Bern Station, southwest of the center of Charlotte, Fountains Southend apartment complex is being marketed for its transit connection. Residents can wait in the lobby, following the progress of the next train on a monitor. The station platform is just outside the building, which appears in the background of figure 3-11.

Perhaps the most spectacular recent example of the potential transformative power of transit-oriented development has been created by the extension of the Washington Metro System through Tysons Corner in suburban Virginia on the way to connect with Dulles Airport. Tysons Corner grew up after the completion of the Washington Beltway in the 1960s at the junction of the Beltway with local routes 7 and 123 as well as the access highway to Dulles. Tysons Corner, not so long ago a rural intersection with just a convenience store and a gas station, now covers 4.25 square miles (11 square kilometers)

**Figure 3-10** The Portland Streetcar, the downtown distributor for the region's light-rail system, has helped energize the mixed-use Pearl District in downtown Portland, Oregon.

**Figure 3-11** The New Bern station of the light-rail Blue Line, which follows an existing rail right-of-way southwest of Charlotte, North Carolina, is beginning to generate residential development in what had been a predominantly industrial corridor.

and accommodates 105,000 jobs and 17,000 residents, more than many traditional downtowns. Joel Garreau, in his 1991 book *Edge City, Life on the New Frontier*,[5] enthusiastically presented Tysons Corner as a new kind of urban place that might not meet the expectations of city planners and might not even be liked by the people who use it, but it was nevertheless what was really happening.

Garreau helped people understand "edge cities" as a new urban phenomenon developing all over North America. More critical observers have commented that these new kinds of cities are spectacularly inefficient because of their total dependency on automobiles for access. Now Tysons Corner is about to have four transit stations on the Washington Metro's Silver Line to Dulles Airport. According to the comprehensive plan for Tysons Corner, recently prepared by Fairfax County in anticipation of the new transit, almost 1.5 square miles (3.9 square kilometers) of the land at Tysons Corner has been occupied by parking, most of it at grade.[6] Figure 3-12's aerial photo of existing development in the county's plan with the four new station locations superimposed on it shows the way that office parks, shopping malls, and apartment clusters are surrounded by parking lots as they spread across the Tysons Corner landscape, a familiar pattern but at a much larger scale than usual. There is market demand for denser development at Tysons Corner, but the regional road system has become too congested to support it. Transit access will unlock this growth. The plan is for 100,000 residents and 200,000 jobs by 2050, and the county is already approving substantial increments of new development within walking distance of the new stations. The master street plan (figure 3-13) shows the street and block pattern that Fairfax County is establishing around the four Metro stations. The smaller blocks make pedestrian movement easier and let people access buildings directly from a sidewalk rather than by crossing a parking lot. Retrofitting the area for transit that runs on an elevated line instead of underground does not permit the same integration of transit and buildings that can be found in downtown Washington. It will be a

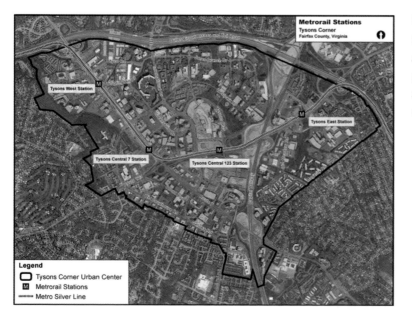

**Figure 3-12** Four new Washington Metro stations, for the line that extends to Dulles Airport, are shown superimposed on an aerial photo of Tysons Corner, Virginia. The photo also shows how automobile access required much of the land to be devoted to parking.

**Figure 3-13** Fairfax County's plan for a network of new streets for Tysons Corner creates traditional urban blocks that will accommodate denser, walkable new development.

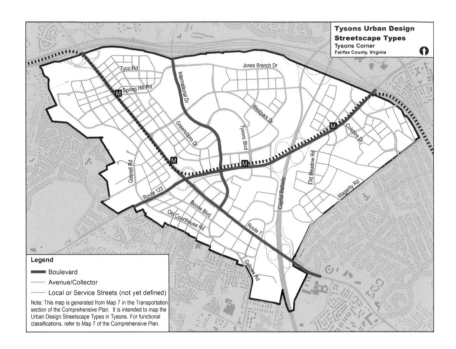

long time, if ever, before the walk from a Tysons Corner station is a completely urban experience, but a short walk will bring transit passengers to urban destinations. The first proposed buildings look like downtown development anywhere, but in the context of Tysons Corner they are a radical new departure. Even when the comprehensive plan is built out, cars will still be a primary way to go to and from Tysons Corner, but the access system will be balanced. More people will live there and be able to walk or take transit to their destinations, people can commute to work on the train, and going out to lunch or doing an errand won't always require getting into a car.

## Restructuring Suburban Corridors with Bus Rapid Transit

The way that transit is transforming Tysons Corner suggests that adding transit could also transform other suburban locations. Although rail transit is too expensive to be built in most suburbs, BRT could perform a similar role. The photomontage of a proposed express bus system for Staten Island, a borough of New York City, shown in figure 3-14, illustrates how exclusive bus lanes can fit into an arterial street lined with small commercial buildings and parking lots, a "commercial strip" such as can be found in cities and suburbs all over North America. Although the buses pictured are typical city buses and the rendering doesn't show any special boarding platforms or ticket machines, special vehicles and other elements of BRT service could easily be added within a similar configuration. Ordinary bus routes do not usually generate real-estate investment because it is so easy to change a route or move a bus stop, but BRT represents a serious commitment to rights-of-way and stations. Much of the development along suburban commercial strips consists of small retail buildings surrounded by at-grade parking, a very inefficient use of land. The same corridor could accommodate apartments with ground-floor retail and possibly some small office buildings. Such development types can also support parking garages, which would allow the land to be used more effectively than with commercial strips. With good transit access, development at a more urban scale could be attracted to commercial strips.

An interesting thought experiment about the ways that BRT service could transform the typical commercial strip was prepared by noted transit expert Robert Cervero and four colleagues at the Institute of Transportation Studies at the University of California, Berkeley.[7] They selected an operating bus transit line in Stockton, California, and looked closely at one of the station stops. Within the five-minute walking distance of the stop, they found a typical suburban pattern, with commercial buildings surrounded by at-grade parking. Similar development continues to the south within the ten-minute walking distance. The properties along the street are developed at such a low density that they can be considered to be a land bank. The study made simulations of potential development along the corridor, including one that showed a Curitiba-like bus system with amenities for bicycles and pedestrians, which would enable the development of apartments along the street fronts including ground-floor shops. The building types pictured are like the four- and five-story apartments with ground-floor shops that are currently being built along commercial streets in many cities. It would take a generation to complete such a transformation, and it is much easier to consider it as a possibility than it would be to achieve it in reality, but the potential is there.

Cities and suburbs are beginning to build BRT lines that run through commercial corridors. One example is the Health Line that runs east from downtown Cleveland along Euclid Avenue, a street where the development was already relatively dense, and connects downtown to the University Circle area and the hospitals that give the line its name. In the Seattle region, King County's Metro Transit has introduced six RapidRide lines. RapidRide offers ten-minute headways at peak periods and fifteen-minute headways most of the day, seven days a week, with message signs available at stations to let passengers know when the next bus is coming. The stops have well-lighted shelters and fare-card machines so that passengers can enter the vehicles at the midbus doors, thus reducing the amount of time needed for boarding at each stop. Once on the bus, there are comfortable seats and free WiFi. There are no exclusive bus lanes, but buses can use high-occupancy-vehicle lanes,

**Figure 3-14** Illustration of a proposed express bus system running on bus-only lanes in suburban Staten Island, a borough of New York City. With longer vehicles and raised platforms, this route could become a true BRT system. This photomontage shows one way that BRT lanes can fit into typical suburban commercial strips.

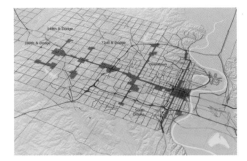

**Figure 3-15** Map of the major commercial corridors in Omaha, Nebraska, which could be served by BRT, with a main, east-west line connected to lines along the north-south commercial streets.

and extra lane space has been added at stations to allow a loaded bus to go around another bus that is still picking up passengers. In addition, the bus driver can signal traffic lights to hold the green light longer, or switch a red light to a green light faster, so that the buses can keep moving through heavy traffic. The intent is for RapidRide to offer a service that is comparable to light-rail or a complete BRT system.

The RapidRide service is expected to stimulate real-estate investment along the routes. The B Line, for example, runs from downtown Bellevue to downtown Redmond. Although much of the route is already densely developed, new transit-related development has already taken place at Overlake, about the midpoint of the route, and near the Redmond terminal. A regional Bus Rapid Transit and Land Use Initiative Partnership has been created to help capitalize on the opportunities created by the six RapidRide lines.[8] Comparable improvements in bus service are within the reach of many communities. Figure 3-15 shows the most important commercial corridors in Omaha, Nebraska. Such corridors could become the map of a future BRT system, and the transit, in turn, could promote denser, more walkable development in the commercial corridors. People along the corridor would need fewer car trips, and the new development could reduce some of the growth pressures that are causing Omaha to keep annexing and urbanizing farmland at the edge of the city.

## Enhancing Traffic Safety, Walking, and Cycling

Most urban and suburban streets today have been designed to facilitate traffic; to put it another way, they are designed for speed. There has been a tacit assumption that some proportion of pedestrians and cyclists are going to be hit by cars, trucks, and buses and that some occupants of vehicles are going to die in collisions. Although being on a road in developed countries is much less dangerous than it is in countries where driving is still a relatively new experience, there are still a great many deaths every year. In 2010, according to the World Health Organization,[9] there were 35,490 traffic-related deaths in the United States, 2,296 in Canada, 3,992 in France, 6,625 in Japan, and 278 in Sweden. The number of deaths per 100,000 people was 11.4 in the United States, 6.8 in Canada, 6.4 in France, 5.2 in Japan, and 3.0 in Sweden. Sweden had the lowest number of traffic deaths per 100,000 population of any country other than very small places like San Marino, which has a population of about 30,000 people and reported no traffic-related deaths in 2010.

Sweden adopted a national policy in 1997 that any traffic-related death or serious injury is unacceptable and that the country should aim to have no traffic deaths at all. This policy is called Vision Zero. Implementing Vision Zero requires seat belts and air bags but also computer-aided collision avoidance. Other important implementation measures include reduction of speed limits, severe speed limit enforcement using cameras, and changes to the configurations of streets and highways. One major street-design change in Sweden has been the placement of collision barriers to separate traffic traveling in opposite directions on major streets. Many other changes are required for local streets, bicycle paths, and sidewalk designs.

Mayor Bill de Blasio has adopted Vision Zero in New York City, although implementing street designs that reduce traffic fatalities actually began under his predecessor, Michael Bloomberg. Increasing seat-belt use, requiring air bags, and safety education efforts have brought down traffic fatalities substantially in New York City since 1990. According to the city authorities, at locations where the Department of Transportation has made major engineering changes since 2005, fatalities have decreased by 34 percent, twice the rate of improvement at other locations. De Blasio's goal is to implement fifty comparable street intersection or corridor improvements per year.

Changes already implemented on First and Second Avenues in Manhattan provide one example of a configuration that can reduce traffic fatalities. The two avenues form a pair of one-way streets. The new configuration adds a dedicated bus lane; a buffered bicycle lane at curbside, with parking outboard of the bicycle lane; very clearly marked crosswalks; and well-maintained lane designations. At a more complicated intersection in Queens, where one of the streets comes in on a diagonal, the reorganization reduces the number of traffic movements, delays turns to give pedestrians a head start, lengthens and widens medians to define lanes more clearly, and puts strongly marked pedestrian crosswalks on all four sides of the intersection. There do not happen to be bus or bicycle lanes in this location. The New York City Department of Transportation reports that these improvements have eliminated 63 percent of all crashes that result in injuries at this intersection.

Street lighting and traffic signal timing are also important tools in making streets safer. Law enforcement and education clearly have to be another part of achieving Vision Zero. New York City statistical analysis from 2008 to 2012 indicates that 53 percent of accidents were caused by dangerous decisions made by drivers, 30 percent by bad moves made by pedestrians, and the remaining 17 percent were caused by a combination of both. The mayor is initiating a series of law-enforcement improvements, including cameras, and is stepping up education efforts. Because accidents at a low speed are significantly more survivable than those at higher speeds, the city government has successfully lobbied New York State to reduce the speed limit in New York

City from 30 miles per hour to 25 miles per hour (from 48 to 40 kilometers an hour) except on streets specially designated by the city council as higher-speed streets.

Traffic-related deaths have been going down generally because of seat belts, air bags, and other engineering improvements in cars. Thirty states in the United States have also adopted some variation of the zero-death policy goal. These policies have been effective in further reducing fatalities, but the positive trend has been because of better law enforcement and improved emergency medical responses. Few places have yet made a commitment to design-based safety improvements, but there is clearly tremendous potential in making safety rather than traffic movement the highest design priority.

Designing streets for safety rather than traffic movement reinforces another important street design trend, sometimes called complete streets. At a district and neighborhood scale, walking is the simplest and most efficient means of transportation. People will walk for five or ten minutes if the route is comfortable, safe, and interesting. Bicycles are even more efficient—and faster than walking—but cyclists should have access to a safe, separated pathway and to appropriate storage and changing facilities at the destination. Bicycling is also good exercise, although electric bicycles, heavily used in China, are a less vigorous option. Bicycle parking problems can be reduced with bike-share systems so that people can pick up and drop off bicycles at central points. Places that are designed to facilitate walking and travel by bicycle will make a big contribution to sustainability.

Achieving this result requires reversing the usual traffic engineering priorities. It means making pedestrian movement the most important factor, followed by bicycles, transit, servicing for buildings, and finally, in last place, traffic movement by cars and trucks. The concept of complete streets also emphasizes landscaping, well-designed paving materials, environmentally sound stormwater management, rationalizing of signs and street furniture, and lighting that creates a pleasant environment for people. We will have much more to say about the design of such streets in chapter 5.

## Balancing Long-Distance Transportation with High-Speed Rail

Figure 3-16, a diagrammatic map by the U.S. Federal Highway Administration (FHA), shows interstate and other important highways that were congested at peak traffic periods in 2007. Figure 3-17, another map by the FHA, projects the congestion that is likely to be taking place in 2030. If nothing is done to reduce traffic and this prediction comes true, highway travel by cars and trucks between many U.S. urban destinations will be dysfunctional for much of each day. The congestion will be caused by population growth to 368

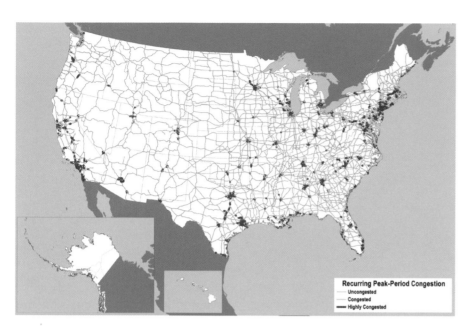

**Figure 3-16** The red areas on the map show peak period congestion on the U.S. National Highway System in 2007. The National Highway System includes the interstates and other highways that together constitute a system of national strategic importance.

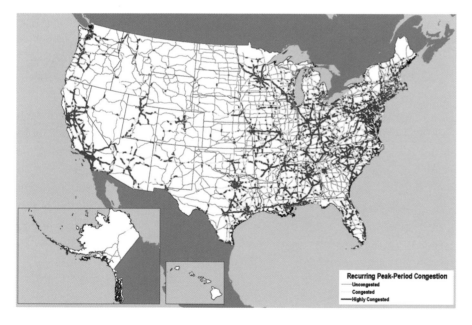

**Figure 3-17** The red areas on the map show peak period congestion on the U.S. National Highway System in 2030 if current trends continue. This projection shows that traffic trends are unsustainable.

million people from 317 million in 2013, more trips, and increasing numbers of vehicles. As noted at the beginning of this chapter, there is likely to be a 21 percent increase in light vehicles on U.S. roads by 2030 and a 27 percent increase in trucks and other heavy vehicles.

Population predictions by county show that much of the future increase in U.S. population will be concentrated in a series of multicity regions, where

**Figure 3-18** Map by the Center for Quality Growth and Regional Development at the Georgia Institute of Technology shows the counties where much of U.S. population growth is expected to take place in the next few decades. This analysis shows urban regions growing together to form multicity megaregions. Not all of each county is urbanized, however, so the map overstates the size of the megaregions in some places, particularly in the Southwest, where counties can be very large.

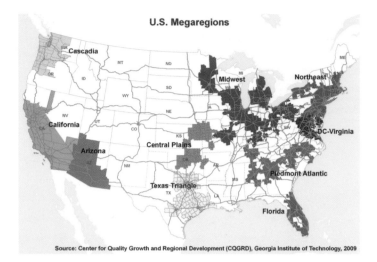

existing metropolitan areas are spreading out and meeting one another. Figure 3-18, a map prepared by the Center for Quality Growth and Regional Development at the Georgia Institute of Technology, shows this development trend forming ten multicity regions, or "megaregions." The map exaggerates urbanization somewhat because it is based on counties, and not all the land in a county that will become predominantly urban by statistical measurements is actually part of a city or suburb. The overstatement of urbanization is particularly visible in southern California and Arizona, where some of the counties are very large. Other demographic studies define the boundaries and numbers of multicity regions somewhat differently. There is no disagreement, however, that multicity regions exist, are spreading out, and will continue to be the places where much of the population and economic growth in the United States will be concentrated. They are also the places where most of the additional vehicles and vehicular trips will be found. The FHA's map of future highway congestion coincides closely with Georgia Tech's map of multicity regions.

The American Society of Civil Engineers gave the U.S. highway system a "D" in its 2013 report on the condition of national infrastructure.[10] There is a big backlog of unfunded repairs needed just to keep existing highways operating. In addition, solving the predicted highway congestion using road improvements alone will require costly highway widenings, double-decking, and other major engineering works, and some of them will have negative impacts on surrounding development.

Most other developed countries do not try to solve highway congestion problems with highways alone. Japan created the prototype high-speed rail intercity passenger system beginning in the 1960s. An international high-speed rail system has been taking shape in Europe since the 1980s, with most major cities now, or soon to be, part of the network. Korea and Taiwan have high-speed rail. China has recently made a massive investment in high-speed rail, linking all its major cities, often over large distances. All these countries have modern highway systems, but they are balancing their systems. Some long-distance trips are more efficient by car or bus, others by air, and at other times it can make more sense to go by rail.

In 2009, President Barack Obama announced funding for high-speed rail in the United States as part of the economic stimulus planned after the fiscal crisis of 2008. Comparing figure 3-18 with the high-speed rail map that President Obama presented (figure 3-19) makes it clear that the future vision for high-speed rail in the United States is about making connections within multicity regions. No one is suggesting taking high-speed rail from New York City to Los Angeles or from Chicago to Houston. Even within a multicity region, if the trip is more than about 500 miles (about 800 kilometers), it will probably make more sense to fly. Although not labeled on figure 3-19, the terminus for the northern New England high-speed rail system is shown as Montreal, and the Pacific Northwest system is shown as terminating in Vancouver. It would make sense for a future Canadian system to connect on the other side of Lakes Huron and Erie from Detroit up to Toronto and on to Montreal and Quebec City, if and when the projected U.S. system is built. The initial reception for

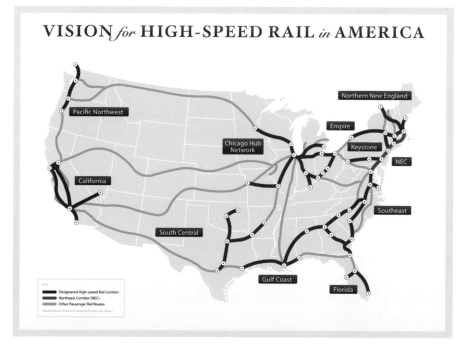

Figure 3-19 President Barack Obama presented this map of future high-speed rail lines at a White House news conference in 2009. The routes make connections within the megaregions shown in figure 3-18. High-speed rail is most effective for distances up to about 500 miles (800 kilometers).

the president's offer of federal transportation money for high-speed rail was not encouraging. To the consternation and dismay of business leaders in Florida, the governor turned down the federal money. The governor of Wisconsin also turned down the money for what would have been a link from Chicago to Minneapolis via Milwaukee. Much of the stimulus money designated for high-speed rail has subsequently been reallocated to California, which is currently the most likely place for true high-speed rail to be constructed in the United States.

Amtrak's Northeast corridor line is the most effective conventional intercity rail system now operating in the United States. Upgrading it to high-speed rail will require "next generation" improvements, which means a new route that uses tunnels to get through Philadelphia, New York City, and into the Boston terminus. The technology is available, and the plan, if implemented, would provide true high-speed rail service to the most densely populated region of the United States. Official plans say that this change won't be complete until 2040 at the earliest.

Building high-speed rail is about balancing the nation's transportation system, which in addition to being too heavily weighted toward cars is also too heavily weighted toward air transport. A high proportion of the flights in and out of U.S. airports are for destinations only a few hundred miles away, trips which could easily be made on high-speed rail if that alternative were available. One report, prepared for the Federal Aviation Administration, projects the capacity needs at U.S. airports by 2025,[11] and of the fourteen airports and eight metro regions shown to need major improvements by 2025, all are within the projected U.S. high-speed rail network. Increasing capacity at an airport often means extending runways or adding new runways, which requires expensive land acquisition and very often must overcome powerful political opposition. There will also always be a limit to how many planes the airspace around an airport can accommodate. Diverting some of the passengers for shorter flights to high-speed rail service could free existing capacity for increases in longer-distance travel.

There is relatively little political controversy in the United States about spending money to improve airports or widen highways, although there have been recent shortfalls in the money for highway repairs and construction that comes from taxes on gasoline. Federal taxes on gasoline have not been raised since 1993. This repair backlog clearly needs to be funded to avoid more highway collapses like the 2007 failure of the Route 35W bridge in Minneapolis, but there have been major political obstacles to raising the money for road repair, and finding the money needed to avoid projected highway congestion will be even more difficult. Some of that highway money could be spent more effectively on high-speed rail, and the overall costs of avoiding congestion would be reduced. The benefits for the construction industry would still be there; it should be a win-win trade-off for the public. Right now, that logic does not translate into political reality.

## Providing Connections to High-Speed Rail in Cities and Airports

What happens to the land immediately around high-speed rail stations will be important for the success of high-speed rail when it is built in North America. The opportunities are comparable to those around transit stations. They will be particularly useful for business, such as being able to have a back office in a lower-cost location one station away from a big-city main headquarters building. A report by SPUR (the name comes from the organization's original name as the San Francisco Planning and Urban Research Association) urges that California not make the same mistake that was made when the BART system opened with few plans for development around the stations. The SPUR report recommends that there should be a detailed design and development plan for every high-speed rail station in an urban center. Conversely, SPUR is also concerned that development should not be drawn to rural areas near stations planned in California's agricultural Central Valley and urges regulations to limit new development there.[12]

Another major issue will be connections between trains and airports. Many of the people who take short airplane flights are making connections to longer flights. If high-speed rail is going to relieve congestion at major airports, it needs to go directly to them. Figure 3-20 shows the high-speed rail platforms at the Frankfurt airport, which is a major hub for international travel. Frankfurt is easily accessible by rail from many cities, and coordinated tickets can be purchased for train/plane journeys from several major urban centers in Germany. The high-speed rail stop at Charles de Gaulle Airport near Paris also allows for coordinated train/plane travel. Shanghai Hongqiao International Airport is another example of an effective high-speed rail interface with a major air terminal. If the Florida high-speed rail line is ever built, there would be train-to-plane connections at the Orlando, Fort Lauderdale, and Miami airports. If the line between Chicago and Minneapolis is built, there ought to be a stop at O'Hare, which could make a big difference to airport operation in the midwestern United States. High-speed rail in California is planned to connect directly to the San Francisco International Airport and also to two regional airports near Los Angeles: Burbank, north of the central city, and Ontario to the east. In a second phase, the southern terminal of the line will probably be at the San Diego airport.

In the Northeast corridor, there are already connections from the Amtrak line at Marshall Baltimore/Washington International Airport and at the

**Figure 3-20** Airports and high-speed rail systems work together in parts of Western Europe. This photo shows the high-speed rail station at the Frankfurt airport.

Newark Liberty Airport. Unfortunately, not every train stops at these airports, and frequent delays on the railroad lead to uncertainty about making connections. After the rejection of high-speed rail in Florida, private investors have proposed a conventional rail line, All Aboard Florida, to connect the Orlando airport to downtown Miami via West Palm Beach and Fort Lauderdale using existing rights-of-way. The service is intended to be similar to trains currently running along Amtrak's Northeast corridor. Amtrak's long-range plan for the Northeast corridor envisages Frankfurt-style direct connections at the Philadelphia and Newark Liberty airports from high-speed trains running in a tunnel under the terminals. This kind of connection would permit true integration of air and rail service.

Right now, however, it doesn't look as if high-speed rail will be available in the United States by 2030, except perhaps in California, and thus will not be a means to ease intercity highway congestion. The federal government, however, is continuing to fund incremental improvements to existing passenger lines that will speed up railway operations and make them more competitive with both highway travel and short-distance airline flights. In the Northeast corridor, Amtrak already diverts substantial numbers of passengers from taking planes or driving. As incremental improvements take hold around the country, railway trips will become more competitive with other modes. For example, conventional train service from St. Louis to Kansas City at speeds comparable to those attained in the Northeast corridor would be faster door-to-door for central destinations than either driving or taking a plane. The same can be said for the Toronto-Ottawa and Ottawa-Montreal rail services in Canada. Local transit systems within the multicity regions also have the potential to take many vehicle trips off the interstate highways, clearing the way for longer-distance travel.

## Creating Consumer Preferences for Balanced Transportation

Rebalancing transportation to make improvements in urban organization will require substantial government investments, which we suggest can be diverted from funds that would otherwise be spent on futile attempts to make highways less congested and on the construction of hugely controversial new airport runways. The political feasibility of this change and the effectiveness of new transportation alternatives, however, will depend on whether the alternatives can compete with the appeal of cars. Competition includes relative convenience and costs, but it also has to do with the design of the trip: its comfort, safety, attractiveness, ease, and the contribution it makes to a person's self-image. The whole experience of these alternatives has to be widely appealing to people, who should feel relatively neutral about the type of transportation and make their decisions based on the nature of the trip. If the destination is close by, walking or biking will be the natural choice; if people are in a hurry or have a disability or infirmities, they will need a car or a taxi; for the everyday commuter trip, BRT or rail rapid transit will naturally be preferred; and if you are going grocery shopping, on holiday, or to an out-of-the-way location, your car will still be what you want. For trips of a few hundred miles within urban regions, rail—and especially high-speed rail—can become a better alternative if the door-to-door time by rail is shorter than going to the airport, going through security, and waiting for the plane and then taking the flight itself. As a result of these natural and spontaneous choices, the shifts will be achieved between the high-impact and lower-impact modes so that both environmental and civic repairs will become practical.

# 4. Making Cities More Livable and Environmentally Compatible

**C**urrent development regulations in the United States and Canada are derived from laws and practices that began more than a century ago. The people writing and enacting these laws saw their job as solving specific problems; they did not believe that they were being asked to understand or manage the great variety of considerations that create a successful city. The result is a hodgepodge of standards and requirements. Early regulations were responses to industrial pollution, the tall buildings that new technology introduced into cities, and the unsanitary conditions that had been created by a previous century of almost unregulated urban growth, which created more and more situations in which property owners caused problems for their tenants and neighbors. Later, rapidly growing car ownership produced another wave of regulations to accommodate parking and faster-moving traffic, generally erring on the side of automobile needs when trade-offs had to be made. Throughout this period, regulations that recognized the natural environment were noticeably absent, primarily because the implications of ecological impacts were not yet widely understood or valued.

Essentially conceived as policing mechanisms, these laws sought to bring order to the complexity of the city by regulating a short list of key physical variables in perhaps inevitably simplistic ways. They succeeded in preventing the worst that could happen to a city or town, but they also often prevent the best. Almost nothing can be built today without some kind of regulatory permit or approval. Although most regulations were amended in the 1960s to allow more tall buildings and add special procedures for large properties, they also multiplied the number of separate zones, making unnecessary distinctions about lot sizes and types of commercial activities. Most development regulations have become seriously out of date and increasingly unrelated to current development trends but are so deeply embedded in property values that administrators can be understandably hesitant to review and change them.

Supposedly objective, these regulations have distorted the shape and character of urban life in ways not predicted or understood when they were first applied. Who thought about the impact on walking through a neighborhood when the wide street-corner radius needed for fast-moving traffic became dominant in local street design (figure 4-1)? Who thought about the impact on lively streetscapes when rigidly applied ratios for the number of restaurant washrooms limited or denied permits for extra sidewalk seating on pleasant days? It is not that traffic circulation and providing restrooms are not important, but that design criteria for cities should not be set by optimizing a single factor.

The extraordinary diversity of historic cities that most people enthusiastically admire, such as the part of Quebec City shown in figure 4-2, would not meet regulations in many places today; in fact, such diversity would be patently illegal. Another major problem is that governments continue to issue permits for the next new area in a city or suburb although the adverse effects of conventional development on the natural environment are now widely understood (figure 4-3). Regulatory authorities also seem uninformed about

Figure 4-1 Because of street standards that only consider traffic management and fire access, this street scene, which could be anywhere in suburban North America, is completely distorted from the tree-lined street with sidewalks and bikeways that residents would prefer.

**Figure 4-2** The intricacy of this lovely historic area in Quebec City would not be legal if proposed in today's cities.

**Figure 4-3** Because of regulatory requirements, the standard pattern of suburban sprawl continues to spread with little reference to the natural environment.

what happens to land values and the economics of development as a consequence of regulations. They are surprised when regulatory action either stymies development or offers excess, windfall profits. The relationship between regulations and urban land economics needs to be coordinated and managed to facilitate preferred development or forestall undesirable development. We have more to say about this issue in chapter 6. Not understanding the consequences of a government action does not relieve government of the responsibility for the result.

It may be tempting to say that if regulations are hampering desirable development, it is time to get rid of them, but managing development in the future city and suburb is not about deregulation. Regulations continue to be essential for managing the relationships among urban activities and between settlement and setting. In a free and energetic society, government is needed to coordinate private development to maximize benefits and minimize unnecessary costs and undesirable side effects; there is an important public interest to be satisfied as we all go about pursuing our private interests. Indeed, a wider scope for regulations may be needed to deal with the environment and the effects of climate change, as well as other emerging considerations now important to the public. To improve the ability to choreograph development, we certainly need to reform regulations so that they do the job that is needed while leaving maximum flexibility to individuals and businesses to express themselves and realize their own objectives. A balance between necessary regulation and good development is definitely possible. One example of a carefully planned and regulated environment in Amsterdam that is nevertheless informal and accepts a variety of ways to live is shown in figure 4-4.

In this chapter, we look at the blind spots in current regulations. Then, we explore how new kinds of regulations can shape cities and suburbs to meet consumer needs and expectations in better ways and how regulations can also be made to recognize the natural setting and keep development compatible with it. Finally, we review the prototypical areas of metropolitan regions—from downtowns to historic inner-ring suburbs, to newer postwar housing tracts, to current community subdivisions in the outer suburbs—to identify what regulatory changes can improve these places and help preserve the natural environment.

## Three Blind Spots in Today's Development Regulations

Development regulations in North America today have three major blind spots. The first is that regulations treat land as a commodity to be divided among different uses rather than as a living, complex, integrated ecosystem. Regulatory maps usually show land without contours and devoid of specific

**Figure 4-4** New living patterns are being explored in the Netherlands within a responsive regulatory framework. This photo shows a good example from Amsterdam.

soil and hydrological conditions. There is often a serious mismatch between what is permitted—or required—and the actual ability of the landscape to survive such changes. For example, the usual limit on how steep a street can be is a 5 percent grade, which often mandates that bulldozers be brought in, the land stripped of all trees and vegetation, and the earth moved around in ways that substitute engineering for the natural ecology, as in an example from Colorado Springs, Colorado, shown in figure 4-5. This kind of radical regrading inevitably sets off a chain of consequences elsewhere in the ecosystem. Tolerable at a small scale, such blindness to natural systems becomes more and more of a problem as urbanization spreads out over the landscape, causing erosion of hillsides and streambeds and more frequent flooding. Rising tidal surges, sinking water tables, and growing forest fire dangers as a result of climate change will make currently unsustainable regulatory requirements even more of a problem than they are today.

The second blind spot is the almost universal prescription by regulators that both uses and densities should be separated, a requirement that is contrary to the natural human complexity of cities and particularly does not make sense in modern development situations. For example, regulations generally separate shopping from areas zoned for different types of houses. It is difficult to go from one to the other without a car, although the distances would be very walkable if the plan were different (figure 4-6). Separating industry from

**Figure 4-5** Conventional suburban development regulations not only permit radical stripping and regrading of the natural environment, they often require it.

**Figure 4-6** As shown in this aerial photo, this typical modern suburb separates uses and densities. This zoning practice is standard throughout North America.

**Figure 4-7** In Regina, Saskatchewan, lot and home sizes are the same throughout the subdivision, as is the practice in almost all North American suburbs.

residences and some businesses was necessary in the 1920s, but the degree of separation of different uses found in most zoning codes is not needed today because of changing technology and the dispersal of industry away from urban centers. Regulations that also segregate buildings by size as well as use make it even more difficult to build new compact, walkable centers, where a mix of retail and offices with townhouses and apartments would be appropriate. We now know clearly that urban success is about mixing uses and densities in an almost endless variety of ways.

A third blind spot is a system of zones based on arbitrary categories rather than functional segments of a city, such as neighborhoods, business centers, or campuses. Most zoning codes have many different residential zones, each requiring a single specific size for building lots, perpetuating social distinctions accepted in the 1920s but not acceptable today, spreading out urbanization unnecessarily, and contributing to making much of new housing unaffordable for ordinary families. Separating residential buildings by lot categories makes it difficult to create new versions of the walkable neighborhoods with mixed housing types found in older parts of cities and suburbs; instead, there is a seemingly endless succession of similar houses (figure 4-7).

A big part of the recipe for suburban sprawl can be found in same-sized-lot zoning and the narrow commercial corridors zoning establishes along major roads.

## Government Concerns versus Consumer Needs in Development Regulations

The regulatory framework and many of the specific regulations now shaping our cities were conceived and promulgated by public officials and local legislatures with very little input or overview by private citizens. There was little questioning of the implications that came with the oversimplification of city patterns because of the narrow way that regulatory interests were defined. The complexity of the city is engendered by a lively marketplace driven by consumer preferences (figure 4-8). Consumer attitudes are constantly

**Figure 4-8** Most people would like the intimacy and diversity of this street scene in Auckland, New Zealand, but it challenges the regulatory framework in North American cities.

changing, and in recent decades, consumers have become more and more demanding that the city deliver not just the basics of health, safety, and efficiency but also characteristics and qualities that offer a fulfilling urban experience on a day-to-day basis.

## The Need for an Experiential Perspective

In the contemporary world, the demand for desirable experiences is shaping all aspects of product offerings and services. This demand is about quality and style, but it is also about ethics and social and environmental responsibility. Responding to consumer demand requires an understanding of what the whole urban experience is about rather than just being concerned with basic functional requirements. Although following ecodesign principles absolutely requires professional expertise, it also needs to integrate the consumer perspective into the regulatory equation. It requires substantial and sustained involvement of people in the original design and ongoing management of regulations, not just as citizens, participating in a political process, but also as consumers, involved in a design process, shaping the kind of ambience and character that they want in the city. Just as citizen preferences and support are, in turn, shaped by the political experience, consumer preferences and support can also be shaped by the design experience, and can be shaped in positive directions. Including the design experience takes a new kind of planning and a new way of conceptualizing development, with an emphasis on how we perceive and engage with the city every day, and how the city affects our well-being. Just as experiential learning means lessons from firsthand involvement, we might call this process *experiential planning*. In any event, the objective is all about facilitating the very best that the city can offer so that it delivers feelings, sensations, and interactions that are meaningful and memorable for the most number of people, with opportunity for all to participate, as well as providing the basics of health and safety for all citizens.

## Building Demand for Sustainable Cities and Suburbs

The sustainable urban region, a whole metropolitan system compatible with its setting and offering economic and social opportunity, will only be a dream unless it is widely and happily embraced by an overwhelming majority of average consumers who are prepared to use their buying power coupled with their voting power to make it a reality. In Western Europe, particularly in the Scandinavian countries and the Netherlands, it appears that well-designed and sustainable development is becoming normal practice, not just because of government and developer initiatives, but also because of strong consumer support and acceptance of a sustainable lifestyle (figure 4-9). In North America, even with all the progress made in core cities and older suburbs over the

**Figure 4-9** A sustainable lifestyle in Rotterdam in the Netherlands is still the living situation of only a minority in North America.

last several decades to draw people back, only about 5 percent of the housing market has been shifted away from less-sustainable alternatives. As many as 70 percent of North Americans still prefer the familiar car-based suburban development of large lots, commercial corridors, and widely dispersed destinations (figure 4-10). Although there is often a lack of affordable housing in sustainable settings, a bigger factor is the simple preference that so many people have for what they see as the benefits of suburban life and that so many of those benefits are not replicated in the more sustainable alternatives now on offer. Existing suburban development represents a huge investment of wealth, energy, and loyalty by residents, and it is there for people who really want it, but, as we saw in chapter 2, continuing this kind of development to meet population growth and also to draw people farther away from urban centers is not going to be sustainable. A big job for the upcoming generation of city builders is to develop as little dispersed suburbia as possible, and thus bring people back to the many development opportunities within places that

**Figure 4-10** Most North Americans say they prefer this suburban pattern, although building more of it is not going to be sustainable in the future. This typical North American example is in Sacramento, California.

are already urbanized, by tapping latent demand for more compact mixed-use centers and walkable neighborhoods. More important, attracting people to more compact, sustainable development requires building new demand from household sectors that have shied away from such alternatives in the past. How do cities, and also suburbs, build such consumer demand?

There are two directions that have great potential. First, we have to think how we can marry the consumer aspiration for good day-to-day experiences—things like safety, privacy, reasonably priced homes of an adequate size, good schools, and spacious landscape—with the urban forms that secure environmental compatibility, such as improved transit, walkable places, complete neighborhoods, diversity, and a basic urban level of housing density. Second, we have to find better ways for the public and private sectors to work together, because successful urban regions need to have a tight integration of public and private realms, public and private activity, and public and private energy. Cities and suburbs will need to use public initiatives to create incentives for the right kind of private investment, while private investments can and should be building blocks toward implementing public plans, to the benefit of both. Well-crafted development regulations can be the means of moving in these directions.

To address consumer aspirations, we have to get back to designing the physicality of cities as was done in the past. Over the years, the planning profession has moved away from an emphasis on the physical shape of cities toward a seemingly more objective, policy-based way of regulating:

substituting floor-area and open-space ratios for more specific requirements, for example, or for physical urban design plans for buildings and public spaces. Fortunately, this practice is beginning to change. Planners have again become much more interested in shaping the city, but the way today's regulations are written deprives them of some of the tools they need.

Increased density, housing diversity, and transit are not widely popular with North American consumers, primarily because these qualities were implemented poorly in the past. Many contemporary dense developments, from garden apartments and townhouses to towers, are oppressively banal and utilitarian, partly because of overly categorical zoning and partly because of a limited number of standard building formulas used by developers. Transit systems often offer only slow trips and infrequent service along with crowding and a lack of privacy or amenities. It is no surprise that they are seen as second-class alternatives, and they certainly don't possess any hip or style factor.

What if planners and developers bring a strong component of enjoyable experience into all dense and mixed-use situations through very careful and very artful urban design? What if suburban commercial corridors can be rezoned to permit walkable, mixed-use development around bus rapid transit (BRT) stops as we described in chapter 3? These places could provide a range of more affordable housing than the typical suburban single-family home, and with the right amenities, they could compete more successfully with the attractiveness of a private house and yard. These alternatives can be achieved if development regulations are rewritten to encourage mixed uses in the right places and to permit higher densities in places served by reliable transit. Design excellence, use of better materials, safety and privacy measures, richer landscape, and other amenities can be brought into regulations and would make these housing choices more naturally appealing. What if these kinds of objectives became the driving agenda for the regulation and development management of cities and suburbs? There are no fundamental barriers to these possibilities.

Even if regulations change, however, we still face the hard job of actually making development happen that is both sustainable and popular. Here is where new expectations for public and private collaboration are going to be needed. Just building a few rows of townhouses within walking distance of a transit stop is not enough to move development toward more sustainable patterns, but what if planners and developers bring a strong agenda for creating desirable public places to reinforce better private development? What if we shift from meeting minimal functional requirements to encouraging beauty, complexity, and even caprice across the whole fabric of the city, within both the private and the public realms?

The traditional division of responsibility is for the private sector to build homes, workplaces, and commercial outlets on private land. The public sector builds the utilities, community, and recreational infrastructure on public land. Sometimes, the developer builds infrastructure to government standards and then turns it over to the local government, but there is seldom sufficient cooperation or coordination between their efforts. How many times have we seen housing tracts build out without a school or even a park, even if they were included in the original plans? How many times have we seen a street grid fully outlined on the landscape before a single private building has been constructed within that grid? The consumer wants and needs the whole package: not just the building and the street, but the sidewalks, bicycle paths, and landscaping along the streets, as well as the parks, schools, and other amenities needed for an inviting lifestyle. This demand becomes stronger as densities go up and people need resources beyond their own house and yard. If the whole experience cannot be delivered, people with choices stay away, and retrogressive urban patterns and practices are perpetuated.

To build consumer demand in the marketplace, development regulations have to both permit and encourage products that consumers need and prefer, and public-private cooperation has to facilitate the delivery of these products.

## Relating Development Regulations to Nature

Although there are laudable programs that have developed within the private sector to rate green buildings and neighborhoods, such as the Leadership in Energy and Environmental Design, or LEED, program popular in North America, the most direct and comprehensive way to reconcile the relationships between development and its environmental setting is by incorporating ecological considerations into the regulatory framework. A discretionary and transactional approval framework should not only codify the essential environmental performance to be secured; it should also provide the offsetting incentives to make it happen. When Ian McHarg first suggested using environmental factors to channel and limit development, he had to use hand-drawn overlays on tracing paper to map different environmental conditions. The lack of regional information at this level of detail meant that local government could only go forward on a site-by-site basis. Today, governments almost everywhere have GIS programs that can organize necessary information about the natural environment as layers on a single map: contours, hydrology, underlying soil types, sun angles at various times of the year, and prevailing wind patterns, plus streets and buildings, lot lines, and taxes. Development regulations have traditionally been administered using maps based solely on street patterns and property lines. Figure 4-11 shows a conventional street and zone map from the development regulations for Penn Township in Lancaster County, Pennsylvania. Figure 4-12 shows the same area mapped in GIS, displaying some, but not all, of the many layers of information organized on the map, including buildings, property lines, and an aerial view. The terrain and hydrology are on another layer of the GIS map. Adopting the GIS maps as the zoning base map would make it easier for a local government to incorporate detailed information about both the environmental and the development context into the regulation and approval process.

Some local regulations already recognize places like steep slopes and wetlands as subject to additional controls, but the procedures still date from the days when local governments had no reliable information of their own and had to rely entirely on surveys made by the developer. Local planning provisions require the developer to submit a map of steep slopes and wetlands on a property as part of the development application. There is then a discretionary decision about the extent to which the presence of these geographic features should modify the development. The basic development rights have probably been predetermined by the zoning district without considering the natural ecology, according to the "billiard table" method, which makes the assumption that the land is completely flat and featureless. Having ecological information as part of the regulations would enable the local authority to map steep-slope and wetland overlay zones in advance of development and to restrict buildings and roads in all such areas in accordance with an objective set of criteria based on minimizing flooding and preventing the destabilizing of the natural environment. Establishing such policies generally, rather than for individual properties, makes sense because steep slopes and wetlands continue past individual property lines.

Incorporating GIS-based information into development regulations also provides a basis for implementing a policy proposed by Lane Kendig in his 1980 book *Performance Zoning*.[1] Kendig suggested that the underlying zoning should be discounted for areas that are obviously unbuildable, like wetlands, or places where disturbing the existing landscape needs to be minimized, like steep slopes, rather than determining development rights as if the land were the top of a billiard table and then transferring the development from unbuildable areas to other parts of the site. Zoning ecologically sensitive land in accordance with its carrying capacity for development would do much to reduce the adverse consequences of urbanizing new areas. This concept has been implemented in Bucks County, Pennsylvania, and Lake County, Illinois—both places where Kendig was the planning director—and in a few other places such as Irvington, New York, but it has needed the general availability of GIS to make it an effective part of public policy.

**Figure 4-11** A portion of the official zoning map for Penn Township in Lancaster County, Pennsylvania. This legal map provides only limited information to decision makers.

**Figure 4-12** This aerial map, part of the Geographic Information System for Lancaster County, Pennsylvania, shows clearly both the development and the environmental context for the zoning in figure 4-11. More information, such as terrain and hydrology, is also available on other GIS layers. Making the GIS maps the legal maps could improve the way development decisions are made.

Regulations for one-hundred-year and five-hundred-year floodplains usually govern what needs to be done if the property owner wishes to qualify for flood insurance. Incorporating these floodplain maps into development regulations and then zoning such areas in accordance with their carrying capacities would bring the two sets of regulations into conformity with each other. GIS provides a simple way of relating zoning and floodplain maps. Coastal flood and velocity zones that restrict permissible land uses in exposed locations can also be incorporated into local GIS maps, and these issues will become an increasingly important part of regulation as climate change makes flood surges more likely to encroach on previously buildable areas.

Who should be responsible for environmentally protected land? Property that has been protected from development for environmental reasons can end up being deeded to a public park system, it can belong to a property owners' association, or it can become part of an individual lot. It is often easiest for the developer to simply apportion protected land to individual lots, which makes their owners responsible for its maintenance. Wildwood, Missouri, has strong environmental protection provisions in its subdivision ordinance because the soil is unusually sensitive to erosion and because the city's location is subject to sudden powerful thunderstorms. The city planning department proactively sends out a letter to every new property owner in Wildwood who has a lot with a protected area within it. The letter clearly explains what the preservation is all about, why it is necessary, and specifically what it means, as well as what an owner can and cannot do on the protected portion of the property. It tells exactly who can answer questions and how they can be reached. It calls for a partnership between the property owner and the local government to manage the situation for the benefit of each owner and all citizens. It is a model example of the need for ecodesign to be based on strong communication and support.

How do we best relate development to watersheds as natural zone boundaries? In chapter 2, we discussed the way that development relates to watersheds using the example of Lancaster County, Pennsylvania. Steep slopes, wetlands, and floodplains are all constituent parts of watersheds, which are the framework for the natural environment and create a series of definable zones. Development in Lancaster County has tended to be located on higher land that forms the boundaries between watersheds, which means that a single watershed is likely to be part of several different local government jurisdictions. The criteria for mapping parts of a watershed will be similar from one jurisdiction to the next, making it relatively easy for adjoining towns to coordinate watershed management. A typical objective for regulating property within a watershed is that the amount of stormwater leaving the property and flowing downstream should be as close as possible after development to the rate of flow that would have taken place before. Implementing this objective often requires detention areas in places where the natural retention characteristics of the landscape have been altered by development. The most effective retention systems need to be designed to serve clusters of properties so as to apportion the requirements among property owners, and conform to the boundaries of the natural drainage system, rather than property lines. The complex interactions of all these factors clearly require discretionary approvals within predetermined limits.

Solar access is increasingly seen as important to meeting future energy needs without the pollution from conventional fuels. Requiring buildings to set back from the property lines to protect access to light and air for adjacent buildings has long been a traditional part of development regulation. Height limits and building setbacks above a certain height are also traditional for the same reason, although there is an argument that these provisions are less necessary today because everyone can have artificial light and mechanical air-conditioning. However, the growing importance of solar collectors to provide an alternative source of energy has made height and setback regulations more important than ever. The orientation of site plans and street layouts for subdivision also have to be considered as a way of maximizing solar access. For example, Boulder, Colorado, has a solar access code that outlines the required parameters and sets up a procedure for a zoning applicant to determine whether a proposed building meets the positive solar requirements. The availability of GIS technology can now provide data to determine the most favorable arrangement for solar access of the streets and buildings in a specific area.

Larger buildings are beginning to incorporate wind turbines as the problems with noise and vibration are being solved. In the future, cities may map zones for tall buildings to take the best advantage of prevailing winds, and tall buildings that might obstruct this access may be discouraged in other locations.

Ian McHarg's well-known injunction to design with, not against, nature will have to become a basic principle of development regulation. It is certainly a fundamental tenet of ecodesign.

## Restoring Compact, Walkable Development

In the early twentieth century, urban downtowns included offices, theaters, hotels, and streets of shops and restaurants. These downtowns were the hub of local rail and transit lines, and all major roads led there. Warehouses and factories were close to these urban centers because both depended on access from railroads. There were houses and apartments among the businesses and warehouses, although they were generally not very desirable places to live. Downtown was surrounded by close-in neighborhoods, a few of them exclusive, unfortunately, often literally. Other neighborhoods were middle and working class. Some were so badly deteriorated that they were lived in only by people who had no other choice. Distances between destinations were small, easily negotiated on foot or on a short trolley or bus ride. In bigger cities, there would be a distinctive financial district, which was mostly office buildings, and a midtown area with a mix of offices, hotels, and retail.

These centers evolved gradually until construction was stopped by the Great Depression of the 1930s and then by World War II. Urban downtowns were far from perfect; they were dirty and noisy and incorporated all kinds of inequities. Many suburbs excluded factories, any business that employed a large number of people, and low-income residents. The virtues of these urban and suburban areas were compactness and walkability; and their diversity of buildings and uses made them lively places.

What happened next is a familiar story: sprawl and more sprawl. The growth process began with widespread car ownership and the trend to move goods by trucks as well as trains. Government subsidies for home ownership enabled many families to move out of cramped urban apartments and narrow city houses and buy new homes with front and back yards in suburban tracts.[2] Shopping centers were built at major intersections, so retail businesses could follow their customers to the suburbs. The increase in suburban dwellers made it easier for offices to move out of cities, especially as more women entered the workforce. Fewer urban jobs and fewer central-city residents led to decay and abandonment in many urban neighborhoods, leaving people with the fewest alternatives in the oldest and most deteriorated parts of the city. Downtowns just went to sleep at night, parts of them frightening hangouts for the disaffected, the disenfranchised, and the dispossessed. Cities took on a bad name, which they still have in the minds of many people to this day. The downtown revival we are seeing around North America is a recent phenomenon.

The role of development regulation in facilitating and cementing the evolution of the early twentieth-century city into today's decentralized metropolis is not as well known as the story of its growth. Before the middle of the century, regulations were mostly about separating large categories of uses, such as keeping industry away from residences, and about general principles like preserving light and air for neighboring properties by means of height and setback regulations.

When development and construction began again in the 1950s, there was a strong move to modernize development regulations to bring them into line with new thinking in planning and architecture and to extend regulation out to the formerly rural and suburban areas that were rapidly becoming urbanized. Architects and planners saw the tall tower as the characteristic modern building for offices and apartments. By the time free-standing towers became a normal part of development regulations, public housing and the towers and plazas of downtown urban renewal districts were already well established and had already been cogently criticized by Jane Jacobs.[3] Replacing urban setback regulations with floor-area ratios[4] gave designers more freedom to shape the permitted density into towers. It also resulted in substantial downzoning in many places, setting absolute limits on what could be built for the first time and was favored by planners as a way of relating building size to transportation access and other planning considerations. Adding open-space ratios to the regulations is a way of making sure that new towers keep their distance from one another. It also provides a quantifiable measurement of something that was still considered to always be an advantage for the public, again despite Jane Jacobs's well-argued criticisms of useless urban open spaces. Because much new construction is only reachable by car, increasing parking requirements also pushes buildings farther apart.

Land uses in these ordinances are carefully catalogued according to their potential impact on other activities, with the least potential impact being the most desired condition. What is obvious now, but evidently was not obvious at the time, is that by demanding rigid separation to achieve the least potential impact of one use on another, the ordinances also eliminate the valuable connections among urban activities. Industries are categorized as light, medium, or heavy and are separated accordingly, and an ordinance can have as many as ten or twelve commercial districts with differing permitted uses, floor-area ratios, and parking requirements. Hotels and motels are categorized by size and may be permitted in some commercial districts and not in others. Residences are often not permitted in commercial districts, a particularly damaging requirement because twenty-four-hour use is an important component of urban vitality and safety. Office parks, hotels, shopping centers, and destinations like arenas and stadiums are all zoned to be in separate locations disconnected from one another and disconnected from places where people live. Commercial zones used to be mapped in narrow strips along streetcar routes in older urban neighborhoods and suburbs, where stores often occupied the ground floors of apartment buildings. That precedent has now been extended out along arterial highways through the rapidly developing suburbs, accompanied by new parking requirements that must be satisfied on each individual site, leaving only a fraction of each property available for buildings that are allowed to contain only certain commercial uses. The result is downtown-type shops set within nothing more than parking lots (figure 4-13). The familiar suburban commercial strip with its small structures surrounded by parking

**Figure 4-13** A normal North American strip mall with local shops, this one in Las Vegas, Nevada. There is no urban experience between the car and the store.

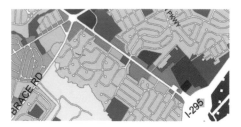

**Figure 4-14** Portion of a zoning map for Cherry Hill, New Jersey. Red is commercial zoning, olive is small-lot single-family housing, yellow is large-lot single-family housing, blue is institutional zoning, and the brown zone permits apartments. All the ingredients of a neighborhood are here, all separated and scattered. This pattern is typical of conventional zoning categories and maps, and it explains what you see almost everywhere.

is very much an artifact of regulation. There is too much land zoned for commercial use to provide an incentive for denser development, the commercial zones are usually too narrow to create any kind of center, and the use restrictions prevent adding residences.

The familiar image of a typical modern housing tract with hundreds of single-family houses, all the same size, is also created by regulations. An ordinance can have as many as eight or ten residential districts, mostly for single-family houses. The key variable is the size of the lot, although height limits and floor area ratios are also used. In older neighborhoods and suburbs, houses on different-sized lots could often be found side by side, often with small apartment buildings next door or not far away. Under the new regulations, not only are house lots with smaller frontages in a different zone from houses with only slightly larger frontages, but a concern for fairness and uniform administration requires that each such zone has to be mapped to cover a substantial area. Figure 4-14 shows a typical suburban zoning map, with large areas zoned for the same kinds of houses backing up to a narrow commercial strip zoned for only a small number of retail uses.

## Pushing Back against Decentralization and the Rigidity of Regulations

Another regulatory blind spot, now partly corrected, was an underlying assumption that older buildings were likely to be obsolete and thus open to replacement. The laws gave no recognition to historic buildings and neighborhoods. Today, buildings and districts can be designated as historic landmarks, but even with new laws to protect them, the underlying regulations may still make historic buildings more valuable dead than alive by permitting much larger structures.

Some very unfortunate demolitions, such as the destruction of Pennsylvania Station in New York City, and a growing appreciation for the architectural merits of the old, fashionable urban neighborhoods helped give historic preservation its start. Many of the original inhabitants of fashionable urban neighborhoods had long moved out to suburban country-club districts, and their elegant old houses had been broken up into apartments and small offices. These buildings and places were still attractive, however, and at first many old mansions could be bought for bargain prices. Instead of a setting for people leading a stuffy formal existence supported by servants, these houses became homes for energetic younger people who were often prepared to do much of the necessary renovation themselves (figure 4-15).

The Main Street Project of the National Trust for Historic Preservation in the United States and other, similar organizations in other countries found

**Figure 4-15** This street in Washington, D.C.'s Dupont Circle area is an example of an older neighborhood that has attracted many people looking for the coherence and location advantages of a traditional urban life.

ways to restore economic vitality to neighborhood commercial districts and old downtowns in suburbs. In bigger cities, business improvement districts were created by municipalities that added a small tax on downtown or neighborhood commercial businesses to finance additional lighting, street cleaning, and safety patrols above what the city could provide and to advocate for policies that favored downtown development and commercial revitalization (figure 4-16).

Many old warehouses and loft factory buildings near downtowns had lost their tenants to new, more efficient buildings in the suburbs. Considered obsolete, these solid, well-built structures were demolished to make room for urban renewal or just for parking. Then the architectural merit of the buildings that survived began to be appreciated, and their cheap rents were another

**Figure 4-16** Walnut Street in Philadelphia is now a successful retail street because of the management of the downtown area by the Center City Business Improvement District.

attraction. Warehouse and loft districts became another form of historic district; a good example is the Bricktown District in Oklahoma City, with a mix of shops, offices, and residences (figure 4-17). Development regulations had to be changed to make it legal to live in these buildings. New York City led this movement with changes made in 1971 to an industrial zoning district to permit artists to occupy lofts in the landmark buildings in what was then called the Cast Iron District (now called SoHo, for "South of Houston Street"). Today, urban loft living is so popular that developers have run out of old buildings to renovate and are constructing new lofts.

At first, the historic neighborhoods were mixed income, but the renovation process—wryly called gentrification in Great Britain and later in other English-speaking countries—tended to price out the low-income residents or businesses that had moved into these neighborhoods when the original owners decamped for the suburbs. Rising rents and house prices were not so bad for property owners, although rising property taxes could be a problem, but they made these places unaffordable for many tenants. However, the old neighborhoods that attracted the new investment were usually part of larger school and urban service districts with a wide variety of residents. The new "gentry" could not live the narrow, protected lives of their fashionable predecessors.

Old, fashionable neighborhoods, historic main streets, business improvement districts, and repurposed loft and warehouse districts became living laboratories for urban, walkable, mixed-use communities. Their success has

**Figure 4-17** This updated warehouse district, Bricktown in Oklahoma City, is now part of a special design district and houses offices, loft residences, shops and restaurants within restored handsome nineteenth-century buildings. The design district gives more flexibility than a historic district, which can be both a good thing and a problem, according to the sensitivity of the various developers.

meant that they can now be found in almost every city center, and developers have been inspired to create new mixed-use centers in suburban downtowns. The Legacy Town Center, in an office park north of Dallas, Texas (figure 4-18), is one example.

## Regulations for Compact, Mixed-Use Urban Centers

Regulations that will preserve or create compact, mixed-use building complexes and urban districts, such as the Ruoholahti development on a formerly industrial waterfront in Helsinki (figure 4-19), need to be based on several interacting principles that should apply not only to zoning codes but also to building codes and parking regulations. Regulations should allow a richly compatible combination of activities, directed toward the totality of the place that is being created rather than just the integrity of any one use. They should also manage the interfaces among different uses, moderating negative impacts and fostering positive connectivity so that the contradictions of use that were seen in the past will not be replicated. In this respect, the concept of "neighborliness" is very important. Finally, they need to foster a natural evolution of activities so that there are ranges of acceptable uses that do not require ongoing approvals. Unfortunately, the result of the current nature of

**Figure 4-18** This new mixed-use suburban center, the Legacy Town Center north of Dallas, is a walkable precinct within a large office park.

**Figure 4-19** Inside the compact, mixed-use Ruoholahti district in Helsinki, Finland. Apartment buildings face the inlet and the promenade in the foreground. You can see a high-tech research center in the background, a few blocks away. Shopping, other housing, and offices are close by, as are the Helsinki Conservatory and other institutional buildings.

regulations, along with the design and building practices that emanate from them, is to create highly tailored buildings that do not easily convert to other purposes. It could be relatively easy to change the zoning, but the size and shape of the building and provisions in the building code can present bigger problems. Even if one regulation is fixed, many others can stop an action or distort it, to the point that people become ambivalent about following through. What we tend to do, rather than fix all the relevant regulations, is to bypass them in some special way. The specific project gets to the finish line, but it remains an exception. Building reuse is like a Gordian knot, but we never undo the knot, and we don't cut it either. We just find a way around it, and we often lose the spontaneity of the city, which is what we really want.

We can learn a lot from the reuse of the historic buildings in many cities that had a first life as warehouses or department stores or manufacturing. Because these buildings were structured to provide full-floor open spaces for storage or sales or industry, they turn out to be suitable containers for many different activities—workshops for artists and artisans; offices for architects, lawyers, or start-up companies; good places for retail stores and restaurants—as well as being good multiple dwellings, with more flexibility for living arrangements than conventional apartments. All these uses can coexist within one of these old large-format buildings. The first reuse and mixed use was done by brave people illegally, like the artists who occupied enough lofts in SoHo that New York City decided to recognize them, and the contributions they were making to a valuable historic district, and make them legal. As in SoHo, conventional regulations classify such buildings as light industry. To permit most of these new uses, they have to be rezoned, such as has been done not only in New York City but in Portland, Denver, and many other cities. A good example is the repurposed warehouse in the Pearl District in Portland, Oregon, shown in figure 4-20. In places where some industrial tenants remain, there are potential conflicts that still need to be managed.

**Figure 4-20** A historic large-floor-plate building reused in the Pearl District in Portland, Oregon. This building, once a warehouse, now contains apartments and shops.

Successfully regulating mixed-use buildings, or districts, requires attention to details. A good example is enabling housing to be built over shops and restaurants (figure 4-21). Interface issues of noise and fumes can limit compatibility. These problems can be solved by such modest requirements as setbacks of the housing above the commercial spaces, inclusion of something as simple as an awning to screen apartments from the noise of people coming and going from the commercial spaces, and careful location of garbage handling facilities and venting of kitchens to manage fumes and odors. Another potential conflict can arise when housing is adjacent to offices or there is a mix of housing and offices within the same building group. A typical issue is

**Figure 4-21** In Vancouver, building bases hold the street line, in this case shops on the ground floor with apartments above. A terrace forms a setback, which limits impacts from restaurants and shops on the housing.

the messy domestic image of housing balconies in the context of a decorous business precinct. Looking out at a balcony filled with bicycles, barbecue equipment, and storage boxes can upset office users because they say it diminishes the business feel that they prefer. Possible solutions include requiring opaque residential balcony railings, requiring that residential balconies not face office frontages, or requiring the use of enclosed storage facilities accessible from the balconies. Another issue is security for residents in a mixed-use building when employees, customers, messengers, and others need access to offices in the same structure. One solution is to require separate entrances and elevators, but regulations should also permit use of a single lobby and bank of elevators if there is an appropriate security system to control access to each floor. These are just examples among many possible use mixes and hundreds of interface relationships. If we want to take advantage of the obvious benefits of mixed-use buildings, such as shared parking and amenities, and close association of home and work, these issues have to be anticipated, regulations written, and solutions identified in design guidelines, a much better strategy than simply banning mixed use.

Density diversity will require even more disentangling of existing regulations. In conventional practice, a single density specification for an area expresses itself in different-sized buildings according to the size of the development sites. One can always build less than the permitted density, but can never build more. Uniform density districts, as proposed in Transect-Based codes, are just as arbitrary as uniform use districts. There is no reason that townhouses should not occupy the same block as apartment towers or that a small office building should not be next to a larger one. In fact, the easiest way to build respite into a dense urban scenario is to vary densities among sites, opening up vistas and offering distance for privacy, based on specific conditions.

Because density and land value are so intimately tied together, a big problem with varying density in regulations is ensuring fair and equal treatment among property holders. The principle should be to allow a density on each site that fits the particular cluster of demands on that site and the context in which it is located, which means that mixed-density districts should be mapped in accordance with a conceptual urban design plan. Doing this allows the shaping of buildings to meet variable urban design expectations and preferences, which are articulated as general principles in the code and developed in detail by administrative design guidelines. One implementation method is to allow an increase of density for larger sites. If design specifications are also changeable with different site sizes, even greater diversity is possible, and the cause and effect can be deliberately designed into the regulatory framework. Another approach is to set a base density and then allow increases in density above this base according to developer performance, which will naturally vary over time and from site to site. A third approach is to allow transfers of density from one site to another, subject to a careful urban design assessment that ensures that the receiving site can comfortably manage an increase in building size. These last two approaches are usually tied to some form of bonus program so that the density is offered for preferred performance, but the implication is the same: The city gets more diversity of building sizes and shapes.

## Regulations to Keep People Comfortable in Downtown Housing

Residents in mixed-use downtowns are critical for their success, but it can be tricky to attract them because of skeptical consumer attitudes toward density, diversity, and mixed use, as well as a lack of housing affordability. Having people around twenty-four hours of the day improves public safety; supports restaurants, entertainment, and a variety of available retail establishments; and offers a population of workers living close to jobs. Single people, couples without children, and older people who are tired of maintaining suburban houses are strong candidates for downtown living, but a truly vital downtown needs families with children as well (figure 4-22).

Vancouver has made it a top priority to include families with children in downtown developments, with clearly articulated guidelines and unit

**Figure 4-22** Parents and children play in Emery Barnes Park, a popular downtown gathering place for residents. A truly vital downtown needs families with children, and that has been a top city policy priority in contemporary downtown Vancouver.

requirements for families coupled with a strategy to secure low-income housing and, more recently, middle-income housing. About 30 percent of new households in developments downtown now are families with children. Not every family will want to live in a downtown, but development regulations can help families that appreciate the convenience and liveliness of downtown living find this choice an attractive option. Providing for the needs of families with children touches every aspect of a building program and becomes more and more important as densities go up, because a family's skepticism about living downtown seems to go up in proportion to the density. The experience of multiple living for families bringing up children has to be competitive with their single-family alternative. How can we make the multiple-family home a surrogate for the single-family home? We can say that the city offers more cultural opportunity, walkability, and time savings with the avoidance of the commuter trip, but the city must also have housing that families can afford, as well as schools, community facilities, and childcare centers (figure 4-23). It must also have a general ambience of safety, and, because few families want their children to grow up in isolation, it has to have what sociologists refer to as a "society of children." A typical family also needs an apartment that supports their demanding way of life. Vancouver's *Guidelines for Housing Families at High Densities* offers a good indication of what needs to be considered (figure 4-24). The nature of unit floor finishes, privacy of laundry facilities, availability of protected play spaces, natural supervision potentials for children by neighboring adults in the building, and many other specific concerns have to be addressed.

**Figure 4-23** A childcare center in Vancouver's False Creek North Neighborhood. Nearby are a school and community center along with other public amenities, all necessary parts of a strategy to attract families.

**Figure 4-24** Vancouver's official Guidelines for Housing Families at High Densities mandates children's play yards close to family units, even on roof terraces as illustrated in this example in the Yaletown neighborhood. Guidelines deal with aspects of the unit, the building, the street, and the neighborhood as determined by research with urban families.

Managing the experience of density is important to the image of that density and its viability in the marketplace, especially for residential consumers. This is another job for thoughtful regulations and guidelines. Vancouver provides further illustrations. For example, as densities increase, there are always consumer concerns about household and project security, personal privacy, and noise mitigation in multiple housing. Vancouver's clear urban design guidelines reinforce its family housing guidelines. These guidelines offer many options to resolve concerns for families and other tenants, such as grade-separation of open spaces from the street and minimum distances between windows in adjoining buildings for privacy, plus construction standards for noise control. Their policy directions also assist with the more endemic realities of living in a city. Urban design requirements for animation at the sidewalk level and prohibition of blank walls help create a safer atmosphere along the streets.

A vital mitigation factor for density is landscape. Single or double rows of street trees along with grass boulevards soften the impacts of massive construction (figure 4-25). Small landscape gardens along street frontages offer a domestic feel that moderates the anonymity usually found at higher densities (figure 4-26). Lush courtyards and pervasive roof gardens provide respite and simple visual pleasure for the tenants of individual buildings (figure 4-27). A simple matter of massing so as to set back the base of a tall tower behind a three- or four-story streetwall of lower buildings will dramatically change the oppressiveness of towers for people along a sidewalk (figure 4-28). All these

**Figure 4-25** A double row of trees along the sidewalk offers a visual barrier to adjacent tall buildings and creates a sense of protection from cars on the street. This photo shows a normal Vancouver sidewalk that results from this planting requirement.

**Figure 4-26** A private door at the sidewalk offers convenience and personal identity at high densities. A small terrace and a modest change in grade from the street create a sense of privacy and permit individual gardens that offer variety. Vancouver has hundreds of modern townhouses with this kind of design.

**Figure 4-27** Lushly landscaped courtyards within groups of apartment towers offer privacy, neighborliness, and a safe place for children to play. Vancouver housing's shared courtyards are often on a raised level above a garage and street-front shops.

**Figure 4-28** Integrating the base of towers within a podium of townhouse frontages along the sidewalk cuts the impact of tower scale on pedestrians. The tower/podium scenario is typical of Vancouver's high density.

amenities and design moves are relatively inexpensive and are not difficult to include in legislated requirements.

Vancouver also limits the floor-plate size of residential towers and separates towers (but not their lower floors, which should form a continuous frontage that holds the street line) to create significant space between them. This requirement offers wider view opportunities, provides a sense of openness, and improves the composition of the skyline (figure 4-29). Cities can manage public view protection with zoning overlays and can review design proposals to protect private views and cushion the feel of density. Even the specification of materials for buildings can enhance the acceptance of density because so many people worry about maintenance problems as well as the image of their home. With some reform of regulations, parking in a multiple dwelling could easily replicate the security and flexibility of the garage in a suburban house, with a door and storage for each space, instead of open spaces in huge underground caverns (figure 4-30). Also, more typical garages in apartment buildings can be equipped with automated security gates. Because urban garages are expensive, people who don't want to pay for them should have the option of doing without, relying instead on car sharing or bicycles. Developers should be permitted to lower parking ratios as much as they think the market will permit.

All these concerns are about improving the quality of the living experience, which is at the very heart of consumer demand for living in a place that

**Figure 4-29** Managing the massing and spacing of towers is a key requirement for making high density more comfortable. Tall Vancouver towers are required to be thin and well separated.

**Figure 4-30** Underground parking in the form of a private garage with a door is provided in some Vancouver buildings. It can be a useful inducement for households converting from single-family to apartment living.

**Figure 4-31** A typical Vancouver block of townhouses, sometimes called row houses, integrated with a tower. These units offer housing variety and appeal to people who are averse to apartment or high-rise living.

people enjoy and where they can develop a sense of ownership and belonging, and, of course, affordability is an important consideration. There seems to be a chemistry for success in terms of consumer acceptance when density and design quality are tied together at a price within reach. The architectural solutions allow the density to work; the high density generates enough value to carry quality construction, great on-site amenities, and a very nice contribution to the neighborhood infrastructure; and the supportive neighborhood draws all kinds of people back to a truly urban lifestyle, making for a vibrant city with new economic and social opportunities.

Downtown living cannot just come in tall high-rises; it also needs to include townhouses or row houses with a ground orientation (figure 4-31). For example, there are people who don't want to live in a high-rise apartment with their large dog, or want their own front door image, or are afraid of heights, or do not want someone living above them, so the tower apartment scenario does not work for them. Sometimes, modern households want to put home and work together for financial reasons or ease of child rearing, so higher density needs to include lofts and live/work units with regulations and even tax assessment rules that support this lifestyle (figure 4-32). Sometimes, households want to live in extended family arrangements, so higher density needs to include cohousing or shared housing. Sometimes, two single people want to share a unit and share a mortgage to build individual equity, so higher density needs to include units with multiple master suites, sometimes

**Figure 4-32** A new building with live/work lofts in mixed-use downtown Vancouver, an alternative to live/work units in converted warehouses.

called "mingles" units. The contemporary multiple-housing market has barely touched the range of options for dense housing that needs to be provided to build strong and sustained demand and to convert consumer skepticism about downtown housing into support and loyalty.

## Achieving Social Diversity

The question of social diversity and affordability of housing is more complicated than just reform of regulations (figure 4-33). It is also often a matter of public investment and a question of public policy. Unfortunately, the usual way the real-estate market works tends to homogenize housing and push social diversity out of the city. The more demand there is, the more prices tend to rise. Rising prices edit out people by level of income as well as by household type simply because some kinds of households, such as families with children, need more space at reasonable prices. Even if developers are well intentioned, the private market cannot deal with this reality, and some form of public intervention or participation is required. One reason for so much homelessness in cities is that the idea of public involvement in the market to secure housing affordability has become unpopular. Public investment in social housing has been withdrawn or dramatically limited, and the unavoidable effect is a scarcity of affordable housing. We need to recognize that housing for everyone is a benefit for everyone.

**Figure 4-33** An example of housing for low-income people in Vancouver. This building also includes a component of low-end-of-market worker housing. It is good-quality housing well integrated with other activities and is certainly "more than a roof."

A first step toward a balanced and equitable community is a strong municipal policy statement of the public intention to secure social diversity in proportions that reflect regional norms. The statement might be about security for various income levels; low-income housing targets are not unusual, middle-income housing targets are rarer but just as important. Other parts of the statement might be about securing various types of households, such as housing for seniors, families with children, or those with special needs. A policy statement simply expresses that some form of intervention in the usual market process is being planned in that particular community. To turn policy into reality, several mechanisms can be used. The most obvious is to protect the modest-income rental housing that is already there. Rate-of-change provisions in zoning can forestall new development approvals if the stock of existing modest-rent housing is in jeopardy. A provision to ban demolition of what are called single-room-occupancy units in old, downtown hotels, used almost exclusively by single poor people, is another popular measure. Of course, the most typical initiatives are driven by public investment. Sites are purchased or portions of private projects are subsidized so that units are built for a specified segment of users.

However, there never seems to be enough public funding. As an alternative, some low-income and special needs housing can be leveraged through rezoning processes. Many cities have tried what is called inclusionary zoning, whereby a certain amount of low- or moderate-income housing must be provided in a new development or contributions to an off-site housing program must be made instead. Because this provision can be very expensive, especially in new construction, even to the point of stalling development, inclusionary housing policies can be backed up with incentives. For example, a bonus provision within zoning or implemented as a policy through rezoning can offer a greater level of development opportunity in exchange for security for some level of affordability or for a type of tenure that opens up affordability, such as market rental, rent-specified rental, or nonprofit home ownership. A variation on this strategy is to use both public investment and density bonuses.

As we learned from the experience of the public housing ghettos of the mid-twentieth century, mixing of incomes in multiple housing is essential, but this mix also has to be carefully arranged. The expectations of people at different income levels are different, and it takes a special social accord for people with different requirements to live together. There is a natural mix that is important to support. It is offered in mixed-income co-ops, where people sign up for a cross subsidy that these co-ops organize and are motivated to live together with mutual support. In most contemporary nonmarket housing, there is a policy of social mix that is built in from the beginning, including low-income households and at least low-end-of-market or worker households. Experience shows few problems in these situations because all residents are there through free choice or see the housing opportunity as a benefit. Mixing income levels at a larger scale, for an entire urban neighborhood, for example, takes more management and preparation because residents in some buildings may believe that they are participating in something that they hadn't expected. Some policies target income mix within market buildings, whereas others look for the mix among closely associated buildings (figure 4-34). Regardless of the specifics of the policy for neighborhood social mix, several principles are important. First, the differences in building quality, finish, scale, and appearance need to be minimized. Second, there needs to be equal access to facilities and amenities. Third, there needs to be equal treatment in management and programming. Such principles can help everyone understand and enjoy the benefits of social mix.

## Regulations for Walkable, Mixed-Density Residential Neighborhoods

"Neighborhood" is a term everyone uses, but it can mean different things to different people, from geographic proximity to ethnic identity (figure 4-35). Many have argued that the notion of neighborhood organization for cities is no longer relevant. They talk about the geographic spread of the modern

**Figure 4-34** Subsidized and market housing next door to each other along Pacific Boulevard, a prime location in Vancouver. Only the residents know which is which.

**Figure 4-35** The bottom line for shaping cities is that neighborhoods matter. This pub is the "local" for Vancouver's Kitsilano neighborhood.

city that frustrates face-to-face engagement and the pervasiveness of Internet access that fosters digital "clusters of interest" that can be spread all over the globe. Real geographic neighborhoods nonetheless persist, and people seem to continue to find them appealing (figure 4-36). We can take advantage of this natural consumer inclination by shaping more walkable cities and

**Figure 4-36** People identify themselves as living in a neighborhood and are inclined to socialize in this context and to help one another as neighbors. This sign indicates a local celebration to come in a downtown Vancouver neighborhood.

suburbs. Mixed use, density, and social diversity can be synthesized through both the physical geography and social consciousness of neighborhood. More importantly, a fulfilling consumer experience can be artfully delivered in the neighborhood context. It is prudent that both the policy and regulatory framework of municipalities and the marketing story of development be shaped and, indeed, differentiated, by neighborhood specification and identity. Regulations can reinforce neighborhood structure and organization, and edit out the factors and influences that are pulling neighborhoods apart.

The neighborhood as a significant component of city development was defined by Clarence Perry in a well-known essay published in 1929 as part of the first Regional Plan for the three-state New York City metropolitan area. A critical parameter is that the neighborhood should be largely contained within a five-minute walking radius, which translates into approximately 160 acres (65 hectares). It should include a mix of housing types and sizes and access to public open space. According to Perry, each neighborhood should also be a short walk from a shopping district situated where the corners of four neighborhoods meet, and the density of the neighborhood should be determined by the population needed to support an elementary school that would be within walking or cycling distance for all the children (figure 4-37). When Perry wrote this essay, he was simultaneously defining the way most cities had developed up to that time and reacting against already visible trends toward the thinning out and dispersing of cities and suburbs because

**Figure 4-37** One of Clarence Perry's diagrams of a neighborhood, from the 1929 Plan for the New York City Region by the Regional Plan Association.

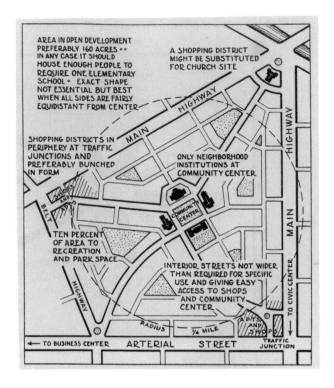

of rapidly increasing car ownership. The inspiration for his diagram was the model community where he lived, Forest Hills Gardens, in the borough of Queens in New York City, which had been developed by the Russell Sage Foundation, where Perry also worked. The development had been designed by Grosvenor Atterbury and Frederick Law Olmsted Jr., and it took the form of a charming English village, with denser, more urban buildings around the station square (figure 4-38). Even in 1929, the kind of neighborhood that Perry was proposing was exceptional, but there were many other garden suburbs like it on the fashionable side of most big cities, and it was plausible to present the neighborhood, as defined by Perry, as a necessary basic element of cities and regions.[5]

After World War II, there was a strong modernist reaction against the kind of scenic streetscapes and historical architectural inspiration found at Forest Hills Gardens. Urban renewal districts and public housing projects were planned as orderly rows of plain, straightforward buildings surrounded by flat plazas or lawns. They were also single-use areas, in keeping with modernist thinking about cities, and single-use zones were being translated into development regulations at the same time. As single-use regulations were adopted, with their commercial corridors and large residential districts that permit only one kind of building lot, the neighborhood as defined by Perry became

**Figure 4-38** Forest Hills Gardens, the planned community where Clarence Perry lived, was developed by the Russell Sage Foundation, where he worked. Meant to be a model affordable neighborhood, it soon became a coveted and expensive place to live.

impossible to build, and the whole idea of neighborhood as a planning concept fell into disuse.

In cities, neighborhoods began to be important to planners again when community participation in planning became widely accepted in the late 1960s. Neighborhood organizations also grew up at this time to help residents deal with local governments about plans or about proposed new buildings or roads or failures to provide traffic management or services.

The neighborhood revival in the suburbs is often credited to the example of Seaside, a resort village in the Florida panhandle designed by Andrés Duany and Elizabeth Plater-Zyberk and developed by Robert Davis beginning in the early 1980s. Duany and Plater-Zyberk were well aware of the Clarence Perry diagram; their street plan and basic organization create a walkable neighborhood with a mix of different-sized buildings, although the whole development is only half the size of the 160 acres (65 hectares) in Perry's formulation. They also admired garden suburbs like Forest Hills Gardens, with their scenic mix of buildings inspired by historical examples, their lawns, and their tree-lined streets. Seaside takes its inspiration from Florida resorts like Key West and DeFuniak Springs rather than an English village, and the sandy southern landscape is very different, but the charm of the development derives from its evocative images of clapboard houses with pillared porches. The Duany/Plater-Zyberk firm soon went on to design walkable neighborhoods with a

**Figure 4-39** A street in the Kentlands/ Lakelands development in Gaithersburg, Maryland, a suburb of Washington, D.C. The designers, Andres Duany and Elizabeth Plater-Zyberk, have re-created the kind of neighborhood built before World War II, using standard developer's building types from the present-day Washington metropolitan area.

mix of different housing types for developers who controlled large tracts of land, almost always in suburban locations, notably the Kentlands and Lakelands developments in Gaithersburg, Maryland, designed in the neo-Georgian style favored by developers in the Washington suburbs (figure 4-39). Duany and Plater-Zyberk were also instrumental in founding the Congress for the New Urbanism in 1993, which has brought together proponents of neighborhood planning and traditional design and is a strong voice for good planning and sustainable development at all scales.[6] There are now several hundred developments that follow the precepts of the Charter of the New Urbanism. Almost always, these developments have been built by a single investor who has secured approval from the local government by using planned unit development, traditional neighborhood development, or other exceptions to the usual regulations, exceptions available only for large sites controlled by one landowner. Even these neighborhoods, which are internally walkable, can still be isolated because of a lack of transit, to the point that car use is still endemic. Many of these neighborhoods are also very expensive, with limited social diversity. In any event, they are enabled through special approval mechanisms. Creating a walkable neighborhood with a mix of different housing types and income levels continues to be difficult under typical regulations, especially if a developer has to go it alone without government partnership and cooperation. Omaha, Nebraska, is an example of a city that has a walkable neighborhood zone that can apply to multiple ownerships as part of its ordinance, but at present it is only an option. Such zones need to be adopted for specific locations before they can truly become a template that coordinates and shapes development.

## Adding More Housing to Successful Urban Neighborhoods

Older, usually pre–World War II, streetcar suburbs and garden suburbs exist in every North American city, and comparable residential neighborhoods can be found in most cities and suburbs in the developed world, although usually with a higher ratio of apartments to individual houses. They already have many of the features for complete neighborhood life, but in too many places, current development regulations would no longer allow them to be built if construction started today. They are compact, walkable, and have a high, but comfortable, residential density. They almost always have a mixed-use "main street" pattern for commercial development, plus corner convenience stores and the occasional institution or attraction. They accommodate some mixing of generations and incomes because of changes that have occurred over time—conversion of larger houses into multiple units, addition of secondary suites, in-filling of garden apartments and townhouses, small complexes of housing for seniors, other special needs residential facilities—yet they protect single-family homes as well (figure 4-40). They usually maintain a walk-up

**Figure 4-40** In-fill can be a way to diversify housing options in a built-up neighborhood. Here is an example from Vancouver.

scale of three stories or fewer in height for houses and a few floors higher in neighborhoods where apartments are permitted. Because their buildings developed over many years, these suburbs have a variety of architectural styles, a valuable heritage that offers local character.

Although in-fill housing is a very good way to revitalize these existing neighborhoods, doing so can be tricky because of the high potential for unwanted impacts on existing residents and therefore the tendency for local opposition to in-fill proposals. Usually, such in-filling is best facilitated with very strict and clear urban design guidelines, such as the ones Toronto uses for well-established areas within the city. These guidelines generally cover how new buildings fit within existing commercial streetscapes and residential streetscapes as well as how slightly different types of housing can be made compatible. Toronto's guidelines for in-fill townhouses are illustrative of what is needed. These guidelines indicate how new townhouses can be placed carefully within existing single-family and duplex settings while having regard for existing neighborhood character. Key aspects are considered, such as street or open-space orientation of front façades; adjacency conditions for neighborliness, including heights and setbacks; sensitive handling of servicing areas and auto access; parking arrangements; landscape patterns, including saving mature trees; and streetscape improvements to contribute to walkability. With such guidelines, neighbors can have some security that new townhouses will not clash with the existing ambience, rhythms, and scale of nearby development. These guidelines facilitate approval of such housing through the political process, which is especially important as we think about sustainable and affordable housing alternatives for families with children as an alternative to the single-family home out in the far suburbs. The results not only sit comfortably within existing communities, but also offer excellent ground-oriented housing options for families (figure 4-41).

Older neighborhoods usually have an interconnected grid of streets that disperses traffic and offers an excellent network of sidewalks for walking. Streets are relatively narrow, so traffic and speed management come naturally; a three-and-a-half-lane cross section for local streets is not unusual, with parking on both sides and only one and a half lanes for two-way traffic (figure 4-42). Sometimes, there are back lanes or alleys, so there can be a proper, welcoming front-door presence for homes, with garage doors shifted to the rear side of the property. Usually, these neighborhoods have at least bus transit that is convenient, and sometimes rapid transit is accessible. There is an elementary school, built before elementary schools became so big that they required larger districts. There is relatively close access to middle and high schools. There are community facilities. These places are dense enough that most public services can be delivered in an economically viable way. Most

**Figure 4-41** Townhouses are in-filled behind two single-family homes in Toronto, the result of careful guidelines for densification in delicate existing neighborhoods.

importantly, if you ask typical suburban dwellers to draw their ideal place to live and describe its attributes, the results will generally look like one of these neighborhoods, which are very appealing and, in fact, should be inspirational for new neighborhood design out at the urban fringe.

The major defects of these neighborhoods are that the housing stock is old, the rooms may be small, and the houses may not have the luxurious bathrooms and kitchens people look for today. Such problems can easily be solved when homeowners have the resources. One problem encountered in some of these neighborhoods is that regulations permit much larger structures than the prevailing house type. "Tear-downs" have become an issue. An urgent task for cities and suburbs is to review the regulations currently in force in desirable neighborhoods to make sure that they haven't been rezoned into single-house-type districts that are incompatible with what is there already, creating nonconforming buildings whose future is restricted, and allowing inappropriate new structures.

It is often hard to find a place to live in these desirable locations. In 2009, Vancouver initiated a policy of permitting a second, smaller dwelling to be built on individual house lots facing the service lanes in older neighborhoods. Although these laneway houses are small, from about 500 to 1,200 square feet (46.5 to 111.5 square meters), they are carefully reviewed to make sure that they meet city guidelines intended to preserve the character of the existing neighborhood (figure 4-43). They do not immediately answer larger regional

**Figure 4-42** This three-and-a-half-lane street in the Mount Pleasant area of Vancouver works perfectly in a residential setting, calming traffic, offering valuable parking, and giving all the access that is needed. Unfortunately, it is substandard to contemporary street specifications and would not be built today.

problems of housing affordability because, on a cost-per-square-foot basis, they are not inexpensive. They do broaden the housing choices available; for example, they are attractive to smaller households, which prefer a ground orientation—a single parent needing a play yard for a child or a senior who loves to garden. They have excited particular interest in part because the profits of this housing stay with the resident homeowner. If laneway houses continue as a city policy for a generation, they could add substantially to Vancouver's available housing supply.

Accessory apartments, often called granny flats or in-law suites, are an old idea that had been zoned out of existence in most communities. Such units, built over attached or detached garages or in day-lit basement areas, have

**Figure 4-43** Laneway houses, a second house on a once-single-family lot, are proliferating in Vancouver. They bring housing diversity and a better level of affordability into existing stable neighborhoods with little disruption. This example also has advanced sustainability features.

been included in some New Urbanist residential developments as a way of adding to the variety of housing options available. Although these units are a very useful idea to facilitate diversity, regulatory and enforcement issues have to be handled carefully. Some communities require that these units can only be rented out by the owner-occupiers of the principal house, presumably on the theory that if the tenants are unruly and make a lot of noise, an owner living on the same property will be one of those most affected and will have to deal with the problem. Sometimes, these units can only be rented to extended family members. Such limitations are difficult to enforce.

## Creating New Neighborhoods at the Urban Fringe

The neighborhood as formulated by Clarence Perry and now tested in many communities actually lends itself to development regulations. The 160 acres (65 hectares) that Perry picked as the size of a walkable neighborhood is one fourth of the square mile (2.6 square kilometers) that has been mapped as a street grid over large areas of the United States, so each square mile potentially could contain four walkable neighborhoods. A similar framework exists in most of Canada. There is usually an intersection every mile (1.6 kilometers) along the main streets of the grid, and this area could be the location for a BRT stop, or perhaps a light-rail stop, and a small commercial center. Within each square mile, green spaces could be reserved and shared by each neighborhood, their location determined by the character of the local landscape.

**Figure 4-44** In portions of North America laid out on a 1-mile-square grid ( 1.6 kilometers on each side), commercial centers 1 mile (1.6 kilometers) apart, shown in red on the map, have four neighborhoods within walking distance at the 160-acre (65-hectare) size that Clarence Perry proposed.

Figure 4-44 shows how this arrangement could be mapped. Each red square is a commercial center serving four Perry-sized neighborhoods. Figure 4-45 shows how this pattern could be applied as regulations for the urban fringe of Omaha, Nebraska, a city that is continuing to expand by annexing agricultural land. Properties being annexed can be made to accept the city's zoning as a condition of receiving urban services under the annexation agreement. Where cities continue to spread out because of growing population, managing growth in this way can provide structure instead of sprawl.

The neighborhood should be a basic building block of cities and suburbs. It is a physical place, a social place, and an economic place both in high-density residential areas as well as in low-scale residential environments (figure 4-46). A neighborhood has emotional associations and geographic convenience. It is understandable and memorable. Its application at higher densities diversifies the appeal for a wider variety of potential residents. Its application at medium and lower densities can provide structure and meaning to what all too often has become a dispersed random pattern.

Older areas of a city or suburb will have some kind of neighborhood structure already. It may not conform to Perry's diagram, but these places will be perceived by their residents as neighborhoods and are likely to have some of the characteristics that Perry advocated: walkable streets; a mix of different house types, often including small apartment buildings; neighborhood institutions; and some local shops.

### Creating Neighborhoods from Housing Tracts and Commercial Strips

The places farthest from having a neighborhood structure are the large tracts of suburban land zoned for a single lot size, which produce big areas of similar houses, often at very low average densities. Threading through these areas are the commercially zoned arterial streets. As we saw in chapter 3, the

**Figure 4-45** A grid of neighborhoods and commercial centers that could apply to portions of the agricultural land around the city of Omaha, Nebraska, that are likely to be annexed. The city has the power to require this pattern as part of annexation agreements.

**Figure 4-46** Neighborhood is a physical place, a social place, and an economic place; it is relevant to developers and naturally appeals to consumers. This neighborhood party in a Vancouver park was organized by the nearby residents.

commercial corridors are so underdeveloped that they could be rebuilt to support a mix of stores and apartments if they were served by transit. The transit should be part of a comprehensive system, such as is being constructed in the Toronto metropolitan area, that would allow people getting on to the transit vehicle to journey to many other destinations in the metropolitan region. BRT technology could be used in these relatively underdeveloped corridors because it requires much lower upfront investment than a rail system. As we discussed in chapter 3, the preferred distance between stops for this kind of local transit is 1 mile (1.6 kilometers) so that everyone along the corridor is within a ten-minute walking distance of a station, that is, within about 0.5 of a mile (0.8 of a kilometer). At the station stops, there could be a concentration of commercial development and apartment houses, a less intense version of the kind of mixed-use, transit-oriented development that already takes place in cities (figure 4-47). This scenario would produce something very like the Perry neighborhood diagram. Every mile there would be a mixed-use center with stores and apartments, which would be within a ten-minute walking distance of four districts, each of about 160 acres (65 hectares). If this potential situation were recognized and encouraged in the development regulations, walkable neighborhoods could be expected to evolve in these areas within a generation after the opening of the transit.

Cities and suburbs seeking to introduce or reinforce neighborhoods will need to start with a coherent policy framework that clarifies three aspects of neighborhood formation: structure, amenity provisions, and form. To

**Figure 4-47** Transit-oriented residential development at the Joyce Station on Vancouver's Skytrain system. The station has drawn housing, offices, and shops all within a short walk.

forestall the tendency for ad hoc patterns and incomplete provisions, these neighborhood concepts need to be enacted as regulations, with everyone working toward the same goals.

Regarding the structure of the neighborhood, regulations will include a preferred size of the neighborhood zone, which, from our own experience, can be stretched from the Perry minimum of a five-minute walking radius to a maximum seven- to ten-minute walking radius. Regulations will permit at least the minimum number of people required to support basic local commercial provisions, including a food store and pharmacy, which would be zoned to occur at intervals of about 1 mile (1.6 kilometers) along the arterial street. The arterial street should also, if at all possible, be a transit corridor, so these mixed-use centers would be at a transit stop. The regulations should permit at least 20,000 residents within the approximately square mile walking distance around the center (just less than 8,000 residents per square kilometer), the density ultimately necessary to make commercial development work. That averages to thirty-two people per acre, or about twelve families per acre (about thirty families per hectare). This density is about twice the average density for suburban tract development today. Much of the additional development should take place in apartments within the commercial corridor, however, so changes to existing houses and lots, if they happen, will take place very gradually. These neighborhood densities are attainable in metropolitan regions that are growing, but only if continued urbanization and annexation is reduced at the urban edge. Reducing the pressure to urbanize farms and forests just outside the existing urban area will be one of the benefits from getting better use of land that is underused in existing commercial corridors. In writing neighborhood regulations, there should be a target mix of unit types, including both household types and income levels. There may also be a workplace or jobs target. Widening the alternatives available for housing makes it easier to provide affordable accommodation for retired people, young people just leaving home, and service workers. The building types that should be permitted under these regulations, a ground floor of shops and parking with four floors of apartments above, are already being built in many markets.

In addition to a walkable scale and transit availability, each neighborhood should be planned with a list of amenities—the neighborhood amenity package—and for each local amenity there should be standards and targets. Along with a hierarchy of parks, clusters of neighborhoods should include a neighborhood school that can be reached by children walking or riding bicycles, at least at the primary school level. There should also be a neighborhood branch library, recreation center, senior center, and childcare facilities. When costs prohibit separate facilities, combining facilities is a good option, and such groupings can be strategically located to serve up to four neighborhoods, creating an efficient and cost-effective arrangement. Although there can be problems with sharing facilities among separate budgets and administrations, there are now places where these kinds of synergies and savings have been obtained. A notable example is the elementary school that shares a building and playing fields with a YMCA center in the Lake Nona community near Orlando, Florida. Public policies and development regulations can promote sharing the location of public services to reinforce neighborhoods, and it may be possible to secure at least some of the amenities through zoning bonus provisions. Targets can motivate completion of amenities at specified levels as a new neighborhood is completed, or an older area turns into a neighborhood as the commercial corridor is redeveloped.

There should also be urban design guidelines for the form of a neighborhood, the relationship of buildings to streets and public spaces, and walkable streets as well as standards for bikeways and walkway networks. There should be provisions for heritage preservation and an incentive program to facilitate reuse of these buildings. Sophisticated guidelines will include targets for public art.

A city or suburb can have a wide variety of densities within its constellation of neighborhoods. The lower-density neighborhoods will tend to be farther away from the traditional core city, but this natural pattern can be broken down with denser neighborhoods clustered closer to transit nodes and other places with strong development energy, even if these points are a long way away from the original city center. Regulations that encourage compact development are important for several interrelated policy reasons: to take pressures off of the agricultural lands and natural landscapes in rural areas by making better use of urbanized land, which we consider a fundamental issue; to make a transportation alternative to the car more viable and affordable; to improve efficiency of community and utility services; and to promote social, cultural, and economic opportunity. Density, to be popular with consumers, also has to reflect unique situations and be conceived to support different tastes and preferences that engender special character and identity.

Basic density targets will deal with both the social ecology of the neighborhood and its performance for sustainability. In many suburban areas in the United States, zoning specifications set densities at less than two units or families per acre (about five units per hectare). In Canada, recent suburban densities clock in at about six units or families per acre (about fifteen units per hectare) or less. Minimum average densities to support transit within a ten-minute walking distance of a station-stop need to be at a level of ten to twenty units or families per acre (twenty-five to fifty units per hectare), but much of that density can be accommodated close to the station stop, grading down to single-family lots at the edges of the walking circle. At this density, neighborhood schools probably need to serve more than one neighborhood, although having a multiuse park, school, senior center, and library building can make a smaller school easier to finance. As mentioned above, at thirty to forty units or families per acre (about seventy-five to one hundred units per hectare), we begin to see support for higher levels of amenity, including the possibility of a neighborhood school within a single neighborhood walking circle. At this density, civic costs start to break even, and a greater variety of day-to-day shopping options is viable. Above these ranges, variations in built form and character will offer differing experiences to diverse groups of consumers, but forty units or families per acre (about one hundred units per hectare) seems to be a pivotal threshold for a true urban experience and basic sustainability. At this scale, they are also desirable places; one example is the Mount Pleasant neighborhood of Vancouver (figure 4-48).

There should also be other kinds of local differences and anomalies. Each neighborhood has to be designed or retrofitted to reflect both the basic template and the unique and special conditions of the setting, people, and history of the place. So, if there are people already living in an area that might be augmented with facilities and public realm improvements, as well as diversified in its housing and commerce to become a fully sustainable neighborhood, the residents already there need to participate in planning the changes. They can

Figure 4-48 Older inner-city "streetcar neighborhoods" such as Mount Pleasant in Vancouver offer a viable sustainable model as they have evolved and diversified over the years. They illustrate the forty units per acre (one hundred units per hectare) threshold that works from environmental, social, and economic perspectives.

visit successful neighborhoods to see for themselves what the advantages of neighborhood living can be. They can then become active designers of the neighborhood regulations together with city officials and professional urban designers. A concentrated multiday workshop, often called a charette, is a way of getting all interests together to reach a consensus about what should be done. This process accommodates setting the standards, but also fosters the inclusion of subtle consumer expectations, and highlights the special attributes that can make the neighborhood unique. These features might include a cluster of historic buildings, a major park, a waterfront, or unusual views. One consideration will be how density and building massing express themselves. Some communities will embrace the transit-oriented development model, which focuses higher density and higher-scaled buildings at transit stations and leaves other areas at lower scale. Others may target higher density and scale along local retail spines with housing over shops. Still others may zero in on anomalies within the area where there are larger sites that were passed over by earlier development and now can be used to introduce alternative density and scale. Or, there may be a preference for subtle densification throughout the built fabric of the residential district, lot by lot.

To round out a smart neighborhood strategy, a social kick start, such as the event shown in figure 4-49, is helpful. This can be the result of a community development strategy that fosters the formation of neighborhood

**Figure 4-49** This Children's Day in a local downtown park in Vancouver was well attended and also carefully planned. For complete neighborhoods, a social kick start is sometimes necessary, driven by government or by citizen action.

organizations and institutions and proposes programs to pull people into the local activities and society. There may also be need for an affordable housing strategy. These measures are the way that neighborhood social networks are formed and how mutual aid is set off. This is how neighborhood stability is engendered.

## Restoring Older, Deteriorated Neighborhoods

Unfortunately, no discussion about neighborhoods and local business centers is complete without referring to places in cities where high numbers of residents are living in poverty and having to deal with pervasive crime, particularly drug-related crime. Some of the buildings in these areas have been kept up by their owners, and others may have been abandoned and become crack houses or squats; some structures may have been allowed to deteriorate so far that they will eventually have to be demolished. Vacant lots are filled with rubbish as summonses for code violations are ignored, and sanitation departments often do not dare come into these violent neighborhoods to enforce a cleanup. These kinds of problems can be found in only a small number of neighborhoods, but most cities in the United States have such places. Many of the deteriorated buildings in these distressed areas are capable of restoration into good housing, with in-fill development going into the vacant lots. They could even attract new residents who see depressed building prices as a special opportunity. Civic and nonprofit neighborhood development corporations such as Habitat for Humanity can have a big role in such restoration projects. Before anything like that can transform such a neighborhood, however, the underlying problems have to be tackled with a coherent social development strategy targeted to the particular problems in the area.

One such approach, pioneered by the police in High Point, North Carolina, with advice from David Kennedy of the John Jay College of Criminal Justice in New York City, is to intervene in the neighborhood drug market, which is always a source of violence and danger to the rest of the community. The leaders of the local drug market, who are inevitably a small group and always known to the police, are invited to a meeting at which they are assured that they will not be arrested. Instead, they find themselves talking to community people, relatives, and ex-offenders about the impacts of the drug trade, alternatives for their lives, and services that would be available to them. License plates of people driving into the neighborhood to buy drugs are also identified and the car owners sent warning letters. The result in High Point is that drug dealing and related violence and danger decreased dramatically. The people in the West End neighborhood were able to come out of their houses and reclaim the community. Neighborhood volunteers began to clean up empty lots, and people began to fix up their houses. Once people reestablished control of their street corners, they took turns occupying them by congregating in lawn chairs and making it clear that they would not tolerate anyone coming in to their community to deal drugs. This type of intervention is being repeated in other places through the National Network for Safe Communities, an organization run out of the John Jay College of Criminal Justice.

More profound programs to limit the effects of drug addiction are under way in several proactive cities, such as Geneva, Zurich, Frankfurt, Vancouver, and Sydney. These programs are moving away from the war on drugs and approach drug addiction as an illness rather than a crime. In such programs, there is usually what is called a four-pillar approach, which includes harm reduction for addicts with such things as safe injection sites and needle exchanges; prevention, including aggressive education with young people; treatment, with even direct prescription of the necessary drugs in advanced programs; and enforcement, focusing policing efforts on dealers rather than addicts. Such programs are still quite new, but initial results show a dramatic reduction of drug users on city streets, a drop in overdose deaths, reduction in infection rates for HIV and hepatitis, and, where drugs are directly provided, a drop in random property crime. These results significantly change the ambience in public places and the levels and sense of safety in communities.

If law and order can be restored in challenged neighborhoods, and particularly if the impact of the drug culture can be moderated, it is then possible for other housing and social service programs to take hold. Comprehensive transit systems that help people in all parts of a city commute to jobs, increasing affordable housing choices, and more effective education are all important factors, but no city can be truly successful economically, or ethically, as long as parts of it exist outside the normal legal and social systems.

## Summarizing the Essentials of Compact Downtown Centers and Walkable Neighborhoods

Walkable places are experiencing a comeback in most cities, both in and around the downtown, and in suburban centers, some old and renovated, some newly constructed. Their attractiveness is their mix of activities and high levels of convenience. The lifestyles among young "singles" and older "empty nesters" are helping energize this phenomenon, but if buildings and places are appropriately designed and coordinated, and the right amenities and services are included, the mix, convenience, and walkability can also appeal to other kinds of households. Reinforcing this trend requires the right strategy of development regulations and public policy incentives along with public-private collaboration.

The mixed-use building format has proved itself financially viable where regulations permit it. Mixed uses are practical, are land conserving, and can contribute to creating more identifiable places. Market synergies can create a balance of commercial, residential, and entertainment uses. Development regulations should permit and promote the arrangement of the "high street" or "main street" retail frontages accessible from sidewalks, not parking lots. Appealing to consumers, street-front retailing is enabled by the mixed-use building. Heritage preservation and reuse can be facilitated in this scenario because there is room in the pro forma to use incentives, and because it is architecturally interesting to integrate the old and new in a single development. Cities can reinforce these places with alternative parking standards and shared auto programs.

With the right development regulations and carefully administered design guidelines, areas surrounding stations along commercial corridors equipped with improved transit systems can evolve into walkable mixed-use places with enough intensity and scale of development to create a coherent neighborhood ensemble. Surface parking lots in commercial districts can be screened from the experience of the street, and the economics of apartments can permit secure garage parking. Apartment towers can be visually anchored to the sidewalk with a low-rise podium containing townhouses, shops, or offices instead of being surrounded by parking or formless plazas. Higher-quality materials can be used for areas close to pedestrians. Even big-box retail formats can be integrated into this kind of urban scene, so that they become a contributing part of the energy and a benefit to the massing of the area. Some of the parking for big-box stores can be provided below grade or on the roofs of the stores. Through guidelines, these features can be choreographed among building complexes along a street and in the surrounding neighborhood. Through discretionary allowances and transactional approvals, incentives can be created to implement the preferred patterns. How to attain these objectives will be discussed in chapter 6.

The compactness and convenience of traditional downtowns can be re-created, with far greater amenity than before. Walkable neighborhoods once only available in the older parts of cities and suburbs can become a standard throughout the metropolitan region.

A reinforcing public realm strategy can bring all uses and activities together in traditional urban centers and suburban downtowns, in new business centers, and in neighborhoods of different density, creating a continuous positive experience. We will discuss public realm strategies in chapter 5.

Compact business centers and walkable neighborhoods supported by transit are more sustainable development patterns than the conventional separated uses reachable only by car, and their additional density and efficiency can become an alternative to suburban sprawl. Together with development regulations that recognize that the natural environment is a complex ecosystem and not just white spaces on a street map, these measures, within the reach of all local governments, can make big improvements to the future of the whole built environment.

# 5. Designing and Managing the Public Realm

**T**he public realm is a term borrowed from philosophy and social science. When talking about city design, it refers to all the spaces in the city that are more or less available for public use (figure 5-1). The public realm includes land owned by the public, such as streets, public squares, and parks, as well as waterfronts, freeway rights-of-way and their verges, and back lanes and other utilitarian places that represent great potential value but are often forgotten. It also includes the sites and forecourts associated with public buildings. Another public realm component, accessible

**Figure 5-1** In this typical urban street, the public realm extends from property line to property line, encompassing the street, the sidewalks, and the grassed area for trees in between. This is the heart of the public domain, which also includes parks and public building sites. Public experience extends right to the face of the buildings, so even within the property lines it is important to have consistent, compatible treatments to those out in the public right-of-way.

to a greater or lesser degree by the public, exists on private property, including shopping malls, building lobbies and atriums, plazas, courtyards, roof gardens, arenas, and stadiums. Thus, there is a range of public, semipublic, and semiprivate space that, together, comprise the places where there is a public interest in how they are designed and how the public is allowed to use them. Embracing the completeness of the public realm, while acknowledging that methods for its design and management are different depending on its public or private ownership, is an important principle of ecodesign. When we experience the city, we are often unaware of the lines of ownership, but we are very aware of the continuous impressions we receive. The best public realm offers a connected experience that includes both public and privately owned spaces.

The great cities of the world have all been shaped by programs that put the public realm first. Think, for example, about Paris, where the boulevards, squares, and parks were rebuilt from the seventeenth through the nineteenth centuries to form a cohesive public open-space experience for the entire historic city. It was a conscious government strategy to make the city a cultural and commercial magnet. The idea was to create ceremonial places, improve traffic connections, and open up light and air, but it also created a public experience that has been attracting people ever since (figure 5-2).[1] A more recent example is Copenhagen, where the entire street and public open-space

**Figure 5-2** On the Boulevard Saint-Germain in Paris, a rich diversity of activity occurs on the street and along the adjacent sidewalks. Paris invented the boulevard, which is still a vital street model; here, it has been modified to accommodate a busway.

system has been reshaped incrementally since the Strøget, an important shopping street, was made a pedestrian mall in 1962. Copenhagen's policy is to give primacy to pedestrians and bicycles. There are still trucks and automobiles on the streets, but they have their place, just as pedestrians and cyclists have theirs (figure 5-3). Consider also Savannah, where the original network of squares had become decrepit and dangerous but has now been revitalized with landscape and embellishments to again become the outdoor "living rooms" of the city (figure 5-4). Although each of these cities has its problem areas, their overall prevailing image is determined by how well they accommodate everyday experience through their public realm. People visit cities with well-designed and managed streets and public spaces just to be there because life is so much more pleasant than it is at home. The same coher-

**Figure 5-3** Copenhagen has made itself into a great pedestrian city. This street view shows that cars, bicycles, and pedestrians have their equal places. The hard stone surfaces of Copenhagen's street design, with light fixtures hung inconspicuously over the roadway from wires, follow a different aesthetic from the greenery and ornamental street lamps along Paris boulevards.

**Figure 5-4** A view from one of the historic squares in Savannah, Georgia, which have become the outdoor "living rooms" of the city.

ence, character, and connectedness can be created in all cities and suburbs in the developed world that already have the necessary wealth, design resources, and social understanding. The key to improving the lives of the millions of people who live in informal settlements throughout the world also lies with providing public infrastructure and a network of streets, public spaces, and public services, although the resource problems are going to be much more difficult to solve than when there is already an established governmental system.

Sometimes, for important public places, the public realm is given special attention, such as the very elegant streetscape of Confederation Boulevard in Ottawa. Creative designers look at specific needs and design for the specific situation. When that happens, the public is almost always consulted and becomes party to finding the design solutions. Many North American cities have made major public realm improvements in recent decades. New York, Boston, Chicago, Charleston, Washington, San Francisco, Portland, Oregon, Montreal, and Vancouver are notable examples, and there are many others elsewhere in the world. Unfortunately, such improvements do not happen often enough. In any modern city, one can count the special initiatives, and they stand in vivid contrast to the hundreds of other standardized public realm "improvements" that are included in the annual budgets of every municipality.

When specific design by architects, landscape architects, or urban designers does occur, we get those few places that stand out and become beloved, places that can compete with the lovely historic spaces that claim most of our attention in today's cities. Unfortunately, in most cities, the character of the public lands, including streets, public spaces, and even parks, has been determined by decisions made for reasons not related to creating good, coherent public places. We find the same contradictions and blindness that we wrote about in chapter 4 when describing the policies that have so often misdirected the regulation of private property in the modern city: the drive for efficiency related to single purposes, public safety defined narrowly, extreme risk-averse management, minimum cost as a governing criterion, and what seem to be endless arrangements and accommodations for automobile traffic. The result is not design at all; instead, it is a routine layout based on the given specifications. In many cities, we see schemes in which parklands are the leftover places where other types of development have been found to be impractical, and we see traffic lanes that have been incrementally widened to the point that there is room for no other user than the private car, not even a modest sidewalk.

Cities may look accidental, but they are formed by official actions. We have to remind ourselves that what seems chaotic and unplanned is actually closely determined. The form of public spaces is set by application of standards and requirements for every aspect of the use of the place: street and sidewalk standards, fire access requirements, health standards, recreation standards and sports templates, utility standards, liability parameters, and limitations because only certain elements are stocked by city agencies, such as particular types of streetlights or paving materials. These procedures create utilitarian, homogenized places; they are forgettable places (figure 5-5). We see endless examples in our cities, big and small, through new construction or retrofits, of the trade-off between rich human experience and the efficiencies and expediencies that might make sense in and of themselves but make no sense in terms of the totality of human engagement, character, or place-making.

This emerging dull quality of public space, especially streets, seems to now be taken for granted by government; it is the status quo. People seem to cope the best they can and complain the least they must. They tune out the dissonances: the overhead utility wires, glaring signs, traffic signal booms, narrow, broken sidewalks, and ragged fringes of parking lots. People just get used to these surroundings, but they are still a constant negative influence on their lives, a pervasive irritation. If we are getting the public realm required by regulations and standards, we should be able to change the rules to get the public realm we actually want.

The quality and diversity of the public realm is probably more vital today than it has ever been in modern times. Public realm improvements can bring

**Figure 5-5** In this typical modern suburban arterial street scene, the public realm may look unplanned, but it is nonetheless the product of governmental setback and sign regulations and official construction and drainage standards. Unfortunately, such places, found everywhere in the newer parts of North American cities, are banal and forgettable.

with them significant competitive advantages and environmental benefits. In the modern city, both social and economic development are driven by drawing people to the place and building their attachment and loyalty to the place. In large measure, this happens in public places where you want to be and may carry away a fond memory. We also now understand clearly that, as densities increase, the contribution of public space to livability and health is more essential than ever. It has been demonstrated again and again that high-quality public spaces enhance private property values. Walking, cycling, and transit within public spaces also help balance the transportation system, reduce capital costs for roads and highways, and reduce the fuel costs and air pollution from traffic jams and excessive auto use.

The most sought after and successful places are the ones that are efficient, well landscaped, and easily accessible. They generally offer mixed use and serial use, alternate uses at different times of the day. Encouraging trees to grow within a public landscape improves air quality, and public plazas and parks can be a part of a stormwater management system that is also a natural ecosystem threaded through the urban fabric.

We will begin by looking at some of the special situations where a specific design has produced extraordinary places. We will go on to discuss the principles that make these designs successful and then consider what can be done to make a well-designed public environment possible everywhere.

## Correcting a Disrupted Public Realm, Especially Intrusive Highways

What is the single worst condition disrupting the entire urban experience around it? In many places, the answer to this question is elevated railways or highways. The rebuilding of downtown Philadelphia after World War II began with the removal of the elevated railway tracks into the old Broad Street Station in the heart of the city. A new business center grew up on the land that became available when the station was moved back to 30th Street and the downtown tracks were removed. In New York City, many of the elevated transit structures, "the Els," running through the center of Manhattan came down, setting off real-estate booms, especially along Third Avenue and Sixth Avenue. More recently, Boston's elevated Central Artery was replaced by the "Big Dig," the Central Artery Tunnel Project, completed in 2006. This project was part of a comprehensive highway reorganization, but the public realm improvement has been substantial: the Rose Fitzgerald Kennedy Greenway, which is a chain of city parks, plus the opportunity to knit the downtown street network back together (figure 5-6). Comparable public space improvements have taken place in many other cities, including the landscaping of old industrial canal systems in Richmond, Virginia (figure 5-7), and Indianapolis; the replacement

**Figure 5-6** The new chain of parks, the Rose Fitzgerald Kennedy Greenway, built over the Central Artery Tunnel, Boston's "Big Dig." Some may find the landscaping disappointing, but the parks and streets are a big improvement over the elevated expressway that was there before.

**Figure 5-7** Creation of the Canal Walk in Richmond, Virginia, in 1999 was part of a construction initiative that also involved the relocation of a major sewer pipe.

of the earthquake-damaged elevated Embarcadero Freeway in San Francisco with a surface street, plaza, and promenade; the Cross City Tunnel in Sydney, Australia; the new park that forms a cap right over a freeway in Dallas (figure 5-8); and the Tom McCall waterfront park in Portland, Oregon, created by the removal of Harbor Drive (figure 5-9).

### Seoul's Cheonggyecheon

In Seoul, the capital of South Korea, a stream—the Cheonggyecheon—flowed through the center of the city. The city grew up on both sides of this waterway, but by the middle of the twentieth century, after years of neglect and the

**Figure 5-8** Klyde Warren Park in Dallas, Texas, built as a cover over a freeway, knits the two sides of the downtown back together. It has created an elegant focus for new development.

**Figure 5-9** Tom McCall Park in Portland, Oregon, replaced a major road along the riverfront, creating an attractive amenity for downtown workers and nearby residents.

horrific damage from the Korean War, the stream was little more than an open sewer, and the city decided to put a cover over it. Then the streamway became the site of the elevated Cheonggye Expressway, completed in 1971. By the late 1990s, the highway was so badly deteriorated that large vehicles had to be banned. The highway was also blighting the areas around it and confining the expansion of the central business district, which was losing ground to a new business center on the south side of the Han River. In 2002, Seoul's Mayor Lee Myung-bak decided not to try to repair the highway and not only tear it down, but also remove the deck over the stream, restore the water quality, and create a public amenity 6.2 miles (10 kilometers) long. The original pattern of tributary streams had been greatly changed as the city developed, so except during floods, the Cheonggyecheon's water is augmented by water pumped from the Han River and by drainage from the subway system (figure 5-10). The finished project was opened in 2005 (figure 5-11). Critics had predicted that removing the expressway would produce catastrophic traffic congestion,

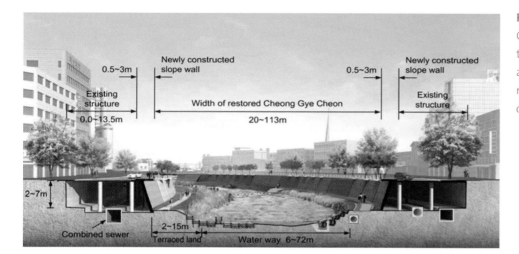

**Figure 5-10** This sectional view of the Cheonggyecheon in Seoul shows that the apparently simple design is actually a complex work of engineering with multiple purposes, including emergency drainage for major storms.

**Figure 5-11** Looking along the newly accessible Cheonggyecheon in Seoul shows how it has become one of the most important public amenities in the city. Turning a sewer topped by an elevated highway into a clean stream in a linear park is an inspiration for all cities.

but the transportation system has adjusted to the change. There has been a 12 percent reduction in the average traffic speed in the center of the city, but there has also been a 19 percent reduction in the number of cars coming into the city. Bus ridership has increased as much as 10 percent and subway ridership as much as 9 percent. There has been a big improvement in air quality and a substantial decrease in hot weather air temperatures along the stream.[2] The Cheonggyecheon is a good example of what we are calling ecodesign, uniting principles of good urban design with restoration of the natural landscape, although that restoration has required some artificial means. The new

**Figure 5-12** The Madrid Rio Park along the Manzanares River in the center of Madrid is built over highways along both banks that have now been enclosed in concrete structures, correcting the serious urban design mistake made when the highway was first built in the 1970s and cut off the city from the river.

ecosystem created by the stream now supports several species of fish, and its surrounding landscape now includes varied bird life.

## Madrid Rio

The Madrid Rio project is even more ambitious than the Cheonggyecheon as it kept the highway in operation and rebuilt it underground. Highway M30 had been constructed along the Manzanares River in the center of Madrid during the 1970s on both of the banks. Beginning in 2003, the highway was rebuilt in concrete boxes or underground on both sides of the river, and an international competition was held to design the park spaces that were becoming available atop the highway. The competition was won by a team directed by Burgos and Garrido from Madrid with West 8, a landscape architecture firm from Rotterdam. The construction of the chain of parks along the river is now complete, with the landscaping in place (figure 5-12). Landscape restorations like these are big and expensive, and they can take a generation or more to implement, but they can transform the public realm and the experience and image of the city.

## Turning Viaducts into Parks

One alternative to removing an elevated viaduct that is no longer needed is to reuse it as a linear park. In areas where there is not much parkland, the addition of a continuous open space may be more valuable than the light and air created by demolishing the structure. Many cities are looking at the possibilities for making unused elevated structures an active part of the public realm.

## Paris' Promenade Plantée

The prototype for adaptive reuse of elevated railways is the Promenade Plantée in Paris, built atop the former viaduct for the Vincennes rail line (figure 5-13). The old viaduct is handsome. The arches along its base are being filled in with stores that relate it to the buildings across the streets on either side. The goal has been to fill the spaces with restaurants, galleries, studios, and other arts-related businesses, making it into "Le Viaduc des Artes." Landscaping along the promenade by landscape architects Jacques Vergely and Philippe Mathieux is like a traditional park (figure 5-14).

**Figure 5-13** The Promenade Plantée in Paris is an adaptive reuse of the former Vincennes railway viaduct and was the world prototype for adaptive reuse of this kind of nineteenth-century rail infrastructure. The arches of this handsome structure are being filled with galleries, shops, and arts-related uses, making it "Le Viaduc des Artes."

**Figure 5-14** The formal gardens on top of the viaduct in Paris are a lush embellishment for the city. Jacques Vergely and Philippe Mathieux are the landscape architects.

## New York's High Line

An obsolete elevated freight railway in the lower west side of Manhattan serving now long-gone piers and waterfront warehouses seemed destined for demolition until it was retrofitted as the now famous High Line Park (figure 5-15). People and businesses colonizing the gritty old warehouses liked the trees and plants that had taken root along the abandoned tracks, giving the impression of a path through wild nature. Led by Joshua David and Robert Hammond, a group called Friends of the High Line was formed in 1999 to raise money for improvements and to advocate for a new kind of linear park. Ultimately, the New York City government found a way to finance restoration and development of the park by committing $50 million of public capital funds and creating a special zoning district where developers would buy the air rights to portions of the viaduct and transfer the development to sites along the line. There were also substantial contributions from private donors. The design was prepared by architects Diller Scofidio + Renfrew and landscape architects James Corner Field Operations. The first section opened in 2009, a second opened in 2011, and the third, completed in 2014, connects to massive new development over the 30th Street railway yards just to the north.

The High Line certainly embodies many of the principles we are highlighting in this book. It is a major design intervention that is transforming an entire district of the city, and it is introducing elements of the natural environment back into an area that was almost entirely composed of structures. It has been a huge success, with throngs of visitors and many new buildings drawn to this increasingly chic area, which still retains much of the character of its industrial past.

**Figure 5-15** View of the High Line Park in New York City, looking south from 20th Street. The design of the park recognizes the industrial origins of the area, which now has a mix of old warehouses and expensive new development. It is a green spine in an amenity-deficient area.

### Chicago's Bloomingdale Trail

In Chicago, the Bloomingdale Park and Trail has been designed by Michael Van Valkenburgh Associates along 2.7 miles (4.3 kilometers) of an old viaduct that runs parallel to Bloomingdale Avenue on the northwest side of the city. The design seeks to maximize connectivity with streets and parks at ground level and will offer a variety of spaces and activities.

### Turning Waterfronts into Parks and Neighborhoods

Container shipping made many traditional urban piers obsolete because there wasn't sufficient land area associated with these piers to store the containers and to then transfer them to rail lines or trucks. Because of rationalization efforts for railway operations and to cut access and warehousing costs, inner-city rail yards that once occupied key waterfront sites near shipping operations have also now been replaced by yards much farther from the center. Many cities have now rebuilt such waterfronts as public parks and esplanades or as entire new neighborhoods.

### Brooklyn Bridge Park

A particularly interesting example of a transition from industrial waterfront to public use is the Brooklyn Bridge Park across from lower Manhattan. The plan distinguishes between upland areas, which can be turned into natural

**Figure 5-16** View from the Brooklyn Bridge showing the completed first phase of the Brooklyn Bridge Park. In the background, construction is beginning on recreation buildings on the former pier structures. The design for the whole park complex is by Michael Van Valkenburgh Associates.

landscapes, and the piers, which are structures that can be rebuilt for more intensive recreational uses. The overall plan, by Michael Van Valkenburgh Associates, allocates the waterfront land and piers among different uses. The configuration is layered, with the existing Brooklyn Queens Expressway on a series of cantilevered structures and the famous Brooklyn Heights Promenade built above the expressway. Back down at the waterfront-grade level is Furman Street, which used to be the access to the piers and will now be the address for apartment towers. Proceeds from this real estate will help pay for the park. The land mass of the park is built up as a shield from the noise generated by the expressway. Lighter landscaping and structures are built over the piers (figure 5-16).

## New York's Battery Park City and Vancouver's False Creek North Neighborhood

There are opportunities to transform industrial and commercial sites no longer in active use in every city and suburb. Sometimes, there is enough land along a waterfront to plan and develop a whole new district. Other large pieces of land in a single ownership—perhaps an old freight yard, a vacant factory, or a failed shopping mall—could also be an opportunity to re-create a natural landscape and bring in new uses. There are sometimes good economic development reasons for maintaining an inventory of vacant industrial sites,

**Figure 5-17** Composite photo forming a panorama of Battery Park City in New York: high-style inner-city living on the water, close to financial sector jobs.

but often land in developed urban areas is going to waste. Battery Park City in lower Manhattan (figure 5-17) and False Creek North in Vancouver (figure 5-18) are large-scale waterfront developments that offer useful lessons about the importance of the public realm in creating successful new parts of a city.

Battery Park City is the smaller of the two developments at 92 acres (37.2 hectares) compared with False Creek North's 166 acres (67.2 hectares). Battery Park City began in the 1960s with the excavation for the twin towers of the World Trade Center. Rather than cart the soil and rocks away, they were used to help create new land to replace obsolete piers along the Hudson River just west of the Trade Center site. To develop Battery Park City, the State of New York created a public agency, the Battery Park City Authority, which owns the land.

**Figure 5-18** False Creek North in Vancouver, a gracious new waterfront community that has transformed the image of the whole city.

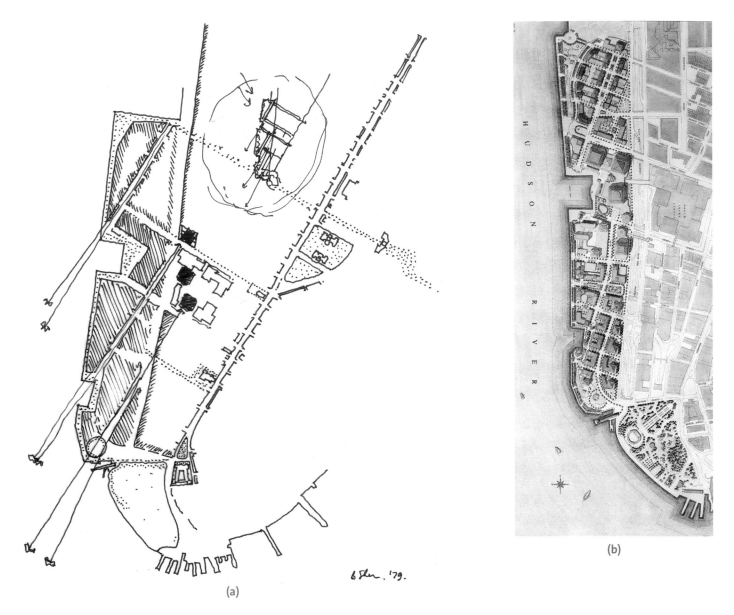

6 Shea. '79.

(a)

(b)

**Figure 5-19** Diagrammatic Plan for Battery Park City (a) showing the network of connections to existing streets, creating a framework for subdistricts that reflects the scale of the Manhattan grid as seen in the fully developed illustrative plan (b). Planners and urban designers are Cooper-Eckstut. Drawing by Brain Shea.

False Creek North is built on the site of obsolete Canadian Pacific Railway yards. The land was purchased by the Province of British Columbia as the site for a world's fair, Expo '86. The exposition opened up public access to the north side of False Creek, which until then had been a purely industrial area. After the exposition closed, this waterfront land was sold to the Concord Pacific

Group, a private international development company, which worked closely with the City of Vancouver to design and build the district.

The original Battery Park City plan was for a series of massive buildings on large superblocks. Public areas were limited to a narrow series of plazas along the river, negotiated with the City of New York to satisfy its demands for public access. The developer's original False Creek North plan, which was not approved by the City of Vancouver, proposed to cut a channel close to the already built-up areas of Vancouver so as to make the new development appear as a series of self-contained islands. In both situations, the ultimate plan has reversed direction and welcomed the public.

Battery Park City was redesigned in 1979 by the firm of Cooper, Eckstut, after the original project had run into severe financial difficulty. Figure 5-19a is a conceptual diagram of the redesigned street and waterfront configuration. The diagram relates the new development to historic Broadway, Manhattan's original main street. The most important downtown streets connect to Broadway and are extended directly into the new waterfront development. It wasn't possible to connect all the blocks because of an existing highway, Westway. The blocks within Battery Park City, shown in the illustrative site plan in figure 5-19b, are designed to be similar in size to the prevailing historic blocks nearby and are organized along three new north-south avenues designed to focus on views of the Statue of Liberty, across New York Harbor. The waterfront forms bays at important locations and includes a public esplanade. Not including the streets, there are 36 acres (14.6 hectares) of parks and public open space in Battery Park City serving market-rate housing and office blocks.

The basic plan for what was originally called Concord Pacific Place by the developer but is now commonly known as False Creek North was prepared by a truly integrated public-private multidisciplinary team of urban designers and planners. The Concord Pacific team was led by Stanley Kwok with prime designers Rick Hulbert, Graham McGarva, Barry Downs, John Davidson, and James Cheng. The public team included all departments of the City of Vancouver under the leadership of the planning department.[3] No special authority was used. Instead, the private company owned and would develop the land, but was totally dependent on a development agreement with the city for the right to build. An overall Official Development Plan (figure 5-20), including many individual performance agreements, was approved by the city council in 1990. Then, the public-private collaboration extended into years of detailed area plans and zoning, followed by implementation of both the private development and the public realm. The street and public open-space plan extended the existing principal streets from the adjacent area into the development. The perimeter street, Pacific Boulevard, is an easily crossed traditional boulevard that permits seamless connections between the new and old blocks. The entire waterfront is accessible to the public along a linear park that is part of

**Figure 5-20** Plan for Vancouver's False Creek North, which illustrates how the new area is an extension of the existing inner city, with the addition of a pattern of super-amenities that serve not only the area, but also nearby neighborhoods.

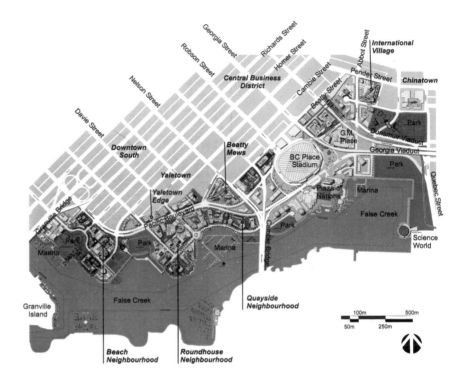

a larger seawall concept, a cycling, jogging, and walking path that extends along much of the downtown waterfront. There are bays and parks at major transition points in the plan. Not including the streets and the waterfront walkway/bikeway, there are 42 acres (17 hectares) of parks and public open space in False Creek North serving both market and nonmarket housing and mixed-use development arranged in a series of small neighborhoods.

## Structural Principles for the Public Realm

The large-scale plans for Battery Park City and False Creek North illustrate some important principles for the structure and design of the public realm, applicable whenever a new public domain is being created in a city or suburb.

### Emphasizing Small Blocks

The street system needs to be relatively fine-grained with many intersections so that there is maximum access from private properties to the public realm, as that kind of accessibility greatly increases the value of the property. A fine-grained street system is also safer for pedestrians and encourages social inter-action. In both Battery Park City and False Creek North, everyone lives or works within a short distance of an attractive, easily accessible public place. The modernist idea of superblocks, part of the rejected original plans for both of these projects, does save some land from being used for streets, but this turns out to be a false economy because it limits space for public engagement and discourse. The trade-off that the designer must keep in mind is making the street system as fine-grained as possible, while keeping development parcels big enough to provide appropriate building footprints for different types of uses, and with enough space for functional parking layouts underground or in a building base. The downtown in Portland, Oregon, with a street grid of 300-foot square blocks (a little more than 90 meters on each side), is often noted as well calibrated for both of these concerns.

## Maintaining Connectivity

The street system needs to be an interconnected network; in general, the more connectivity, the better. The pattern that we typically see in many recent large developments—only one or two ways into the area from commuter streets—should be avoided. There should be enough continuity to offer choice for many different routes. There should also be a hierarchy of streets of varying scales and carrying capacity, but that hierarchy should not prevent flexible uses for any one street. The traffic within the street system needs to be managed, even choreographed, throughout the day to get the most out of it and to broker its use of street space at any one moment of the day. The network does not have to accommodate all modes at all places at all times, but it needs to facilitate a free flow of movement of all modes as much as possible. Dead-end streets can be appropriate in some places. In both Battery Park City and False Creek North, some streets come to turnarounds that are entrances to the public spaces along the waterfront. There is connectivity for pedestrians but not for cars.

As a more general principle, some limitations on through movement of autos at key locations will be justified to reduce traffic impacts on residents. There are some limited places for cul-de-sacs in suburbs and for street barriers or traffic management devices in urban settings, but the fluid movement of other modes should not be cut off. There is an art in finding the balance between barriers and openness that delivers both comfort and convenience. Conversely, to secure the continuity of the network, it is sometimes prudent to have the right-of-way in place even if the use is not yet allocated. Such rights-of-way, ultimately planned for a movement function, can be used in the short term for view corridors or miniparks or can just sit fallow. The potential continuity of the system provides flexibility for whatever use might be needed in the future, because adding components to a street network after development has already taken place can be very difficult.

## Preferring Two-Way Streets

It is better to err on the side of two-way streets rather than the one-way patterns that speed the flow of cars in and out of town during the commuter rush hours. A one-way street limits access to properties, which limits the utility and even the value of that property. Two-way streets facilitate pedestrian safety by slowing traffic, and they enhance visibility for retail.

## Making Multiuse Streets

Streets need to allow for multiple uses. This has been explored best by Allan Jacobs in his influential books *Great Streets* and *The Boulevard Book* (with Elizabeth MacDonald). Jacobs advises that in a well-functioning street, all the demands should be served, but no one demand ought to dominate all other users, or be allowed to push them out. His theme is that everyone has to make compromises.[4] In both Battery Park City and False Creek North, traffic is light except along Westway and on Pacific Boulevard, so the local streets are designed for many uses with a minimum of traffic control devices. As shown in figure 5-21, South End Avenue in Battery Park City accommodates two-way traffic, a jaywalking pedestrian, and a delivery truck making a turn, all without difficulty. A painted safety zone in this portion of the street indicates that normally there should only be one lane of traffic in each direction. There

**Figure 5-21** South End Avenue at Battery Park City in Manhattan accommodates all kinds of traffic and is very safe for people on foot.

**Figure 5-22** Davie Street in False Creek North has a median that makes it easy for jaywalkers while also handling volumes of bikes, short-term parking, cars, and deliveries. This scene embodies the Vancouver priority for pedestrians and cycling on downtown streets.

are no traffic signals. The theory is that the more you differentiate rights-of-way for each mode, the more that mode wants to dominate the space, with people paying less attention and offering less respect for other modes. Speed and sloppiness of navigation create accidents and a sense of danger. Mixing modes slows traffic and increases everyone's attention to everyone else. Davie Street near Marinaside Crescent in the Quayside neighborhood in slightly lower-density False Creek North has a similarly low-key street management system in place (figure 5-22). The design of Granville Island in Vancouver is an early example of this kind of traffic management. This public gathering place with work, education, and commercial spaces was designed by Norman Hotson with a seamless public realm where all modes have access to all public areas from building wall to building wall (figure 5-23). This scenario has been in place since the 1970s without a single significant accident, and commerce on and near the public realm thrives. Of course, all city streets cannot be designed in this flexible way, but such designs do apply to parts of the public realm where walking, meeting, entertainment, and social interchange are equally or more important than auto access and movement.

## Defining Public Space with Buildings

Spaces need clear boundaries to be understood and remembered as space. Streets and public spaces achieve a three-dimensional form that one can easily perceive because of the defining influence of surrounding building walls, a principle that goes back to traditional city design, as at the Place des Vosges in

**Figure 5-23** Granville Island in Vancouver exemplifies the multiuse public realm with cars and pedestrians as well as industry, commerce, and culture all mixed together. It is a vibrant area, and there has not been a serious accident within the wall-to-wall right-of-way since it was built in the 1970s.

Paris (figure 5-24). That is why building façades closely related to sidewalks or park edges are important to both street and park images. The plans for both Battery Park City and False Creek North contain guidelines for the placement of buildings that require them to bring a portion of the building walls right up to the front property lines, but they do it in very different ways.

The Battery Park City guidelines are modeled on typical New York City streets on the Upper East Side. Buildings go straight up from the sidewalk for ten or eleven stories. There may then be a setback, or sometimes there is just an "expression line" along the building façade that acknowledges a horizontal division that is uniform along the street. The bases of the buildings are clad in a stone-like material for the first few floors, again like typical older New York City buildings, before graduating to brick. You can see these guidelines at work in figure 5-21, although the office towers at the end of South End Avenue respond to a different set of guidelines. The philosophy is, let's not try to invent something new; let's use something we know will work.

The guidelines for False Creek North are trying for a much more relaxed set of relationships consistent with the nearby Vancouver pattern. The buildings are a combination of towers and what are called "streetwall" podium structures; making this configuration a public policy was pioneered in Vancouver (figure 5-25). In general, the base of the buildings form a podium three to five stories high, which can contain stores, townhouses, a health club, maybe a

Figure 5-24 The Place de Vosges in Paris, built in the seventeenth century, was the defining example of how public space can be shaped by coherent surroundings of individual buildings. It has a powerful identity that has never been out of style, and it has continuously maintained its financial and social value.

Figure 5-25 In its urban design guidelines, Vancouver pioneered the podium/tower building form that offers a strong consistent and active "streetwall" without cutting off light and while carrying high density in towers that soar above.

swimming pool, and sometimes a core of parking hidden behind. The podium provides enclosure for the streets and open spaces. Often, the buildings along the street are individual townhouses, so there are terraces raised half a story at the property line as a buffer between the public on the sidewalk and the private houses. Figure 5-26, by James K. M. Cheng Architects, shows how the

**Figure 5-26** This plan by James K. M. Cheng Architects, for the Quayside neighborhood in Vancouver's False Creek North shows how lower-scaled podium buildings surround private courtyards and shape the public realm of streets and the waterfront walkway/bikeway. Strategically located towers carry the density.

guidelines shape the public spaces and buildings along Marinaside Crescent. A few steps down from the street are the public walkway and bicycle path along the marina. Interior courtyards are private and raised several stories above the street, but there are public pathways at grade between the groups of buildings, even where there is no street. The whole arrangement shows how it is possible to enclose and organize space using buildings and landscape elements. The heights of streetwalls and space-enclosing walls of between three and six stories are comfortably scaled for people along a sidewalk or in a space. Long experience has found that similarity between the width of streets and heights of bordering walls offers proportions that are congenial to people.

For parks, it can be important to clarify the public domain even further by surrounding them with public streets or walkways rather than having them extend out directly from private development with no expression of separation. We tend to privatize space that is very close to us, especially if it does not seem to have another obvious user. Sometimes, we need to find a way to signal that spaces are truly public places open to all. That can be done by designing a sense of open welcome and entry. Just as with rooms, we perceive open spaces as more agreeable if they display comfortable proportions and human scale. At the south end of the Battery Park City esplanade, tree plantings create the illusion of enclosure within a large public space (figure 5-27). The large parks at False Creek North are accessible from streets on at least two sides and by public walkways and the seawall on the others (figure 5-28).

**Figure 5-27** The trees enclosing this public space at the south end of Manhattan's Battery Park City esplanade create the illusion of a park in a suburban or even rural location, although it is in the midst of a very dense urban environment.

**Figure 5-28** David Lam Park in False Creek North is bounded by public rights-of-way: streets on the land sides and the walkway/bikeway along the shoreline. This scene is typical of Vancouver's waterfront parks, which rarely have privatized edges.

## Highlighting Landmarks and Wayfinding

In the interest of individual perception, there are several key needs for public space beyond simple respite, things that help our orientation and sense of well-being. Public realm design can contribute significantly to understanding where you are and finding your way around. Of course, signs are important for wayfinding, but design can go much further; it is all about geographic memory. We remember location from landmarks. We remember location from the clarity of identity of particular places. We remember location if it touches something inside us that we care about. There are many ways to make a place memorable. Figure 5-29 illustrates a location in Dallas; no one ever forgets where they are in this neighborhood. Memorable places contribute to our sense of belonging or rootedness. They give meaning to the larger surroundings that we call neighborhood. This rootedness then reinforces our definition of ourselves.

In both Battery Park City and False Creek North, a sense of place is created by a succession of public spaces. At Battery Park City, a powerfully designed waterfront esplanade, the work of landscape architect Laurie Olin, provides a

**Figure 5-29** This historic landmark in the Lakewood neighborhood of Dallas, Texas, gives clear identity and direction to the area. No one gets lost in this community.

wide open pathway along the water and secluded, more shaded spaces (figure 5-30). False Creek North, conceptually designed by landscape architect Don Vaughan and detailed by Don Wuori, offers several large public spaces, notably David Lam and George Wainborn Parks (figure 5-31), which form identifiable centers for the whole community, connected by the continuous waterfront

**Figure 5-30** The waterfront esplanade along Battery Park City in Manhattan provides a spacious pathway with spectacular views and adjacent more shaded and secluded spaces along the walk.

**Figure 5-31** The waterfront walkway/bikeway spine throughout False Creek North meanders informally more or less at the water's edge, but all the shoreline is in public ownership and control. This recreation spine connects large waterfront parks and neighborhood destinations throughout Vancouver's inner city.

**Figure 5-32** In Manhattan's Battery Park City, the massive financial towers are clustered around a yacht basin. This design separates the buildings, offers a stylish setting, and creates strong identity.

**Figure 5-33** At ground level along the yacht basin in Manhattan's Battery Park City, the public space is firmly delineated with architectural paving and furnishings. This design reinforces active use and gives this area its unique character.

walkway/bikeway system. At Battery Park City, a series of very large office buildings forms a central landmark, reflecting its proximity to the Wall Street financial center. The financial towers are grouped around a yacht basin (figure 5-32), perhaps evoking the perennial question about the financial industry: Where are the customer's yachts? At ground level, the space is firmly delineated with concrete and stone surfaces (figure 5-33). The waterfront walkway/bikeway path at False Creek North is a more extended organization with a more direct relationship between the space and the fronting buildings (figure 5-34). Orientation is aided by the bridges that traverse the area and by marinas located along the shoreline that alternate with expanses of open water (figure 5-35).

## Incremental Improvements to the Public Realm

Comprehensive redevelopment of large sites creates the opportunity to experiment and implement progressive ideas for all kinds and sizes of spaces in the public realm because there are few landowners involved and because of the freedom of available space. Because most of our cities are already built, it is vital that we also reform obsolete standards and retrofit existing dull places.

The urban public realm of today has profound demands on it that need special attention and for which thoughtful and specific design is essential. There are economic, social, and environmental urgencies and opportunities that, if realized effectively, can make the entire city around these places come vividly to life. There are opportunities to create unusual schemes that contrib-

**Figure 5-34** Fronting buildings along the walkway/bikeway in False Creek North, away from the parks, offer a strong direct relationship between living and public use as well as an unforgettable image of Vancouver.

ute to the uniqueness of a surrounding area. There are ways to reuse spaces that fill the gaps that people feel in the cityscape around them. Incremental improvements of existing places can start with a clear understanding of what and who we are planning for: not just for the car, but for pedestrians and all kinds of activities by and for people. To start, it is insightful to remember one basic truth about the city: It is first and foremost a place to walk.

## Life Takes Place on Foot

A fundamental statement about the importance of the public realm is Danish architect Jan Gehl's formulation that life takes place on foot.[5] When you walk from one place to another through a boring or hostile environment—what Gehl calls a necessary activity—you try to get to your destination as fast as you can. If you walk through an interesting, well-designed environment, you

**Figure 5-35** Orientation in Vancouver's False Creek North is anchored by major bridges that soar over all the activity and marinas that embellish the shoreline between carefully protected open water views.

may also engage in "optional activities": You stop and look in a store window, sit on a bench under a tree for a few moments, or perhaps stop for a coffee or drink in a café. Even if you are in a hurry, you will certainly remember these possibilities for a future time. These optional activities in turn generate "social activities": You plan your walk around meeting someone for lunch, you run into someone you know and stop to chat, or you exchange a few words with a stranger. You discover social opportunities as well as business opportunities. In turn, these social activities generate better public spaces, engendering a virtuous circle of cause and effect. We expect to find such places in Europe, as in figure 5-36, a view of the garden at the Palais Royal in Paris. According to Gehl, who has produced studies of public space and plans for many Scandinavian cities and for London, Sydney, Melbourne, and New York, among other places, these experiences and encounters are what city life is all about, and they can only happen when walking. Use of the Internet has not changed Gehl's analysis. He says that his studies show that increased use of cyberspace reinforces the need for public places, particularly if they have WiFi, and reinforces the inclination to walk.

Walking is one of the underlying foundations for a healthy lifestyle. The current epidemic of obesity is caused partly by the unhealthy food we eat, but also by our increasingly sedentary pattern of living. It has been estimated by health officials that as little as a half hour of moderately

**Figure 5-36** The Jardin du Palais Royal in Paris embodies Jan Gehl's theme that walking creates the circumstance for casual encounters, fascinating experience, and memory. It is the perfect meeting place, gathering place, and play place that can only be accessed on foot.

strenuous exercise a day provides significant health benefits. Walking is defined as one of the moderately strenuous exercise options, and a walkable community can offer the daily requirement for this exercise as a normal part of everyday activity without the need for planning or special effort or cost. Lawrence Frank, a planner and research scientist at the University of British Columbia, has identified an array of correlations between walkable places and better health.[6]

Walking is fundamental to our overall experience of a desirable city. For a municipality, it can also be one of the cheapest modes to invest in for the volume of benefits that it garners. In most communities walking gets very little attention and even less funding. If you compare the proportion of annual transportation funding in almost any municipality among automobiles, transit, cycling, and walking, it will become very evident that walking gets short shrift. If you look at the level of codification, standards, and regulations among transportation modes in any city, you will find that walking standards are almost unspecified because walking is thought about so little. How many walkway plans are in existence for a modern city compared with traffic plans, transit plans, and cycle path systems? An interesting exception is the Rotterdam initiative to enhance walkability, called the City Lounge program. In a cleverly branded strategy, walking is being emphasized by concentrating on making places people want to walk to and stay in to relax.

## Putting Walking and Public Space Ahead of Cars

Mayor Michael Bloomberg's *PlaNYC—2030*, released in 2007, made transportation and streetscape improvements a priority. Implementation was led by New York City's highly effective transportation commissioner, Janette Sadik-Khan. Jan Gehl was invited to New York, resulting in his 2008 study *World Class Streets: Remaking NYC's Public Realm*. Turning Broadway, the diagonal street that cuts across midtown Manhattan, into Broadway Boulevard has been one of the most important outcomes. The design uses the triangular spaces formed where Broadway intersects with the regular street grid to create a series of enhanced plazas and walkways. The project also reorganizes the traffic on Broadway, adds bicycle lanes, and rationalizes the intersections from Union Square to Columbus Circle.

The design proposals for Broadway Boulevard were developed by the New York City Department of Transportation. The first step was to close Broadway completely from 42nd Street to 47th Street in 2009, shown before and after closing in figures 5-37 and 5-38, and, later, from 33rd Street to 35th Street, shown in figures 5-39 and 5-40. At first, these new public spaces were an experiment, but with just a painted street surface, potted plants, and inexpensive lawn furniture, they were an immediate hit with the public. There was a small improvement in traffic flow on the cross streets and on nearby sections of Seventh Avenue and the Avenue of the Americas (Sixth Avenue). There was also a big reduction in accidents at the dangerous corners where the closed sections of Broadway used to intersect other streets and avenues. The next

**Figure 5-37** In New York, Jan Gehl's advice has led to another improvement for a street and a district, closing Broadway at Times Square to all but pedestrian traffic. This view shows Times Square before the closure.

Figure 5-38 Now, New York's Times Square is happily reclaimed by people walking and relaxing. The closing has been made with just paint, signs, and inexpensive outdoor furniture, but a permanent design is in the works. Compare with figure 5-37's preclosure scene.

Figure 5-39 Herald Square in New York, farther south along Broadway from Times Square, before this section of Broadway was also closed to traffic.

year, these closings were made permanent because of the gains in public safety, land values, and retail activity, without having to justify the change as an aesthetic improvement. The Oslo and New York architectural firm Snohetta has been chosen to design the permanent streetscape and newly pedestrianized plaza space for Times Square. Starting with temporary street closures and portable amenities meant that the administration did not need city council

**Figure 5-40** This view of New York's Herald Square shows the energy and vitality that can be tapped with a strategic street closure, again just using paint, signs, and inexpensive outdoor furniture.

approval for a major public expenditure until the changes had been tested and the project had won public acceptance. Before even temporary changes were made, the city held many information meetings with constituent groups, including business improvement districts and community planning boards.

Gehl has recently also been a consultant to the mayor of Moscow, where the public realm in the historic center, once similar to other old and gracious cities, has been completely overwhelmed by parking and access for the car, to the extent that pedestrians must struggle to find pathways and are in constant physical danger from automobiles in motion. The public realm has become an obstacle course on foot. Gehl Architects was retained to make its customary analysis of public life and public spaces in central Moscow, looking at conditions in both the summer and the winter. Gehl's one-sentence summary is, "Freedom from communism doesn't mean freedom to park on the sidewalk."[7]

Gehl's recommendations are starting to be implemented. Parking has been banned on the fashionable Tverskaya Street, more street trees are being planted, and there are fewer billboards than before. The contrast in the experience of Moscow's sidewalks between 2011 and 2014 is significant. At the same time, while the acting deputy mayor, Marat Khusnullin, has said that the City of Moscow was willing to forgo some of the revenue from outdoor advertising and deal with public objections when parking spaces are eliminated, he also said, "The number of roads per inhabitant in Moscow is three to five times lower than in any major city in the world, so we can't just close all the remaining roads and all walk everywhere happily, because this will paralyze the city and lead to a collapse in transportation."[8] Unfortunately, he sounds like many public officials in other countries. There have nonetheless been an increasing number of successes in Moscow in reclaiming parts of the public realm for pedestrians.

## Social Demands for Public Space: Maximizing the Experiential Dimension

Much is demanded of public space at both the individual and the group, or collective, levels. So much around us in modern cities is insensitive to our emotional needs, both as individuals and in relating to others. This insensitivity is relevant at the level of consumption when we are searching for more in the transaction than just exchange, leading to the demand in our interactions with the urban scene for what we call the experiential dimension to designing cities. These experiences are relevant for our more general sense of well-being, both individually and collectively, at a psychological level. In the frenetic reality of the city, being able to walk through a succession of public spaces can offer respite as well as the potential for human interaction that we need more than ever. Therefore, social demands on the public realm, tied to our personal and group psychological needs, are especially important to balance the increasingly frenetic pace of life. It is in the public realm that we can cope with the sense of alienation and isolation that is so prevalent and that is a great irony when people are so close all around us. So much of the city pulls us apart that many of us feel disconnected from our surroundings, from one another, and perhaps even from our inner selves. Our sidewalks, parks, and other such places can offer the opportunity to help us reconnect, but they have to be designed to do this (figure 5-41). Public space is not just something to hold physical things together in the city. It is vital to help hold an individual sense of self together, to hold a group together, and, ultimately, to hold the whole community together. If our public realm works for us, we are beneficiaries; if not, we suffer a negation that can be very dark. It is this ultimate design challenge for the public realm that is at the very core of what ecodesign is all about.

At the group or collective level, even more is demanded of public space. The public realm is the setting for meeting and social engagement, both pre-planned and spontaneous. It is the place for economic exchange, but more fundamentally, it is the place where we pursue our day-to-day lives together, building the social capital that a community is all about. It is the place for

**Figure 5-41** In this new area of Istanbul, the opportunity for people to connect and socialize is carefully built into the urban design and emphasized by the architecture.

casual social encounters, but also the place that we gather to make a community point, to celebrate, or to protest. Certainly, we use parks and open spaces for both organized and free recreation, the outdoor time that is needed for health and fun, and that is a big focus of local government in custodianship of such places. There are so many other things that we do together in the public realm that also need to be accommodated in how these places are designed, furnished, managed, maintained, and programmed. One aspect of ecodesign is to embrace a much more complete range of community activity, as defined by people's diverse creative pursuits, and then to build all these group activities comfortably into the public realm. Doing this requires varying sizes of places equitably located, different landscape and furniture treatments, contrasting domains of use, and active, diverse programming.

## Fostering Third Places

At a personal level, we live and work in private spaces that may or may not meet our needs. Often, they are standardized spaces within a relatively standardized private setting, and in core cities, they tend to be small spaces. For housing, owners can customize, but renters' options are more limited. For workplaces, most of us sense that we are making a daily visit to a place that is owned and controlled by someone else; we often feel the corporate hand. It's easier if we have money because we can explore our personal expression wherever we are and we can buy our way in, with a drink or a meal, to what Ray Oldenburg has called "third places."[9] After home and work, a "third place" is where community culture is created, where there is the action, fun, and the potential to meet people. Oldenburg calls cafés, coffee shops, bookstores, bars, hair salons, and other hangouts at the heart of a community the "great good places." So, we should foster these third places, while remembering that these places all require people to spend money. The public realm is there for anyone, and anyone can engage with it. It is the place we all live in for some part of every day. It offers the pathways and the potential for paths crossing. Public space must be explicitly configured and finished to accommodate its social function (figure 5-42).

## Assuring Safety and Maximum Accessibility

The public realm of the city must be safe. Safety starts with the basics of shared use. Of course, safety is pursued in modern cities with active policing and security. Ecodesign also should include the principle of what is called CPTED, shorthand for crime prevention through environmental design, which involves looking at the design of a space and sorting out the obvious liabilities that foster crime and antisocial activity, things like dark hideaways and blind corners. Research into this aspect of public space has developed into a complete science in contemporary design that can make a big difference in the sense of safety for public areas. The addition of adequate lighting can also make a big difference. In some cases, even the addition of classical

Figure 5-42 What Ray Oldenburg calls "third places" in cities are the essential locations, beyond home and workplaces, where people gather and create their society and culture. A city without many such places will stagnate. This typical street scene in Paris is full of places to meet, mix, and mingle. It is one of hundreds like it, and so we fall in love in Paris.

music has been shown to foster a safer situation. The best, most dependable safety comes from adding other people to a space, which is why cafés and other forms of commerce become important. It is also why an activity agenda, through programming, for a park becomes important. The public realm also needs to be accessible. Ecodesign includes embracing the need for universal accessibility. Movement impairment should not limit use of the public places of the city, which should welcome not just people with disabilities, but also the aged and infirm. Accessibility must be nonnegotiable.

## Furnishing Public Spaces

At a basic level, the public realm needs seating and other furniture to host people comfortably. This need is obvious for parks, but in modern cities, the selection of furnishings is often determined more by concerns about theft, liability, or maintenance than it is by what will be most attractive and convenient for people to use. For example, why do we not all follow the French example of offering movable chairs and tables in parks so that people can define their own patterns for gathering? All our furniture does not have to be fixed. Movable chairs were a favorite prescription of William H. Whyte, who made extensive studies of the behavior of people in public places.[10] He was a consultant for the redesign of Bryant Park in New York City, where movable chairs are a major part of the scene (figure 5-43). Why do we not see the creativity of the artist brought into furniture design more regularly to offer the kind of serendipity that was enjoyed in Victorian parks? Why do we pull away landscape and particularly annuals just to lower park maintenance costs? Why have drinking fountains become so rare? Why is play equipment so standardized? These are the things that bring pleasure into the public realm and these are the things that foster social interaction so that the public realm is a real contributor to community life.

Public space also needs finishes, furnishings, and lighting that evoke memories because they offer hospitality and positive personal experience. That is why public art, well-maintained landscaping, and good surface paving are so important. Well-designed spaces will engage our senses, not just what we see, but the smell of flowers, the rough touch of stone, the sound of water, and, when an event with food takes place, even taste.

Furnishings can also be strategic installations that reestablish public territory in alienated places or set off revitalization in an effort that has been dubbed "tactical urbanism." A great example of tactical urbanism can be found in Dallas, with a group called Team Better Block. This somewhat rogue group of activists pulls many people together, often over a weekend, to create what they describe as quick, inexpensive, high-impact changes that improve and revitalize underused properties and highlight the potential for creating

**Figure 5-43** Movable furniture gives life and a sense of user control to Bryant Park in New York. This is one of the easiest and least expensive ways to encourage people to use a park because they can move the chairs to form groups or take a chair and move away from other people as they please. Movable chairs do require a management system in the park; otherwise, over time, the chairs can disappear. Park redesign by the Olin Partnership.

great streets. The modus operandi is to quickly transform one or two blocks of a streetscape to show what it might be like with permanent improvements. One day, a street will evoke a dull malaise: rundown, with high vacancy rates, a real mess. The next day, it will have sidewalk benches, trees, and landscaping, often arriving in pots; it will have temporary little kiosks and cafés as well as food trucks, with lots of sidewalk presence; there will be art and lighting; there will be all kinds of pedestrian activity; there will be a buzz. The group then invites the neighborhood to experience and enjoy the place, with a lot of music and fun. The result is usually that the community is energized to make the dream a reality. Landlords are offered new faith. Consumers make a new commitment to come back to the place. City officials are charged to make the public realm improvements real and lasting. A happening becomes a force, which becomes a change on the ground, which becomes an inspiration and a lesson for that place and other places.

## Bringing Different Functions to Public Space

Confirming personal perceptual needs of public space reminds us that success of a place is not always signaled by how full it is with people, how crowded it is, or how busy it feels. For escape, calm reflection, and even healing, it is essential to have access to some places that are relatively empty of people at any one point when we want to use them. Such places will offer their pleasures to a few people at a time, and throughout a day, that adds up to many people. This is also true for places that serve different kinds of people doing different things at different points in the day. One thinks of healing gardens and sanctuaries for religious contemplation, but sometimes our tranquility can be served by a simple, quiet backwater in a public park set apart from the actively programmed areas.

## Using Private Semipublic Spaces

The public realm is rounded off by the offerings that are not totally public but that are also not private, the spaces on private property that serve the community needs of people using that property. They are gathering places as well as places of calm reflection. They are the places where we can get to know our more immediate neighbors. Such spaces are essential in a comfortable city. They extend the overtly public cityscape with more variety and intimacy and really bring community life together. As the city becomes denser, these places offer more and more interesting settings and become even more essential. In the nineteenth century in London, some parks and squares were only public to the people who lived adjacent to them and had part ownership in them. We tend to reject this concept today, but there was merit in these spaces. They offered a way for people who knew one another, or at least knew that they were neighbors, to become more acquainted and to do things together within a relatively secure outdoor area. They were private, intimate places even in the center of a metropolis. The same function of semipublic space is served today in the dense city by such areas as roof gardens, courtyards, and play terraces, such as the courtyard on a roof in Vancouver's Yaletown neighborhood shown in figure 5-44. These features make the experience of living in the city much more acceptable. In particular, blank, vacant roofs have been the lost opportunity of modern cities. They offer acres of space for diversified outdoor living activities—from gardening to recreation to children's play—and their greening can offset the heat island effect of the paved city.

**Figure 5-44** As cities densify, they need more and more space for outdoor living, not just in the public domain but also of a more private nature. Roof gardens and play terraces can help make urban living offer something like the spaces found in suburbs, as shown in this view of a rooftop courtyard in Vancouver's South Cambie neighborhood.

### Bringing Public Control to Privately Owned Public Plazas

To be truly inclusive and a useful component of the public realm, a publicly accessible space needs to be under the control of the public, under government authority through ownership or with some kind of guaranteed access agreement. This need is particularly relevant to the ubiquitous plazas that generally accompany modern corporate office towers. These are often vague places, vague in perceptual terms, without discernable shape or scale, so they do not foster refreshing experience or memory. It is especially vague as to whether or not they are truly public and open to all. Sometimes, this vagueness is on purpose with an inclination to control who is allowed in the space, which is why such spaces have to be secured in legal terms for guaranteed public access and use if they are to play a dependable part in the public experience of the city. In addition to securing access through regulation, design moves and management provisions can improve these spaces, especially by adding focal points of furniture, art, or fountains and adding trees for spatial definition. William H. Whyte was an advisor to New York City when it first revised its plaza regulations to make sure that the public had access and could use them comfortably. Like some other cities, New York City's plaza standards can be enforced because the developer receives floor-area bonuses for constructing these plazas which initially had few requirements. Design standards now include size parameters, orientation and visibility expectations, and guidelines for frontage conditions, seating, lighting, signage, and litter receptacles. Operating standards include specified hours of operation, guarantee of access for everyone, and guidelines for adjacent uses and commercial activities such as kiosks and outdoor cafés. These standards foster invitation into these plazas and help them feel truly accessible and comfortable.

### Embracing Beauty

Finally, there should be a basic concern for beauty. Humans relate to beauty, and it is not superficial to try to achieve it in our public spaces. Beauty can come from the planting of flowers or the addition of art, from artful pavement patterns, from water as a natural stream or a fountain, or from sculpting land contours. It comes from protected or even enhanced views. It offers the caprice and romance that disregards functionality but is nevertheless fundamental to the experience of a place. It can come from a large and formal design, like the grand vistas of the Champs Elysees in Paris (figure 5-45), or it can be found in a small and individual corner of a city. Beauty also comes from avoiding the negative features that damage our encounter with a place. Billboards and random third-party commercial signage can be detrimental to the visual pleasure of the public environment. Lack of maintenance or even a deficit of refuse containers can demean the harmony of a place.

**Figure 5-45** The Avenue des Champs Elysees in Paris may be the most beautiful street in the world. Its beauty makes up for many other sins—it takes too much space, it has brutal traffic, and it separates pedestrians from those on the other side—but as this street illustrates so well, beauty matters sometimes for its own sake.

The social offerings of the public realm certainly have strong influence on both our personal tranquility and the richness of our community life. Does the public realm have deeper psychological implications as well? That may be harder to prove. An unfortunate reality of modern life is that some people suffer mental illness and disability whether or not the city is hospitable; one cannot help but believe, however, that even those aspects of the human condition that are harder to understand and manage can be given some moderation or at least a modicum of relief by public spaces whose designs are gentle, respectful, cordial, and salubrious. However, no matter how welcoming the public realm, no one should be homeless, and programs that create supportive housing for homeless people are essential.

## Economic Demands for Public Space: Maximizing Quality, Utility, and Value

The availability of an adequate open-space system brings economic values to a city. The quality of the design and programming of that open space brings even more value. A vibrant market culture, generating wealth and jobs for a community, puts economic demands on the public realm because public space is not just a separate luxury for citizens. Good design of the public realm will embrace these demands, not only to support economic vitality, but also to give wider meaning and practical purpose to public spaces than can be achieved if they are designed with only a narrow recreation focus. Formal streets and parks as well as more informal "found" spaces all have parts to play in the business of the city.

### Fostering Complete Streets

Paying attention to all the things that people want to do in busy places can and should be compatible with the other necessary functions of streets. As mentioned previously, an unfortunate feature of post-1950s development was the simplification of the agenda for streets to primarily serve the movement of cars. Often, even with this priority, streets become congested. We have all heard of the alleged effects of a "congestion index" on economic health. Economic activity is a function of many ways of using streets, however, and congestion sometimes generates more economic activity rather than less, even if the general ease of movement in all modes facilitates more transactions.

If the street is part of a balanced transportation system, it is possible to follow the concept of what has become known as complete streets (figure 5-46). The safety advantages of this concept were described in chapter 3. It is simply a design sensibility and set of principles by which the design of streets accommodates more rather than less of the social agenda of the city, engenders economic opportunity and activity, and supports land

Figure 5-46 State Street, the main street in Santa Barbara, California, is a complete street with mixed use, multimodes of transportation, and maximum landscape with permeability. It is also a very pleasant destination.

values. It turns upside down the conventional hierarchy that puts auto traffic first. In a complete street, the pedestrian has priority, followed by bicycles, then transit, then deliveries, and then traffic movement. Complete streets should accommodate all modes of traffic, but require new cross sections with sidewalks that are wide enough for pedestrians and landscaping (including the landscaping described in chapter 2 which helps restore the contribution of street areas to the natural environment). Streets should also have protected bicycle lanes and clear rights-of-way for transit. Where streets are wide enough, Allan Jacobs advocates the "multiway boulevard." Street tree planting is a big part of a complete street: Think of a line of trees on each side of all streets and, in some cases, even a double or triple row of trees.

A successful street design will deal with all the street furniture in a consistent way: Streetlights, traffic signals, street identification and traffic signs, commercial signage, necessary equipment like fire alarm boxes and hydrants, benches, vending boxes, paving, and landscaping can all be designed to produce an integrated environment. Even with the complicated functional requirements of each component and their complex interactions, it is essential that these elements be visually brought together in a suite that offers a coherent image.

The space between the building line and the pedestrian passageway on the sidewalk, the traditional location for sidewalk cafés, can be the location for many significant urban activities, including outdoor retailing, which bring life and business potential to city streets. A complete street also reflects context. A pairing of the street typology with the place typology of the adjacent area helps integrate the street with its context for mutual benefits.

A proactive program of street closures and animation for special events can add to this contextual fit and provide a natural liveliness. Successful streets accommodate the widest possible array of activities in the widest possible array of street configurations and cross sections, any one of which can offer a fascinating and unique balance of possibilities.

The utility alley or back lane has been edited out of most modern street layouts. The choice offered by these narrow alternative access ways augments the street, allowing services and sometimes parking entrances to be separated from pedestrian access, making the economic use of the whole property more effective.

## Inspiring a Range of Activities in Public Space

Diverse uses are vital to the economic utility of open spaces. All too often, our public realm suffers from the same singularity of activity that affects the private realm of the contemporary city. Too many cities have constrained the social activities of public space because officials worry that many uses have an exploitative commercial aspect or might have an unpredictable consequence, yet it is often this drive of commerce and the joy of the unpredictable that bring vitality to public spaces (figure 5-47). The outdoor café along a street or in a park can have great amenity value. The pop-up market or food truck along a curb can bring people happily together. The localized street dance, community fair, rummage sale, or movie night in a park can build community consciousness and mutual assistance at least as well as recreational programming. A dog run will always be a place where people gather and gossip. Unfortunately, the bureaucratic complications of encroachment agreements, activity permits, health specifications, and permits for public gatherings and other kinds of municipal requirements can make these things difficult, so they do not happen as easily or as often as they should. Although a municipality must certainly take care to avoid negative effects, municipal leaders can also facilitate many more spontaneous happenings by simply deciding to make active use a priority.

With careful design, it is not difficult to allocate many activities to a park or to fit out the space for differing activities at different times. A good example is the sharing of park space and school play areas, which can be a very efficient use of scarce urban land. This setup is well illustrated with the sharing of space between Elsie Roy School and David Lam Park in downtown Vancouver shown in figure 5-48. The same can be said for fairgrounds, where pop-up markets,

**Figure 5-47** This otherwise forgettable small street in Istanbul comes to life because of the spontaneous daily commerce. It draws people to remember it and come back to it.

artists' studios, or other activities might make good use of the space when a fair is not scheduled. Anomalous areas within a street right-of-way can come vividly to life with pop-up uses. Even cemeteries in denser cities are now being seen as recreation places that offer the necessary respite that people cherish. The point is not to take a traditional use for a space or its predominant use for granted. Opportunity awaits when the consciousness of alternative uses opens up.

**Figure 5-48** David Lam Park in Vancouver is a park for general use, but it is also the school yard for adjacent Elsie Roy School and the play space for the children's daycare attached to the school. These school children at recess show that it is a comfortably shared and safe public space.

## Supporting Different Sizes for Public Parks

For parks and open space, diversity of use also requires differentiation in size. The complexity of the city sets up many situations for interface between economic activity and open space or where open space can engender economic value. There is an inherent variation in the size of these places that suits the need and setting. When it comes to parks, many city parks departments think primarily about the active recreation demands that they must satisfy and are skeptical of the smaller open-space options that developers might offer, so they fall back on shapes and sizes that fit the obvious recreation templates. This practice devalues the smaller park space. A well-distributed park network of many shapes and sizes offers the greatest opportunity for a wide spectrum of organized and spontaneous uses and associates more private property with the immediacy of open space, which spreads and shares value. A park or mini-park within a few minutes' walk is one of the key elements of the walkability of neighborhoods. If public space is nearby and attractive, people will use it to the benefit of their interests, which is good for the overall energy of a place. One size does not fit all.

## Installing Useful Fixtures in Public Parks

Smart park design will facilitate maximum utility. For example, a good park will have areas of use that are properly fitted out with infrastructure supports, such as electrical outlets or the ability to install temporary stages or flooring. To accommodate pet owners, it will have enclosures and stations to dispose of dog waste. A good park will also have areas that are designed for active uses, including sports and children's play, as well as areas that are designed for passive use. It will set aside places where a café or other commerce may be installed (figure 5-49). It will have landmarks such as water or landscape features or public art that become places to meet. It will offer opportunities for community expression and messaging. It will accommodate the needs of all kinds of groups: families, seniors, the indigent, dog owners, the disabled, single people, and anyone else who puts a tangible demand on the space.

## Enhancing Retail Streets

A particular issue for modern downtowns, neighborhood shopping, and suburban centers has been the impact of street design on retail vitality. As traffic engineers searched for the most efficient street configuration for maximum utility in moving auto traffic, they often, without realizing it or intending to, also started to endanger the success of the retail that lined the streets. We now understand that a successful retail street is one that both draws pedestrians with its amenity and also slows traffic down so that car users can again be brought into the influence of the shops rather than zoom by without paying attention. The street that is less efficient for cars is a much more successful street for commerce.

**Figure 5-49** This florist stall in the corner of a Montreal park is a local landmark and brings activity to what would otherwise be a forgotten location.

One response to the conflict between retail and traffic has been to create retail streets that are exclusively for pedestrians. This concept has worked well in Europe, where cities are compact, full of residents as well as office workers, and well served by public transit. When tried in North America, pedestrian malls have usually failed, except for a few examples that maintained a transit alignment, such as in Minneapolis and Denver. Somehow, if you can't drive along a street, you tend to forget the retail establishments that front on it. Pedestrian street frontages are enjoying a comeback, however. The evolution of the Third Street Promenade in Santa Monica is an interesting example. There, three blocks were closed to make an all-pedestrian mall in 1965. The design was meant to be the equivalent of a suburban shopping center, but the existing stores along the street were not organized and managed the way retail businesses are managed in shopping centers, where all the store space belongs to one owner. The construction of the Santa Monica Place shopping center at one end, intended by the city planners to help reinforce Third Street retailing, instead put many of the stores out of business. So far, the story is like many other failures of downtown pedestrian shopping malls. Then, the City of Santa Monica started to change things in the mid-1980s. A private business improvement district took over management of the retail street. A special zoning district was passed that encouraged nearby parking garages and added other uses, including cinemas, to draw more people. The Roma Design Group was retained to redesign the pedestrian mall as the Third Street Promenade, with a series of outdoor rooms and a festive atmosphere from well-chosen landscaping and streetlights (figure 5-50). The street became a great success

**Figure 5-50** For the Third Street Promenade in Santa Monica, California, a failed pedestrian mall was transformed by decisive civic action. A business improvement district, special zoning, parking arrangements, and smart design all contributed to its revitalization. Its revitalization also reflects a renewed interest in street-front retail, when it is well managed and attractive.

as a retail location and as a place that had meaning for the whole community. Recently, the Santa Monica Place shopping center has been rebuilt to a new design by the Jerde Partnership that extends Third Street's outdoor spaces right through what had been the interior of the center.

Making the mall more like a shopping street as opposed to making a street more like a mall reflects changes that are taking place in retailing. It turns out that people like shopping along streets. They can find their way to their intended destination without wandering around in a labyrinth of pedestrian passageways. As a result, the interiors of many shopping centers have been rebuilt to look more like streets. A whole new retail category, called "life-style centers," has grown up where the shops front on a landscaped private street system open to automobile traffic and complete with parking spaces, although the streets usually serve an island of retail buildings surrounded by parking lots.

## Exploiting Ad Hoc Spaces

Perhaps the most fascinating economic potential for open space can be found outside the context of street alignments and formal parks in the ad hoc spaces that are associated with other urban activities such as transit access, public buildings, leftover street rights-of-way, and private parcels made available for temporary public use. These often-forgotten, leftover spaces can offer dramatic improvements to the feeling, use, and safety of an area, usually with modest funding. They can be the serendipitous places that offer the surprise, the unexpected amenity, and the fun activity that are usually not integrated into the typical larger, formal spaces. They can be wonderful places for pop-up commerce, the flower stand, or the food cart. Sometimes, all that is involved is planting just one big tree around which people congregate. As small civic projects, these improvements are easy to implement. They offer opportunities to experiment with public or private street activities that make a location more joyful and playful. Their recovery and reuse can set off positive change on nearby private land (figure 5-51).

## Environmental Demands of Public Space: Bringing City Design into Harmony with Nature

Anne Whiston Spirn, in her book *The Granite Garden*[11] (which perhaps should have been called the "concrete garden"), makes the point that just because cities have been designed without regard for natural systems does not mean that cities can exist outside of nature. For the environmental agenda, the public realm represents a vast opportunity to bring ecological systems back into the fabric of the built cityscape. Because of streets, the public realm is a continuous network. It includes a significant component of landscape and

**Figure 5-51** This little ad hoc space in the Nisantasi Neighborhood of Istanbul does great service to humanize the vicinity and provide a local meeting place. It was reclaimed from an overly wide street right-of-way.

could include much more. It accommodates much of the utility infrastructure that must be reformed to be more aligned with natural systems. It is in public ownership. All are vital assets for action on environmental performance. As we become more conscious of the need to make cities compatible with their natural settings, the environment will put increasing demands on public space. The public realm is not just for humans; it is for all the organisms in the ecosystem, and it has to become a host of this ecology and bring harmony into this ecology. Of course, ecosystems do not differentiate between the public and private domains, so solutions in the public realm have to be coordinated and echoed with those on private property. We discussed some of these measures, particularly the advantages for mitigating and adapting to changing climate, in chapter 2.

## Siting Buildings, Spaces, and Utilities for Better Performance

Much can be done with the structure and orientation of our cities to facilitate harmony between the built and natural environments. Buildings can be sited to improve the natural ventilation of cities and suburbs so that prevailing winds help clear away unavoidable air pollution. Sun and shadowing can be considered in designs and regulations to reduce heat islands and cut heating and cooling bills. Artificial lighting, admittedly needed for safety and security, can also be carefully directed, moderated, and even programmed to offer the dark periods that preserve natural rhythms. District energy systems can save fuel and use waste as energy sources. Water can be managed to reduce damage from storms and prevent overburdening sewer systems. We can bring density, mixed use, and diversity into the urban setting that help reduce travel and the use of fossil fuels. We all have to work on these general civic objectives over the next generation, and there are good comprehensively developed examples to look to for direction. A focus on the role that might be played by the vast urban armature of streets, parks, natural reserves, planted areas, and other open spaces, provides insights into just what we can do, and just how far we still must go, before we can be confident that our cities no longer represent the environmental contradiction that is so deeply true today.

Water, light, soil, plants, and animals are all components of the ecosystem, and we must be thoughtful about how they come together in the urban setting so that ecosystems are not destroyed or at least so that a balance between human use and all the other ecological components is achieved. Ultimately, even regeneration of the ecosystem should stand as an aspiration. The initial obligation in any city is to clearly understand the contextual ecosystem: where and how it is thriving and where and how it has been degraded. A holistic, systems perspective is vital before specific decisions start to be made. This perspective can then be used to create a balance between the human activities and constructions of the city, and the functioning of the host natural system, from place to place within the footprint and hinterland of the city.

## Managing Hydrology

To manage hydrology, we might say, "Just follow the water." Patterns and effects of water relating to climate and soil generate the ultimate complex interactions of plants, animals, and bio-organisms that compose the ecosystem. Groundwater, rainwater, and wastewater all play their parts. Management of hydrology in the public realm is essential. Groundwater and stormwater in the urban system must be managed to prevent flooding, erosion, sedimentation, and contamination. The difficulty of modern cities with massive site building coverage and solid paving is that surface water runoff has become a primary utility concern. Engineers used to believe that the correct treatment was to remove this water as quickly and painlessly as possible. This turns out to be the opposite of what is really needed. As surface water runs off over pavement, it mixes with auto waste and other pollutants. At peaks, it floods. Today, historic patterns of hydrology have become irrelevant. How this water might engender the native plant and animal culture has also become irrelevant. Natural filtering and cleansing of this water has been degraded. Water is wasted and contaminated. Although there is no doubt that the intervention of human settlement will dramatically distort the natural hydrological status quo, we can pursue a sensitive alternative system that would repair these damages and gaps.

As we discussed in chapter 2, the first step is retaining as much water as possible where we find it and where it falls. Permeable ground surfaces help absorption and let stormwater follow its natural cycle in an area. For overflows, bioretention arrangements are a practical way to manage the volume of outflows and then filter and cleanse the water for suitable disposal or reuse. Treatments such as bioswales, rain gardens, and carefully designed tree- and plant-growing structures can be built in. With wastewater, a key principle is that receiver waters should not be degraded by inflows, and reuse is a better option than simple disposal. Wastewater can be seen as a resource that permits extraction of constituent components for recycling. Once organic content and suspended solids are reduced, the resulting flow can be used for many secondary water needs or allowed to flow into constructed wetlands that foster ecological regeneration. Various arrangements for managing water not only increase the health of the ecosystem involved, but they can be designed to be positive additions to the amenity and attractiveness of the public lands upon which they are constructed. We have already discussed some of the technical aspects in chapter 2. Swiss water artist and landscape architect Herbert Dreiseitl shows how we can transform the scientific side of water management into a moving artistic expression in his evocative *Waterscape* series of books.[12]

## Naturalizing the Public Landscape

Landscape management in the public realm can help the environment in many ways. The right choice of the landscaping that municipalities constantly plant and renew throughout civic lands can reestablish native species and foster animal life. It can have a particular and significant impact on bird life. Disposal of cuttings can be a fuel source in place of fossil fuels. Streets can be designed in an ecologically compatible way, including pervious pavement, biofiltering landscape on boulevards instead of traditional curbs, and native tree and shrub planting. A popular initiative that also helps the environment is naturalizing of back lanes or alleys by removing asphalt paving, replacing it with pervious paving materials, and adding planting. Because there is continuity in the pattern of public land, enough area can be linked to create viable habitat ranges to re-create the biodiversity that had once been present. Habitat fragmentation through development is a big contributor to loss of biodiversity. Larger protected areas can be designated for what are called habitat patches, corridors between these green sanctuaries can be put together, and the buffering of habitat edge conditions can be designed into the landscape treatments along with careful land use allocations for adjacent property. Connecting parks, green streets, plazas, landscape reserves, and nondeveloped sites into a fully realized, open-space network takes extra effort and funding, but will yield major dividends for animal movements, anchoring native plant growth patterns, and overall species diversity.

**Figure 5-52** Habitat continuity is generally shattered by urban development, but natural networks can be repaired. Dallas and the Trinity Trust have one such initiative well under way in the Trinity River enhancement project designed by Wallace Roberts & Todd and CH2M Hill. The flood corridor of the Trinity River is being reclaimed for much needed recreation, but also to reset biodiversity. Shown is an overall view of the aspiration, now beginning implementation.

One example of such a network is the Trinity Lakes project in Dallas. The floodplain of the Trinity River has long been enclosed between levees to protect surrounding development. Much of the year, the floodplain is open grassland, with the small channel of the Trinity River running through it. The Trinity Lakes design converts this usually ignored space into a great central park for the whole city of Dallas (figure 5-52). Trinity Lakes shows how it is possible to create major new landscapes even within a densely developed central city. A comparable effect can also be obtained by stitching together neighborhood parks, green streets, and the larger regional park system. We mentioned earlier that such a program is being implemented in Hamburg. Rotterdam is considering putting all its green spaces together into a single connected system. The recreational bonus for people from these networks of green space is a parallel benefit. The opportunity for environmental learning and natural experience for children is a further benefit, especially if interpretation is added.

## Harvesting Food from Public Lands

Even food must be in the mix for use of public lands. Food delivery—both production and transportation—is among the most unsustainable aspects of modern living. Some places are even becoming concerned about food security. In addition, because gardening is such a popular pastime and personal pleasure, expanded opportunities for gardening can be a big draw for people to live in more compact development. Food options on public land, including edible landscape along streets or orchards in parks, were discussed in chapter 2. Growing food in urban places definitely involves using semipublic green roofs and underused public areas such as highway verges, bridge heads, or obsolete rail lines for community allotment gardening (figure 5-53). There are even examples of profitable market farming on rooftops (figure 5-54) or on sites at grade that are awaiting more permanent construction. At a larger scale, a reserve system to protect fertile, productive agricultural land from development, by placing it in public hands if need be, is an important contingency plan for the future.

**Figure 5-53** This allotment vegetable garden along a railway right-of-way near Granville Island in Vancouver reflects the keen pleasure that people feel for urban gardening and growing their own food, even in relatively unlikely places.

**Figure 5-54** This rooftop farmer in downtown Vancouver uses leftover semipublic green roofs for commercial market gardens. He has the satisfaction of food production and commercial success.

## Managing the Public Realm

Public property has to be managed. Initial design and development are an obvious focus, but success for public space also depends on facilitating use, coordinating access for many users, and securing renewal over time, which raises the question, who should own and operate the public realm?

### Ensuring Public Ownership as a Guiding Principle

A preeminent principle that underlies a progressive ethos of management of the public realm is that the land for primary public infrastructure must be publically owned. The only way to secure universal access to facilities and amenities is to make sure that they are in public hands. The inclination of some local governments to privatize streets or spaces to avoid maintenance obligations is both shortsighted and irresponsible to those in the society who might be indigent or different and subject to security attention on private property. Public ownership also ensures that every private property will always have access and connection to the public realm. Public ownership provides the armature for a city of enough public lands in a tightly connected pattern to cover all possible activities that might be demanded over a long time.

### Having the Public Help Design the Public Realm

Modern urban environments are basically delivered in final complete form with almost no involvement of people in shaping these places. Inside the home, people are accustomed to the freedom to customize and express their tastes and style and eccentricities however they wish, although they face some limitations if they are not owner-occupants and even more limitations if they are in multiple-family housing. In public areas, people can hardly change anything. They have become alienated from the process of creating these places. There is no reason municipal authorities cannot open up the process of designing the public realm, offering opportunities for personal expression and a sense of responsibility that not only fosters neighborhood loyalty but also lowers the potential for random vandalism and littering. An easy way is to offer personal gardening opportunities for decoration along street boulevards and in traffic islands or the centers of turnarounds. As a gardener, to embellish your neighborhood is a great way to express yourself and enjoy community pride (figure 5-55).

Community volunteer efforts need more support. For example, cleanup campaigns provide a sense of local control, and community watch programs let us participate in our own safety. This area of public realm design and management needs much more innovation in the future.

**Figure 5-55** In modern cities, we have few ways to bring the personal touch to public space. There is untapped potential in gardens in the public domain of streets and leftover spaces. They are inexpensive, they bring care to marginal locations, and they facilitate local loyalty. This public gardening program in Vancouver is a big hit with citizens.

## Marketing and Programming the Public Realm

Often, public space, even if properly designed, languishes because its use is not obvious to people and activities have not been encouraged by the managers who are responsible for the space. Of course, spontaneous activities by people are the most sought-after situations, but facilitating access and activities through marketing and programming is also important. As more users are attracted, it is essential to manage demands among users, including allocation of areas, handling mutual impacts, brokering timing, and mediating conflicts. With use comes wear and depreciation that requires ongoing maintenance and ultimately renewal. Programming for large citywide events is an obvious need, requiring a systematic way to handle timing, policing, crowd control, and infrastructure needs.

It is also attractive to arrange for marketing and programming at the neighborhood scale. Some communities delegate this task to local neighborhood organizations, perhaps based in the public community center. This approach is often very effective because it taps local knowledge, allows quite gentle local brokering among users, engenders mutual assistance and support, and brings a sense of custodianship among neighbors and between neighbors and their own public setting. Similarly, in the interest of commercial objectives, business improvement districts can program events in their areas to make them draw in more people.

## Managing Financing for the Public Realm

For public amenities, the initial capital support is often prescribed by annual capital spending budgets, limits on borrowing, and bond programs for borrowing. Allocation of funds can be quite ad hoc based on political pressures, or it can be systematic with a long-term perspective. A smart municipality will establish a discrete plan or strategy for financing its growth of services and facilities over a given time, taking into consideration the array and timing for public realm investments based on population growth projections and projections of yields from various sources of funding. Operating and maintenance budgets are more prone to variation that does not relate to actual costs but is directed by economic cycles, competing funding demands, special-interest needs, and political preferences. Often, capital spending decisions are not informed by ongoing operating and maintenance cost estimates or advice about how new investments will affect existing operating and maintenance obligations. Uninformed choices help create difficulties later.

A looming crisis in most governmental finance management is the cost of infrastructure replacement and upgrading. North American cities face large-scale costs for renewing obsolete infrastructure. Consumers are often forced to use decrepit and outdated facilities because there has been little thought of funding for renewal, which diminishes the urban experience significantly. A smart approach is an automatic renewal strategy built into capital budgeting as a nonnegotiable component. In Vancouver, a funding program for renewing 1 percent of the public infrastructure each year has long been in place, the concept being that over a century, the entire infrastructure is replaced or upgraded.

## Seeing Public Land as Investment Equity

The public realm is an asset itself and can be subject to careful management to reduce risk and to offer the equity of public lands as a contributor to financial stability for the local government. A municipality can use its public land as an investment equity portfolio, a financial institution akin to a civic-level sovereign investment fund. The Property Endowment Fund in Vancouver is a telling example that has been contributing to civic funding and preferential borrowing rates since 1975. Initially, all public lands in the city were evaluated for future value and utility. Strategic lands were kept, and unstrategic or lower-value lands were sold. Cash generated from such sales was then used to purchase what was deemed to be strategic or potentially strategic property for the future. Holdings not in explicit use for public purposes are managed for profit until they are needed, either to be sold for preferred private development or used for the public agenda. Rents build more wealth, and the resulting fund can be used in difficult financial times for topping off civic operating budgets or can be invested in even more strategic property. The fund can even offer a short-term borrowing source for civic priorities between budget cycles. The entire portfolio offers security to lenders for more forgiving interest rates on civic borrowing. It has become a virtuous circle of wealth creation and project funding for public purposes in the public realm.

# 6. Implementing Ecodesign

**P**roposing big changes in the way real-estate investment and city development are managed invites skepticism. Nevertheless, the proposals we make in this book are critically important to public welfare and can be implemented within existing governmental structures and normal business practices. We have shown by examples that much of what we propose has already been achieved somewhere. The challenge we discuss in this chapter is transforming these isolated successes into general practice.

## The City Is Public and Private, and We All Have a Role in Implementation

Cities are the result of many design and investment decisions made by people and institutions with diverse interests over a long period of time. In the Western, market-based world, the result has come to represent a division of responsibility and control between the public and private sectors. With a few exceptions, the private sector controls, develops, and manages private property, and the public sector controls, develops, and manages the land between private properties that is collectively owned by the local government on behalf of the public.

Government also uses a variety of regulations and policies to shape private development and holds an approval authority over what is built. A municipality often sees itself as policing private activity. According to the specific political history and circumstances of a place, government can take a larger or lesser role, so the private component of the city can be subject to a comprehensive regulatory framework or be largely the result of thousands of individual decisions that serve primarily private interests.

To shape the public environment, government must take direct action and is both the final decision maker and the agent for implementation. In most cases, there is consultation with the private sector in some way, but the decision is made at city hall. Local government is ultimately responsible for what we see on public lands. The relationships between private and public have always been poorly defined and are more or less managed according to the consciousness and inclination of the particular local government.

This situation, which may seem obvious, unfortunately explains many of the problems in contemporary cities. The simplistic separation of responsibilities—and therefore of interests, design-focus, and financing—has become the determining factor in city development. It is why many urban projects end up being disjointed, incomplete, or representative of a lowest common denominator. There are much better results that could be conceived and delivered comprehensively, but, because of the separation of public and private interests, they are seen to be impossible.

To overcome this counterproductive division of responsibility, implementation of new and better ideas for cities and suburbs should become everyone's concern; we all have an essential role to play (figure 6-1). Whether as a citizen or a private developer or a government official, people need to think about how to apply ecodesign principles from their particular perspective, but that will not be enough. Making such big changes in the ways cities and suburbs develop will require new levels of public and private collaboration. Neither side alone can build the livable and environmentally compatible city that we have outlined in this book. We need a system and processes that can bring these essential combinations together into a workable arrangement. As we have seen, necessary public support for better private investment can come from reallocating existing government expenditures. We can use some of the money being spent on widening highways and expanding airports to construct transit and improve train service. We can also save the costs of urbanizing natural land by supporting in-fill of existing developed areas. In this chapter, we will explain how we can also channel land wealth to help carry the costs of public goods and incentivize preferred performance, while remaining open to new ideas and experimentation. It is this combination of public and private investment that can foster outcomes that are in everyone's interest and transform the relationship between the built and the natural environments.

Constituencies will need to mobilize to make this transformation happen. If people do not embrace the forward-thinking examples we have outlined in this book, change will not happen in the free-market, democratic, pluralistic society in which we live. Community participation in planning is now

**Figure 6-1** The CityDesign Studio in Dallas, Texas, regularly undertakes charettes to involve people in the design of their communities. This process taps both citizen and consumer perspectives. We all have an essential role to play in the decisions about our cities, but we must get involved.

standard practice, but it still does not take enough advantage of the kinds of participation made possible by the Internet for sharing ideas and developing positions. There are many organized consumer constituencies that can help start a broad discussion about combining city design practice with environmental preservation, the ecodesign approach for the future of cities and suburbs. These constituencies include environmental advocacy groups, citizens groups, chambers of commerce, residential communities, agricultural cooperatives, historic preservation organizations, and—perhaps surprisingly to some—real-estate developers and investors. All these groups have powerful reasons to support ecodesign principles and could make the examples in this book the general rule rather than special situations.

## Implementing Adaptations to Climate Change

We begin our discussion of implementation with the three challenges identified in chapter 2: adapting cities and suburbs to manage climate changes already in progress, helping reduce the causes of climate change, and redesigning cities and suburbs so that they are in harmony with natural ecological forces and thus sustainable for the foreseeable future.

### Adapting to Sea-Level Rise and More Frequent Storms

Damage from increased coastal flooding and bigger and more frequent inland floods are both new versions of problems that have traditionally been managed by insurance policies on individual properties; by regulations about what individual owners can build on their properties; and, in some places, by levees along rivers, seawalls, and other collective protections. As climate changes make existing protections inadequate and existing regulations obsolete, the threshold question will be how long and at what rates insurance companies are prepared to write policies on properties in the path of floods and storm surges. Insurance in flood-prone areas of the United States has been available from the federal government through the National Flood Insurance Program, but legislation passed in 2012 required the program to charge rates based on the likelihood of flooding, eliminating what had been a subsidized insurance program. Then, in 2014, Congress passed new legislation that repealed part of the provisions of the 2012 act and lowered the costs of insurance for homeowners. However, it is clear that obtaining affordable flood insurance is already an issue in many places and is likely to become much more of a problem in the future.

Once insurance is unaffordable or no longer available, individual owners will either have to take their chances or make their properties as flood-proof as they can, but there are limits to what can be done on individual properties.

Houses can only be raised up on stilts one, or possibly two, stories before the result starts to be unlivable. Local utilities still need to function; without them, the most flood-proof individual building is not of much use.

When adaptation to floods and storm surges cannot be managed by insurance or by protecting individual properties, and when the local infrastructure is no longer reliable, there are two alternatives: comprehensive protection or phased withdrawal. Both choices are difficult to implement because the situation is unprecedented and there are no established policies in place. The sooner the necessary policies are created, however, the less painful the choices will be for individual citizens and businesses.

### Adaptation Alternative 1: Comprehensive Protections for Coastal Cities

In densely populated areas at risk from sea-level rise, making major investments to protect a whole city or district from floods and storm surges makes sense because the overall value of the properties protected will far exceed the scale of the investment in protection. The prototypes are the Thames Barrier, which protects London; the Delta Works in the Netherlands; the recently completed storm-surge barriers for St. Petersburg; and the barrier under construction to protect Venice. It may be that barriers that mimic natural protections, such as some suggested in the Rebuild by Design competition for the New York region, may be a superior alternative to an engineered barrier. Because every urban situation is different, it is important to have sea-level rise and storm-surge potentials calculated for the specific geographic area and then have protection plans prepared in sufficient detail that the actual costs can be estimated. Knowing what is possible and how much it could cost in comparison to potential losses from storm surges and flooding will be essential to making decisions about where and when to build protections.

Because it will take a long time to decide about barriers, it will also make sense to change development regulations to restrict new development in vulnerable locations and to amend building codes to require that mechanical equipment endangered by flooding, like elevator or air-conditioning machinery, be located in the safest possible place within a building. Utilities and transit systems will also need to be redesigned to make them more resilient. At the same time as these interim measures go forward, every coastal city needs to prepare estimates for potential sea-level rise that fit their geographic area. Then there should be an official plan for how to manage potential change, a plan that is understood by every resident and especially by every property owner. If there is to be a comprehensive protection system, such as a flood gate, or a long-term plan to raise land levels, the plan needs an implementation schedule based on real engineering estimates and allocated funding sources. As the Dutch and London experiences clearly show, the sooner a comprehensive protection system is designed and built, the less investment will be needed in interim measures or protections for individual properties, such as raising the structure. A credible schedule for putting protection in place is essential to sustain property values and long-term investment as well as to cut increasing insurance spending.

### Adaptation Alternative 2: Phased Withdrawal

For lightly populated areas in serious danger from coastal flooding, the best option may turn out to be a phased withdrawal. The first step would be new development regulations that restrict building in vulnerable locations. Next, there could be restrictions on transferring existing buildings to new owners in such locations, requiring instead that current owners participate in a government-funded buyout when they wish to sell. Funding such a program will make sense when it becomes cheaper to buy out owners than to provide emergency funds to restore government services such as street paving, water pipes, and sewers after every storm event. Unfortunately, properties will not be as valuable as they were before the effects of climate change began to be evident. It is not likely that taxpayers can give all property owners the value that their properties once had. The owner will have to weigh the value of a buyout offer against the cost of continuing to maintain the property and the changes in the character of the community as other owners leave. In some places, a tipping point could be reached where the community itself is no longer viable because of a decreased tax base.

No one wants to see this scenario happen. When it happens in a particular place will depend on how soon climate change makes it happen. Not long ago, few people thought that such drastic choices would need to be confronted before the end of this century. After Superstorm Sandy, there are places along the New Jersey and New York shorelines that were severely damaged where such decisions may be necessary the next time a similar storm hits.

When a whole area of development along a vulnerable shoreline has been bought out by the public sector implementing a policy of planned retreat, the land can be restored to a natural state and managed as a combination of nature preserve and public recreation area. A new shoreline can take form that will be more adaptable to storm surges and rising sea levels.

### Adapting to Increasing Risk from Forest Fires

Most of the areas increasingly susceptible to damage from forest fires are relatively lightly developed because they are located within an area that is predominantly forest or on the edge of a forested area. Development in a forest setting may need to be treated in a similar way to the less dense areas susceptible to coastal flooding. Some measures can be taken on individual properties, such as clearing flammable material away from buildings and using fire-resistant construction materials, but the buildings will still be in an area susceptible to fire. The limiting factors for continuing to live in such places are the increasingly high cost and danger involved in government fire-fighting efforts, as well as the difficulty of obtaining affordable insurance. There is no national insurance program for forest fires like the one that has been available in flood-prone areas.

Again, the best option in some places may turn out to be a phased withdrawal. The first step would be new development regulations that restrict building in vulnerable locations, fire susceptibility zones. Next, just as in coastal flood zones, there would be restrictions on transferring existing buildings to new owners in such locations, requiring instead that current owners participate in a government-funded buyout when they wish to sell. Funding such a program will make sense when it becomes cheaper to buy out owners than to provide emergency funds for fighting fires. The eventual removal of permanent residents in areas where climate change is making forest fires more likely will permit more flexible fire prevention and fire-management techniques.

Anyone considering buying or building a house in a forest should take a close look at predictions for future conditions. The same advice applies to anyone considering buying a house or lot with a private beach or boat dock.

## Adapting to Inland Flooding

Adapting to increasing risks of flooding along rivers is a different problem from coastal flooding. Some of the sources for the floodwaters are subject to local control. As discussed in chapter 2, water barrels or cisterns to store rainwater from roofs, if used on all buildings in a region, could substantially reduce the flow of water draining into rivers after a storm. Paving that is pervious to water in parking lots and local streets could channel some stormwater to the local aquifer, as could landscaping along major streets, where traffic loads may not permit pervious paving. Again, if the measures we describe were adopted widely, the amount of water draining into rivers after a storm can be reduced. The more rainwater is delayed from entering the drainage system, the greater the likelihood that flooding peaks downstream will be lower. Cisterns and rain barrels can be required by local regulation, as can green parking lots with pervious paving. Local governments can repave small streets with pervious paving and add rain gardens on streets where water flows to the edges.

As discussed in chapter 2, local governments can pass regulations that keep new development away from places that are known to flood and also restrict development in places where it could destabilize the landscape and cause flooding and erosion. The availability of GIS mapping in most localities makes such determinations much easier. Cities and towns can also create watershed associations with neighboring local governments, where they can cooperate in managing a shared watershed to reduce flooding by creating regulations and regional green infrastructure, such as parks and fields designed to flood in a major storm.

For these kinds of measures to be effective, they have to be adopted as widely as possible. All local governments in a flood-prone watershed have to require rain barrels or cisterns, all local paving programs should use porous paving whenever possible, regulations should require green parking lots with porous paving and drainage swales in all new development and in any development where substantial change takes place, and all local ordinances within each flood-prone watershed need to be revised to reduce flooding and erosion.

Many large rivers already have levees for flood protection, but these protections may prove inadequate as the number and size of major storm events increase, even if all the local protection measures we describe are adopted. The Dutch have created a useful prototype for managing flooding along major rivers with their Make Room for the River program. This program, described in chapter 2, relies on levees, but it also permits some predetermined areas to flood. In some places, levees have been moved away from the edge of the river to enlarge the floodplain. Restudying flood management along major rivers and rebuilding protections to new standards are other ways to manage increased flooding risks created by a changing climate. Projects at this scale are generally funded by a national government, and the areas likely to be affected need to mobilize political support for the necessary improvements. A strong argument in favor is the savings that can be realized in emergency flood measures that are no longer necessary and in the costs of reconstruction after a flood that no longer will be incurred.

## Adapting to Drought and Securing Potable Water

Using purified drinking water for gardens or washing cars may be a convenience that will no longer be available in places where water is becoming scarcer. There are many ways of conserving water for individual households and buildings, including modifying showers and toilets to save water and using water-saving appliances. If every building is equipped in this way, the water savings are significant. Building codes can require water-saving devices, and incentives can include raising water rates when usage exceeds a predetermined level. Buildings could also meet statutory requirements by using other water sources, including the rain barrels and cisterns mentioned earlier as a way of slowing down flood events. Water from roofs can be used to water gardens and wash cars, and it can also be circulated in piping systems to flush toilets. Wastewater from sinks and bathtubs can also be used to flush toilets, but the piping required is complicated; the use of garbage grinders, dishwashers, and clothes washing machines is also a complicating factor.

In agriculture, drip irrigation loses much less water to evaporation than spray irrigation and could be required by code. Industrial processes can also be required to reduce water consumption or find water from outside the drinking-water system. Making these prudent measures mandatory may require state, province, or even national legislation.

When water saving does not prove sufficient, engineering measures will eventually be necessary. Desalination plants are an option in coastal areas, although they should be powered by renewable energy so as not to contribute to future climate change and the concentrated salt must be harvested for use or sequestered in environmentally safe ways. Impounding freshwater estuaries as a source of water is also possible, but it is expensive and complicated. As described in the example from Singapore in chapter 2, this option will be most appropriate in places where saltwater is intruding into freshwater intakes because of sea-level rise. Recirculating water from sewage treatment plants is also possible and, in effect, is happening now in communities that take their water from rivers downstream from other cities and towns.

## Adapting to Threats to Global Food Supplies

Cities have historically grown up in the midst of fertile agricultural areas that provided their food supply. Modern urbanization has been spreading cities out over their surrounding food-shed. So far, the global agricultural business has easily overcome the loss of local food in developed countries, although sometimes with a reduction in quality and freshness, but given the stress on world food supplies from increasing populations, which will be made worse by adverse climate changes, it is imprudent to keep sacrificing prime agricultural land to urbanization. Regional governments should act to safeguard agriculture. Prototypes include the Agricultural Land Reserve to protect prime agricultural land enacted by the Province of British Columbia and Oregon's growth boundary legislation. Local governments should be permitted by enabling legislation to zone land for agriculture and should then survey their jurisdiction to make sure that the best agricultural land is protected. Another approach is the creation of land trusts or conservancies that secure agricultural use and forestall other uses through protections on the title deed that do not involve public legislation. This option can involve securing ownership of agricultural property through purchase of gift or, more often, just securing covenants against uses incompatible with or displacing agriculture. Buying up development rights for farms that have already been zoned for other uses can be a necessary remedial measure, but it is obviously unwise for the public sector to confer development rights for inappropriate places and then buy them back, or for private conservancies to have to buy them back. Early action on rural lands before urban development pressures become real is obviously the best course, but it takes a long-term perspective and long-term planning by governments or nonprofit organizations.

Some of the growing area lost to urbanization can be reclaimed by producing food within the urban setting. One approach is greenhouses, which can be built above many urban factories and warehouses. Greenhouses can integrate their supporting structure with the structural frame of existing buildings and can certainly be built in new structures. To facilitate this approach, rooftop greenhouses could be exempted from floor area in zoning calculations. In chapter 2, we highlighted some promising prototypes. Green roofs are becoming more common in cities, although large areas of soil and plants create heavy distributed loads. Retrofitting existing roofs for planting can be difficult, but it is now becoming regular practice to design new buildings for such loads. The potential is to use these green roofs for food production in addition to just recreational or decorative landscape.

Most cities also have expanses of open lands that could produce food. Edible landscapes on public lands, especially fruit trees, can be directly implemented by public landowners. Temporary or even permanent farms can be implemented along freeway verges or by placing portable planting beds in little-used parking lots. For private applications, a flexible zoning allowance has to be adopted, and it has to be easy to secure approvals for this farming, especially for time-limited situations. For public applications, it may be necessary to put a nonprofit organization in place because most public agencies do not have the expertise or inclination to get into this type of farming.

Victory gardens—vegetable, fruit, and herb gardens planted on private land and public parks—were grown in the United States during World War II, illustrating the potential of public lands and suburban yards to add to the food supply. Local ordinances that make it difficult or impossible to grow food or keep farm animals on individual plots can be amended.

## Helping Reduce Causes of Global Warming

Reducing the causes of future climate change is also an urgent priority. The world economy runs on fossil fuels. Because emissions from burning fossil fuels are the principal cause of global warming, reducing them is a matter of international negotiation and treaty as well as national initiatives. Measures are likely to include economic incentives to facilitate limits on carbon emissions such as the so-called cap-and-trade system. Other likely changes include power companies adding solar and wind power plants and cogeneration capacity to their grids and increasing hydroelectric power where possible. Measures that reduce carbon emissions can also be taken closer to home. From an ecodesign perspective, they include creating and building more compact communities that reduce the need for automobile trips and make such trips shorter when they are needed. Balancing transportation systems to make more trips on transit, by walking, or on bicycles can also reduce carbon emissions. We will come to ways to implement these measures shortly, but will begin with measures to reduce the need for conventional power plants.

Having solar collectors provide part of the electrical power for every building is rapidly becoming economically feasible and, with the addition of improved storage batteries similar to those being developed for electric cars, will become more practical as a twenty-four-hour source. As with many of the measures we advocate, solar collectors need to be adopted on a large scale to have a significant effect. Local ordinances need to safeguard solar access, preventing neighboring buildings from blocking sunlight from other properties, a task very compatible with the original rationale for zoning laws. There should be code requirements for solar collectors on new buildings.

Electric cars reduce emissions on highways, but their contribution to reducing overall emissions depends on the power source for the electricity. Recharging the batteries for electric cars with solar or hydro power will be a significant way to reduce emissions from vehicles, a practical possibility when every building has a solar power source or in areas generally served by hydro power.

If adopted at a large scale, geothermal energy is a potential way to boost the efficiency of heating and cooling systems. Fuel-cell technology, particularly if the fuel is derived from biological materials, may also become a way to reduce carbon and other greenhouse gas emissions, again if this technology becomes widely used. In addition, any improvement in efficiency for the engines that burn fossil fuel will have positive value in reducing the amount of global warming.

## Using District Utility Systems to Mitigate Climate Change

Making cities more sustainable requires measures beyond the scale of the individual building or even a multibuilding complex. Planning at the district level can create powerful synergies among heating, cooling, and waste disposal; we described some prototypes at the end of chapter 2. When a new district is planned on a greenfield site on the suburban fringe, or on an in-fill site in an already urbanized area, the plan should require that all the buildings be equipped with energy-saving and water-saving appliances. There should be solar collectors, and cisterns to manage and reuse stormwater. In addition there should be a district-wide heating system that derives some of its heat from a district-wide wastewater system. Recycling and disposal of garbage—which can now be accomplished with a vacuum waste management system with hatches for different categories of waste at every building and the separated waste going to a central collection point—should be managed for whole districts. Eventually, all the districts of a city should have this kind of waste management. The organic garbage gathered in this way can become a source of fuel for a district-wide power plant. It is true that burning organic waste produces combustion products, but this material will eventually decompose in any case, so using organic waste for fuel is generally considered a sustainable practice. Suburban subdivision codes should be amended to require district-wide energy conservation and waste management for developments of more than a designated size, and comparable requirements should be added to development regulations for cities. All cities and suburbs should work with utility companies to prepare long-term plans for reorganizing power supplies and waste management on an appropriately sized district basis.

## Implementing a Better Balance of Cars with Other Transportation

In chapter 3, we noted that auto ownership and use is continuing to grow rapidly. People throughout the world have been liberated by transportation technology and expect absolute freedom and convenience to move around as they please, both for short trips and longer and longer trips. The results are more trips and longer trips, with a strong pervasive bias to use the car. The car, the least sustainable mode of travel, is having the most impact on climate change and the most impact on the humane scale and tranquility of our cities, yet it is here to stay because personal mobility is one of the great benefits of modern life. Although we must all demand and absolutely expect the car to become more environmentally compatible by using new technologies, a city shaped by ecodesign principles should also diversify modes of travel to a much wider range of modal choices (figure 6-2).

### Balancing Transit Systems with Bus Rapid Transit

We discussed in chapter 3 how rapid transit is missing from the transportation systems in many cities and suburbs and how bus rapid transit (BRT) in particular is a new technology, rapidly gaining worldwide acceptance, because it has far lower capital costs than rail transit. BRT can enable transit-related development in the commercial corridors found in every metropolitan area. Having transit available will help accommodate growth by supporting mixed-use development in the commercial corridors, diverting development to places that already have utilities and thus helping to avoid unnecessary

**Figure 6-2** Modal choice is an essential priority for sustainable cities. As you see here, Vancouver is increasingly balancing the availability of the car with walking, cycling, and transit.

urbanization of farms and woodlands. Transit will also enable more trips by bicycle or by walking.

Every metropolitan region should prepare a plan for converting part of its existing bus system to BRT with dedicated lanes along major commercial corridors. At intervals of about 1 mile (1.6 kilometers), corresponding to the appropriate distance between transit stops, development regulations in each commercial corridor should be amended to permit mixed-use commercial and residential development around each stop when the transit becomes available. As discussed in chapter 4, this increase in permitted development should not become effective unless the proposed development meets standards for a compact, walkable design and a development plan is prepared for each station location. These mixed-use centers will be within walking or cycling distance of four surrounding neighborhoods, as shown on the diagrams in chapter 4, enabling many of the advantages of urban living in dispersed suburban locations, whether they include private houses on individual lots or lower-scaled apartments or condominiums.

## Improving Traffic Safety to Enable Walking and Cycling

Achieving zero deaths from traffic accidents is a policy first adopted in Sweden and now being emulated in other places, including New York City. The success of such a policy requires safety improvements for vehicles and tough speed-limit enforcement, but it also depends on major changes in street design: ample sidewalks and easily managed street crossings, dedicated lanes for bicycles, separate lanes for transit, and only then accommodation for vehicles. These policies are the reverse of the changes that have been made in most cities and suburbs to facilitate and speed up vehicular traffic. In chapter 3, we discussed some of the ways that New York City is revising street design to reduce traffic accidents. Reducing deaths and injuries from traffic accidents to as near zero as possible should be a policy goal everywhere. Substantial improvements can be made by redefining lanes with paint and placing temporary barriers. Every city and suburb should study how to implement these changes. Over time, they can be made permanent as streets are repaved. The new configurations will leave more room for street landscaping, which has a beneficial effect on how places are perceived and can help manage stormwater and air quality. Improving the experience of walking, cycling, and taking transit also contributes to making cities more livable.

## Balancing Long-Distance Transportation with Passenger Rail

Passenger rail continues to be a missing part of the transportation system in many parts of the United States and Canada, while investments in intercity high-speed rail have been made in most other developed countries. As discussed in chapter 3, no one expects high-speed rail to connect distant destinations, such as between Chicago and Los Angeles, but at distances of less than 300 miles (about 500 kilometers), rail travel can be more efficient than travel by air or car. High-speed rail is competitive for journeys of up to 500 miles (about 800 kilometers). Proposals for passenger rail in North America are intended to improve connections among cities that are part of the developing multicity regions where most future population growth is expected to take place, such as the Vancouver-Seattle-Portland corridor or Atlanta to Charlotte, North Carolina. High-speed rail requires special tracks and trains and has run into strong political opposition in the United States. So far, the only high-speed rail proposal with any chance of being completed is in California.

Simply giving conventional passenger trains the priority on existing tracks that would enable them to move at speeds attained before World War II would be a huge improvement to current intercity transportation in most parts of North America. Going the approximately 250 miles (about 400 kilometers) from Atlanta to Charlotte on a train that could average 80 miles per hour (120 kilometers per hour), which is the average speed currently attained by fast Amtrak trains in the Northeast corridor, would take no more time than the equivalent trip by car or by air, and it would usually be faster and more reliable. If the trains running at reasonable frequency could also connect via the Atlanta and Charlotte airports, some of the trips to and from the two cities, and for destinations in between, could take place by rail, both reducing the number of flights and taking cars off highways. This reduction is already happening in Germany and other European countries that have good rail-to-airport connections. Improving train service could be financed by not having to fund some of the capacity improvements that will otherwise be needed for airports and highways. Of course, high-speed rail service, which could reduce the travel time between Atlanta and Charlotte to about an hour and a half, would be a far superior solution and will be necessary to remain competitive with city-regions in Europe, Japan, Korea, and China.

Attaining effective intercity rail service in the multicity regions that would benefit from it the most will require alliances among the states and provinces involved. If the chambers of commerce and other organizations of business leaders along these rail corridors become convinced of the usefulness of passenger rail, it could be made to happen.

## Implementing Compact, Mixed-Use, and Walkable Communities that Consumers Prefer

In chapter 4, we turned our attention to the shape of cities and suburbs and the regulations for private development that have distorted urban patterns, making them less livable, more expensive to manage, and insensitive to the environment. We identified the fundamental blindness of current regulations to contextual ecosystems and their equal blindness to the fondness of people for complex places, full of character, in what we called the experiential factor. Current regulations segregate uses and densities, target particular concerns without a holistic sense of urban experience, and do not reflect natural features. These regulations are oversimplified, rigid, and often out of date because of changing needs and expectations. To implement ecodesign requires a much more discretionary and transactional approach.

## Building Demand for Ecodesign

What will encourage more people to think more responsibly in regard to their neighbors and the environment when they consider their living situation? First of all, they have to be able to afford the responsible choices. Although measures to improve the way cities and towns are designed and to improve the way we manage the environment can solve many problems, they cannot by themselves solve all the disparities in our society. If, however, we help reduce locations of concentrated poverty by designing neighborhoods that accommodate people of all income levels, and we create a comprehensive transportation system that helps people get to their jobs from any point in the metropolitan area, many more people will have real choices in pursuit of their individual well-being.

Increasing development density and diversity by in-filling rather than by continuing outward urbanization has not been widely popular. Words like *urban* and *density* alarm people who have chosen to move away from cities. The commercial strips lined with parking lots that have been mapped along important streets throughout the suburbs are effectively land banks, and have all the utilities that need to be constructed when rural land is urbanized. As we saw in chapter 3, they could sustain much more development in the form of midrise apartments and more small offices, along with shops and restaurants, if they were supported by transportation and if regulations were changed to permit residential development in commercial districts, as discussed in chapter 4. The increase in density in those areas would have little direct effect on adjacent neighborhoods. BRT offers a way to add transit to these corridors without the high costs of building rails. There might be resistance to new people moving in, but there would also be opportunities for older people who don't want to maintain a house anymore and for young people just starting out to remain in their suburban communities. In some expensive suburbs, apartments in these corridors would also be a way for people like police, firefighters, and teachers to live in the communities in which they work. Older, now less successful shopping centers and office parks are also land banks that could support more diverse development if regulations are changed to permit a mix of uses. People who like their suburban homes the way they are will continue to have that option. The vast investment already made in suburbia is not going to go away. But using the land banks in commercial corridors, office parks, and shopping centers could add some urban convenience and options to suburban lives while taking much of the development pressure off the surrounding landscape. Many such situations have actually developed, as shown in chapter 4, showing that the demand is out there, waiting to be tapped.

The bigger issue at stake in the way we currently manage development is that we are reinforcing the most unsustainable consumer choices by making it harder to build new consumer offerings that work well with the environment. The reform of our cities rests as much or more on shifting consumer trends as it does on changing government regulations. In chapter 4, we charted the evolution of postwar cities and suburbs away from compact, walkable patterns into massive decentralization. We outlined the themes for reawakening core cities, making higher-density living more comfortable, attractive, and inclusive, and revitalizing older, once gracious inner-city neighborhoods. Arguing that the concept of "neighborhood" remains relevant as the fundamental building block of cities, we have suggested different templates for new neighborhoods at the urban fringe. We also discussed how to bring physically and socially diverse housing types, mixed-use buildings, and walkability back into the vast housing tracts and commercial strips that embody the post–World War II approach to suburban development.

How can we achieve all of these new ideas that so many people warmly embrace? Remembering that cities are the result of regulations and that consumer choices can be influenced by what regulations allow, it is essential that we redesign the regulations to motivate all these desirable objectives. To do so, regulations must be agile and flexible, and they have to integrate innovation and creativity into the regulatory framework, not make them special exceptions. Also, the administration of regulations has to allow dialogue and experimentation that values all views but also values true urban expertise. In other words, regulations and their administration have to be discretionary and transactional.

## Mobilizing to Make Regulations More Discretionary and Transactional

Making many elements of a regulatory system very agile can motivate cooperation between private initiatives and government guidance to handle issues in a more comprehensive and explicitly designed way, as in our description in chapter 5 of the Battery Park City development in New York City and the False Creek North development in Vancouver. The result, also so well illustrated in Vancouver's Athletes Village for the 2010 Olympic Games, can be to integrate ecological and experiential factors in a way that will create a more attractive product for consumers, benefiting both the private investors and the local government. It can tap the natural but often hesitant demand of the more obvious urbanites, such as young "singles" and "empty nesters," but it can also build genuine new demand among the more difficult demographic groups to attract, such as families with children and alternative households.

If the regulatory system can embrace everything the consumer can think of for agreeable everyday living and motivate everything to be done in an enticing way, while incentivizing more environmentally responsible products and practices, there is no doubt that more consumers will pay more attention.

If the development management process can channel land values as a way to carry the costs of public goods, incentivize preferred performance, and keep consciousness open for new ideas and experimentation, development regulation can foster results that consumers really want.

Making a comprehensive revision to the development regulations of a city or suburb is a difficult job. The existing regulations have had a powerful influence on property values; developers and their consultants are protective of the existing system because they know how to work with the current laws, and alert citizens are rightfully cautious about proposals that could result in major changes to their neighborhoods. It is much easier to implement partial fixes. Site-specific tailored development plans and zoning that go by a number of different names in the United States and Canada have become widely accepted as a way to permit more flexible arrangements of land uses and street plans for large properties that belong to one owner. Traditional neighborhood development ordinances are a variant and allow a developer to go back to design standards that were usual before car ownership became so widespread as a substitute for the requirements found in the rest of a contemporary ordinance, again for properties that belong to a single owner. Also, in the United States, specific plans, called official development plans in Canada, are permitted in a few jurisdictions to open up these same tailored development opportunities to multiple property owners within a designated area. It is also possible to revise regulations partially or completely for special districts with limited boundaries, especially where redevelopment is expected to make big changes in an area. Special zoning districts can also be used to reinforce historic areas, requiring that new development remain in keeping with what is already there.

The transect zoning concept has been championed by architect Andrés Duany. Transect-based codes are a way of thinking about development regulation that builds on traditional neighborhood development. The transect is a system of six mixed-use zones based on density instead of land use and requires street plans with traditional, small block sizes. Big developments that don't fit this system, like hospitals or shopping centers, are considered districts and are treated separately. This way of thinking has created a lot of interest because it appears to open a path out of the constricting effects of conventional regulations. Because of the difficulty in making comprehensive changes, however, most development that follows a transect-based way of designing has been approved as a planned development, a traditional neighborhood development, a special zoning district, or a specific plan.[1]

Most of the well-known New Urbanist developments have been made possible because of these ways around conventional regulations, but such changes have also added to the existing regulatory hodgepodge. More important, these special exceptions are a minute fraction of the massive amounts of development that go forward every year under conventional regulations.

To start reshaping the majority of development, a wide array of regulations need review. To regulate private development, there are zoning and related design guidelines or codes, building codes, and subdivision regulations. To shape the public side of the city, there are street standards as well as fire, health, security, and other issue-specific requirements.

Well-drafted development regulations need several essential qualities so that they can get the most out of urban change and avoid the worst consequences. First, there must be a range of performance expectations, including a few mandatory basic requirements, a set of choices for other important requirements, and then a defined range of discretionary approval for other components of the design. The fewer fixed requirements, the more it is necessary to codify the potential supportable outcomes in different forms of performance preferences or specifications. Second, there must be provision for flexibility of requirements to accommodate unexpected but positive potentialities by permitting discretionary approvals. In other words, the law should allow consideration of new solutions not contemplated in the specific wording of a regulation but meeting or exceeding the intent. Third, there must be incentives or bonuses for preferred performance, and these allowances will inherently disincentivize outcomes that are not desirable. In zoning, these concepts come together in discretionary text that is light on outright allowances and heavy on provisional opportunities. These zoning laws are then backed up by more detailed guidelines, or what are often called urban design codes. The same structure can be used for land subdivision, which is already a highly negotiated process because of the need to secure agreement among many operating government departments.

In building codes, where there is more need for fixed requirements, some flexibility can be introduced by adding provisions for equivalencies to handle special cases such as heritage, to cover unique site-design circumstances, or just to open the door for innovation. Examples of these innovations can be found throughout Europe and in quite a few mature jurisdictions in North America, including New York, Toronto, Chicago, and Vancouver. The challenge is to bring them all together into a comprehensive regulatory framework that meets the test of best performance, widest creativity, and effective incentives within all the types of regulation used on a day-to-day basis.

Because of the tolerance for varied performance and open-mindedness for unexpected performance in a discretionary regulatory system, the process for putting regulations in place and approving development in accordance with these regulations will also need to be transactional rather than strictly procedural. An important role for development regulation in today's cities and suburbs is to serve as a broker among competing interests. Assuming this role requires wide participation of involved and interested people in setting the original parameters in place. Then, on an ongoing basis, it requires sophisticated negotiations and decision making based on professional qualifications and experience on both sides of the table, with secure arrangements for inputs from all interests as decisions are made: from neighbors, from interest groups, from other citizens with a general perspective, and from technical and professional peers. Transactional development management is driven by the principle that public and private interests should come to support one another so that all interests are satisfied enough to motivate mutually reinforcing action. It should be a much more specific approach to making decisions than the usual regulatory process.

Something like this kind of transactional system is already widely practiced and has sustained long legal testing. That is the process of rezoning land, which happens in almost every municipal regulatory regime. Because the local government is not obliged to give approval and the private development proponent is not obliged to develop anything, people are motivated to cooperate. As a result, the terms for conferring different development rights, or rezoning, are defined to the specific circumstances of the place, proposal, and participants. At times it is quite systematic and at others very ad hoc, but it is always negotiated to find the balance of interests to be able to move forward. This kind of transactional flexibility and tailoring needs to be extended within regulations, not just when regulations are changing.

The agenda of a discretionary regulatory system and transactional development management process can embrace anything relevant in the modern city; nothing is too complex to be incorporated. It can broker neighborhood conflicts and reconcile settlement and ecology in fine variations that represent the reality of the natural environment and human expectations. It can evolve and change formulas over time and as new understandings emerge. These abilities are especially relevant to fast-evolving requirements of environmental reconciliation, which in the past has had little attention in most civic regulatory regimes. Over time, a city can pursue a better and better agenda that stays constantly at the cutting edge of knowledge and community preferences.

It also has to be said, however, that moving from an entirely predetermined system to a transactional discretionary one can be politically difficult. There are many beneficiaries of the status quo system. Different cities and countries have dissimilar legal frameworks and varied inclinations toward collaboration or litigation. The competence and capacities of government are vastly different from place to place, and there are dramatically diverse levels of trust. The attitudes of citizens in different places can contrast vividly. The regulatory system and the process to operationalize that system can be seen as a continuum, from highly fixed to highly flexible. Each community and each local jurisdiction has to gauge at what point along the continuum the community benefits, public and industry acceptance, and government capabilities are best balanced. Each community has to also decide on the agenda toward which the system and process will be applied. This is a question of community consciousness and the urgency that people vest in different aspects of their current and future will-being. There is not one model for every place. Every community has to find its own fitting answer.

Although the legal frameworks in the United States, Canada, and elsewhere have many variations, developers everywhere are fond of saying things like "Just tell us what we need to do and then get out of the way and let us do it." If developers can negotiate an advantage by changing land to a different district or modifying an existing regulation, however, they are more than willing to ask for it. It is naive to think that a rudimentary rule book is all that is needed as an effective guide for development. Covering all the potential contingencies that can come up in just one project requires extensive legal draftsmanship. The basic principle is that if you want a simple ordinance, you need to permit discretion in administering it. If you wish to minimize discretion, you will end up with a very complicated set of rules that probably won't work because they are too difficult to understand and inevitably will not cover every contingency. The key to writing laws that permit administrative discretion but maintain a legal framework is to set limits within which an administrator or a public body can make decisions about an individual project. Then you back this up by establishing criteria for making these decisions. Successfully administering these laws requires every action to be as transparent as possible.

Having a legal framework that permits administrative discretion in regulating development would actually tighten up the control system in many places. The regulations in many cities and suburbs are so out of step with development realities today that any new project will require a zoning change, a street closing, or some other kind of political decision by the local council. A great many places today are effectively zoned "Come talk to us" because the regulations on the books are out of date or so rigid that almost no development is possible, and they certainly do not embrace the complexity and endless diversity that makes an attractive, successful, and constantly changing city.

Correcting obsolescence in the current regulatory regime is essential to the achievement of ecodesign. Changes are needed in the structure and intention of regulations and in the process through which regulations come together and are applied on an ongoing basis. Regulations should not just avoid the worst consequences; they should strongly engender the best results.

How can more complex objectives be paid for, even if they are acknowledged as rewarding? There is definitely a role for taxes and civic borrowing in the equation, but these sources will never be enough to underwrite the level of quality that people expect today. To some degree, we should expect the regulatory system to create opportunity to do the right thing as well as generate its own wealth as another source to pay for the right thing, above and beyond normal profits. This expectation is a primary aspiration of a discretionary and transactional system.

## Leveraging the Relationship between Development Rights and Land Values

We have described the blind spots in current regulations about the environment that prevent creating compact, mixed-use centers and walkable, mixed-income neighborhoods. But the most profound blindness in the regulatory regimes that determine the shape and content of our cities is the blindness about the cause and effect between regulation and land values. Most local government authorities only vaguely understand urban land and development economics. This is sometimes willful, because they believe that an ethical government does not concern itself about whether a development makes a profit. Private development proponents usually don't want to talk about their finances. They don't want their competitors to know how their deals are structured, or they don't want the public to know how much money they make. These silences do not negate that there is a great flow of wealth in play as cities undergo change. It has to be remembered that, except in the most moribund market, the value of housing and all buildings is not the sum total of the cost to produce those buildings. Rather, the value is based on what people are prepared to pay. In popular markets, people are prepared to pay extensively beyond actual projected costs. The difference creates a pool of wealth that drives the whole industry of development, even acknowledging that real estate is sometimes a very risky business. The role of the regulatory framework in generating and sustaining that wealth is simply not recognized or acknowledged, and is certainly not quantified or directed. Even in the pervasive practice of ad hoc rezoning, there is seldom a strategic approach within city halls to manage the relationship between zoning change and the inevitable shift in the market value of land that results from that change. In fact, many planners and politicians have little sense of how significant the shift can be, what the specific value adjustments are, or who receives these one-time profits. You will often see city hall staff reports that estimate the long-term tax implications of proposed developments, but how often is there a quote for the expected land-value variation? This issue is central to implementing sustainable and livable cities and suburbs because we need the market and ethical building practices to reinforce each other.

Let's pause to remember the basic reality of land valuation. A more complete explanation of urban land economics can be found elsewhere, but here are some of the basic facts. The value of land is determined in cities and suburbs by the zoning specification of what can be built on that land and what it can be used for. A prudent developer, either systematically or intuitively, will determine what he or she can pay for the land under the prevailing regulations by calculating all the costs for the development (including a reasonable amount for the developer's profit for building the product), comparing that against the price for which the resulting built product can be sold, and determining what is left over as the amount that can affordably be paid for the land. This analysis is called a pro forma. Typically, the way the price of land for a project is determined is called a residual land value pro forma. It is easy to see that if government allows a more intensive or more valuable use of the land, more can be paid for the land, which is often called the land-value lift. This windfall sum can be paid to the existing landowner as a one-time gain, or it can represent a second level of profit for the developer.

It is absolutely clear that a developer gets a base level of profit on the building product that is built; otherwise, it would not get built. The developer would have no inclination or motivation to build. That profit can vary in different cities because the risks of development are different, but there is always this base level of profit. Beyond that base profit, it is very enlightening to understand who enjoys the benefit of the second level of profit—the land-value lift—when a city council confers extra development rights over what had previously been understood as the maximum development allowance on a site. The answer is really determined by when and how the new rights are conferred. In principle, whoever controls the land at the time of the regulatory change will expect to be the beneficiary of the land-value lift. The day-to-day transactions of the land market work in subtle ways, however. If it is known or even suspected that a change in development rights is coming (say through an adopted plan or policy or even a strong rumor on the street), existing landowners will expect to share some of the land-value increase even if they are not involved in the process of changing the rights and have no part in underwriting the development that will happen afterward. Because of this, the shares are negotiated as a part of the land transaction. The land market does not work like a perfectly oiled machine; there are variations depending on the level of knowledge, the analytical inclinations, and the prowess of the negotiators on each side of a land transaction. For example, if landowners do not know about a pending change in allowances, or if the change had not been contemplated when they sold the land, they will have been obliged to take less for their land. In the end, however, a sharing generally occurs, and the real developers are often at a disadvantage in such negotiations because they actually want to do something and absolutely must have the land now to do it. In contrast, existing landowners are speculators to some degree in search of greater and greater value for their property, and they can often wait until conditions are optimal for them to make a maximum value sale. The active players want to finalize a land deal, whereas passive players can bide their time.

If availability of development rights can be applied in a strategic way that is cognizant of land-value variations, the land-value lift can be directed so that it can become a source to underwrite a high standard of performance and delivery of public goods. This is fundamentally true as development rights change through rezoning, but it can also be true if differing development rights within a regulation are offered with different levels of performance or delivery of public goods by using discretionary zones. If the land-value lift is bled off by an initial landowner who does not intend to do anything with the land but sell it and walk away with the profits, it will not be available for public goods or to motivate appropriate development. If the land-value lift is channeled into the hands of the developer actually making change—remembering that it represents a source of money beyond the basic profits—some of this increased value can be invested in better performance or public goods, and maybe just a bit of it can also be left on the table until completion as a motivation for the developer to participate in the whole process.

In a rezoning scenario, channeling wealth is best achieved by making the obligations of more profitable development clear as policy upfront and, best of all, conferring zoning when an actual developer is on the scene. A prudent government will not approve additional density unless it is related to public benefits, and it will not approve it casually. This fact is often forgotten. In a rush to put in place zoning that will ostensibly attract the right kind of development, a municipality will prezone and have no expectations for performance or amenity investment. This has a double negative effect. First, it rewards the existing landowner for doing nothing. Second, it deceives the actual developer who negotiates to buy the land by not putting the public expectations on the table. If those public expectations are known clearly, a developer can include them in the "given costs" side of the pro forma analysis, thus being willing to pay less for the land. If they are vague, they get missed in the pro forma, and it appears that more can be paid and is expected to be paid for the land. So, after the purchase, there is no money in the equation for any public consideration. To meet any public expectation that comes along, the developer has to dig into the basic profits, which a developer just cannot do.

In the scenario of development approval within variable-rights or discretionary zoning, funding for the public objectives is protected by carefully articulating the calibration between each level of development opportunity with the nature of performance and expectation of public-goods investment that comes with that opportunity. This method ensures that there is enough land lift at each level of opportunity to cover the costs of the public expectations along with enough incentive to motivate the developer to want to take advantage of the higher levels of opportunity.

One way or the other, a higher level of development opportunity can be seen as an incentive, provided it is still seen as attractive after the costs to access it are covered. Of course, this system can only work to the extent that there is actual demand for higher levels of development. Otherwise, the only incentives that will be attractive, if anything will, will be direct government subsidy. In that situation, tools such as tax-increment finance districts or measures such as investing in a parking garage or closing a key street to focus interest and seed private investment are important. A strategic approach will look past the individual project to the changing attractiveness and value of a larger district. It can include direct subsidies to projects in the beginning, when market demand is not strong. The development itself, if it is attractive, will draw consumers to it, which builds demand. As demand grows, subsidies are decreased, and regulatory incentives tied to real profit drivers will be increased. Until demand is strong, some aspects of desirable development may need to be subsidized. Once demand is strong, it can be leveraged.

The fundamental economic truth of land values underlies a discretionary regulatory system and gives it energy to produce results. This is the reason that a transactional system is necessary because to calibrate land-value increments with development performance takes a subtlety of understanding and negotiations. The bottom line for implementation of ecodesign in the private sector of cities and suburbs is that wealth from development can be explicitly marshaled to underwrite the kind of places we need in the future without touching the base profits that developers must enjoy to survive and thrive in the market.

## Implementing a Public Realm That Supports People and the Environment

In chapter 5, we argued that the essential functionality and fundamental image of a city are set by its public realm. Great cities offer a cohesive and supportive public setting within which the most forward looking ideas of the community are expressed, while also protecting the most historic and meaningful places from the past. Sadly, in recent times, a city's public lands have often been debased. They have been poorly developed and maintained. They have been shaped by standards that do not consider the complexity of human needs. They have been squandered and wasted on single-purpose uses that sprawl unnecessarily. They have been given away. Like private properties, they have been exploited without reference to natural systems, and their potential to facilitate a connected web of ecosystems has been ignored. We have outlined social demands on public space—maximizing the experiential dimension—and economic demands on public space and environmental demands on public space (figure 6-3). We have suggested structural principles to improve and enhance the public realm and have emphasized both incremental improvements and wholesale changes that are sometimes possible and necessary. Two questions remain: How do we change from past practices, and how do we implement a vision for public lands that richly fulfills our collective needs?

## Changing Organization and Processes within Government

Providing progressive design and management solutions in the public realm requires changes in the way we do things in government. It involves building both a constituency and capacity for the designed approach to city building

**Figure 6-3** Public space can provide social, economic, and environmental opportunity beyond the obvious movement and recreation functions we often see. This streetscape in Aspen, Colorado, does the job well and shows that a creative public realm is not limited to big cities or big projects.

as well as changing the legal framework and financial arrangements through which we create and manage the commonwealth of the city. Most aspects of status quo governance are directing us away from both livability and sustainability. We have to shift from applying standards and rules to creating a holistic design, and we have to involve people more in determinations about the common spaces of the city, not just the most important spaces.

We can start by raising everyone's consciousness that this change is important. We can promote ecodesign principles and offer examples so people come to understand that we can do better than we have done in the past. In chapter 5, we showed many individual cases of reclamation and model practices. However, achieving results requires going well beyond promotion. The more that people are actually involved in the decisions that define the public realm, the more they will understand the results, own the results, and advocate for better results. It is vital to engage with people both as consumers and as voters. Doing this will take a strong commitment to public involvement that offers continuous opportunity for conversation, two-way information sharing, learning, and input of people's ideas into government decisions on the cityscape. Many techniques must be used to work with citizens, but there must also be an ethic to embrace the results that come out of the discussions.

A rich legacy of public participation techniques from the middle of the twentieth century have to be brought back into play, now coupled with the use of up-to-the-minute social media technologies that can reach more people and talk with them more directly than ever before. We need to engender creative discussion and motivate people to talk in detail about what they would like for the future, without the kind of bureaucratic critique that tends to constrain ideas. There must be liberation for "collective dreaming" about possibilities before the inevitable limits are emphasized so that fresh ideas have a chance to germinate and be considered. This process needs to include consideration of different scenarios and the use of real examples that people can understand and judge. Working with people in these ways helps open up thinking about the rich potentials in our public realm as well as to bring forward ideas and designs that satisfy personal and group needs in a more fundamental way than they do now.

With growing consciousness and understanding, the stage will be set in our democratic processes for a reform of the rules and management techniques through which we define and operate the public environment. The first step is a fully articulated policy platform that provides the overview and clarity of direction needed to guide hundreds of individual reforms and additions to the legal framework. Then, just like for private development, rules, standards, codes, and regulations need to be rebalanced to incorporate more diverse humane concerns and ecological concerns. Design guidelines for specific situations that cover both humane and environmental performance have to be developed, published, and adopted to shape and energize public places. Then, the format and content of existing laws must be amended to reflect principles and targets as well as an ethos of balancing interests for public places. To avoid bad practices and motivate improvements, we can add even further facilitating measures such as land covenants and property tenure arrangements.

## Maximizing Coordination among Governments

Unfortunately, local government is usually not well situated to fully embrace a holistic ecological approach. The laudable and essential objective of keeping local government as close to the people and responsible to the people as possible has resulted in the fragmentation of system-wide responsibilities for the whole metropolis. Urban regions are usually broken up into many municipal jurisdictions, and there may or may not be an overlay of regional government. Government boundaries generally do not echo ecological zones. Metropolitan governments such as those in Toronto and Minneapolis are often cited as ways to overcome these problems. These amalgamations, however, have created other kinds of contradictions, and, in any event, we do not advocate waiting for a complete governmental reorganization before trying to solve problems that cut across jurisdictions. Sensitivity to the social and environmental geography of a city can lead to joint ventures across municipal boundaries or a formal division of responsibilities between local and regional governments so that the arrangement of actors can fit the geography of solutions for a coherent and dynamic public cityscape. The key is to organize cooperation around specific problems, like managing a watershed, rather than setting up cooperation as an abstract objective. A good example is the Toronto and Region Conservation Authority, which brings collaborative sustainable watershed management to the many municipalities in its region.

## Enhancing the Operational and Knowledge Base of Governments

Because everyone in public service will need new skills, capacity building is an essential prerequisite. The basic precepts and common best practices of sustainable urbanism and the art of city design concepts like New Urbanism have to become common knowledge within municipal bureaucracies. The basic workings of urban land economics have to be understood by the forces at city hall. Promising practices have to be known by political and appointed decision makers, and the ideas behind them have to be translated into themes and terms that a typical civic leader can both understand and communicate to constituents. The workshops and training programs of the Mayors' Institute on City Design in the United States and the Federation of Canadian Municipalities in Canada are good examples of how civic leaders can be helped to make appropriate decisions about urban design.

We have offered many examples of new techniques for conceiving a public realm and, indeed, the whole city. The guiding principle is to undertake multidisciplinary design in teams. Teams can join the technical disciplines of city building with the science of environmental systems, the social science of a humane urbanism, and the arts of three-dimensional expression for a much finer more suitable and satisfying result. This process is not just a liaison activity with disciplines still working in their own studios or offices, as if in separate silos. It involves actual codesign processes, undertaken face-to-face in intensive workshops, often called charettes, that include community and nonprofessional involvement to secure the common-user perspectives. These design formats engender brokering of interests and reconciliation of public and private concerns at a very fine grain to achieve balances through which all kinds of people can see themselves in the resulting design. Where this kind of intensive engagement is not practical, such as in the hundreds of interventions that municipalities do throughout the public realm every year, it is vital to have achieved a similar type of multidisciplinary and multi-interest input, at least on the principal typologies and typical standards, backed up with efficient methods for peer review and public oversight.

As we reshape the public realm, we must monitor and evaluate as we go along. We have so much to learn, and a big part of that will be experimentation and post-occupancy review. For evaluation, it will be prudent to have systematically defined performance measures and targets for benchmarking, including both technical reviews to confirm how complex systems and environmental measures are taking root, gathering consumer responses to see how satisfied users are, and checking to see if modified behavior is also taking root. Unfortunately, monitoring and evaluation are almost never undertaken systematically by either government or the private sector. When such studies are completed in the academic world, their lessons are rarely applied back in government or the private sector as a transformative business or policy practice. There never seems to be enough money or sense of urgency to sustain monitoring and evaluation, but the more we can find a way to do so, the better.

## Finding Solutions through Pilot Projects

A powerful, practical benefit comes from starting to make change. Pilot projects are an excellent way not only to test new ideas in real circumstances, with all their complexities and confusions, but also to gauge public reactions and build public demand. That is why the New Urbanist projects in North America are important exemplars, although they are few and far between in comparison to the great majority of standard development. Once they are embraced by people, innovative projects on the ground tend to set a new standard for all projects after them. They become the new norm for consumer expectations. They become the base from which professionals can challenge themselves to do even better. They become the obvious vehicles for marketing. An excellent example is the improved environmental performance of the Athletes Villages in each succeeding Olympic Games since the 2000 Sydney games. The village construction for each event has been expected to do better from an environmental perspective, and each village has had a big influence on development practices in its region and country. People can be skeptical about theories, but they are easily convinced when they can visit and experience a different environment and draw their own conclusions about its benefits, as well as what might be done better in the next pilot. The innovative public realm constructed for Expo '86 in Vancouver absolutely changed expectations of people for how the whole city should be upgraded. Pilots become standards, standards become norms, and norms become a new status quo.

## Raising the Money

The public environment under local government jurisdiction is shaped and changed by direct investment with funding from many sources—various forms of local taxes; central, state, or provincial government funding; and user fees—enhanced by borrowing. General revenue taxes from property, sales, or other primary tax sources will never be enough to complete the extent and quality of public realm improvements that modern people expect and need. Government funding can be available for one purpose, but not for other equally important objectives. User fees often barely cover operating costs. New forms of revenue will be necessary. There is opportunity to apply more user-based taxes. Local improvement assessments, paid for by the direct beneficiaries over time with a small addition to their regular taxes, can cover costs for local upgrading. Tax-increment financing districts, in shorthand called TIFs, are a way of using anticipated tax revenue from future development to pay for upgrading public infrastructure to support the new development and a whole neighborhood. Special tax assessments for business improvement districts offer management funding and modest capital funding for public improvements. Some jurisdictions are bringing organization and policy into programs for philanthropy. As we already outlined, a very viable source of public domain funding can be derived from the development process itself by offering a discretionary zoning system that enhances the amount, type, or scale of development in exchange for contributions to upgrading the public infrastructure by adding amenities or facilities demanded by incoming residents or workers.

There are also sources of wealth before our very eyes that we are generally blind to. Within the vast property holdings that make up the public environment of any city, there is extraordinary waste of space, with infrastructure sprawled inefficiently across large pieces of land. There is a pent-up equity in these lands that could often be better used. As we turn onto an entrance ramp to a freeway, we are consuming extraordinary acreage for that single activity when compared with land consumption for all the other things we do in the city. Taking that one turn uses many times the acreage of our own home. Think of the diversity of what we accomplish in the home compared with the one activity of that one turn. Utility infrastructure often sprawls over significant environmental assets. An important municipal objective is to find ways for reclaiming this equity and restoring ecological features. We recall the inspiring examples from chapter 5, including the removal of freeways and the underground traffic ways we see in some courageous cities. Auditing of civic land holdings will uncover major public assets sitting under obsolete or inefficient infrastructure that can be reconstructed for public use and leveraged with a component of private development to pay for reconstruction and other improvements. As described in chapter 5, these lands can also be used as the base of an investment portfolio to generate sustainable income or leverage borrowing.

It is vital that these funding sources not be administered in an ad hoc way. There are never enough resources and always more priorities than funds, so governments, particularly at the local level where fund-raising mechanisms are limited, need to plan spending carefully. This means using the best type of funding source for each investment, including having regard for the attitudes of users and beneficiaries. Doing this also means coordinating funding over time so that replacement will not come as a financial surprise or stress. The best way to achieve these objectives is to complete a coherent plan for financing growth that adds this entrepreneurial perspective to the traditional capital budget process, tapping all the sources of capital comprehensively and deploying funds according to real priorities in accordance with a long-term vision. Such a plan can help set the rhythm of spending and borrowing in a way that voters can understand as they are asked to support bond issues and new projects.

There is a strong potential dynamic between a local government's planning powers and its budgeting strategy. On the one hand, an effective way to motivate preferred change is to target public money toward these changes. As we have noted previously, shifting money from roads to transit favors more dense development. On the other hand, strategic, well-planned, and popular change can garner increased tax potentials. For example, in-fill development along existing commercial corridors and underused sites like shopping centers and office parks creates buoyant tax vectors while at the same time forestalling the high costs of new infrastructure investment at the edges of the metropolitan region. This kind of a financial virtuous circle benefits everyone.

## A Final Word

We will always live in some kind of ecosystem. It is now apparent that for the foreseeable future most of us will also live in cities or suburbs. How we reconcile the imperatives of the environment to those of human settlement as well as how we manage the effects of growing populations will ultimately make or break us as a species. Even if the predicted crises do not happen in our own lifetimes, we need to keep this thought foremost in mind. Today, more than half of all human beings live in cities and their associated urban areas, and this proportion will increase continually over the next century.

Every urban region is currently degrading its natural setting, and the potential for natural repair is dropping precipitously as the scale of urbanization increases and the reach into its hinterlands becomes more pervasive. As

**Figure 6-4** More and more people are developing models of new ideas for both the structure and infrastructure of our communities to address environmental and social challenges. This LEED Platinum district in Vancouver, the Southeast False Creek Village, is in the vanguard.

long as our settlements were small, we could pollute and move on, and in time, the situation would right itself. This is no longer true. Now, we absolutely must build the mechanisms for repair directly into urban systems. In fact, the future city should contribute a net positive impact on its host ecosystem. At a small scale, our settlements were much more likely to be livable, sometimes even restorative and supportive. The diversity and flexibility of small-scale development is no longer available. Today, we must be very deliberate in shaping our vast city regions, not only to fulfill the functional needs that we all have, but also to satisfy our emotional needs, and not only to take care of personal requirements, but also to cover our collective social aspirations and expectations.

We face a formidable challenge. It will take change of both the structure and infrastructure of cities on both public and private property. Ecodesign, as an amalgam of environmental responsibility and a progressive urban design ethic and practice, offers the principles and a holistic vision upon which to base this change. Many people are already inventing and implementing solutions consistent with these principles and vision, although not nearly enough to make this the new status quo (figure 6-4). It must become the new status quo. Local government has to be prepared to make dramatic and genuine reforms for better environmental and living performance and for a more equitable and inclusive society, both to hold up its own responsibilities and to offer a model for other people and institutions in society to follow. The same can be said for the development community. Citizens, as individuals and interest groups, have to stay involved and vigilant. In this book, we have articulated a direction that can be embraced by everyone, based on the great and often courageous work of thousands of people. It is a direction that will be elaborated by many more people over the coming years because the ecodesigned city and region must happen. If it does not happen, what will soon follow will be a world that offers a climate and lifestyle vastly inferior to what we experience now. Ultimately, adopting the principles outlined in this book will be part of what ensures our survival.

# Art Credits

**2-23, 2-24, 2-25, 2-26:** Maps by the University of Pennsylvania CPLN 702 Florida Urban Design Studio, 2007

**2-27:** Map courtesy of Metro Vancouver

**2-28:** Map courtesy of the Urban Planning Council, Emirate of Abu Dhabi

**2-29:** Photograph by Aboutmovies, used under Creative Commons 3.0 generic license

**2-30, 2-31, 2-32:** Maps by the University of Pennsylvania CPLN 702 Lancaster County Urban Design Studio, 2012

**2-33:** Photograph courtesy of PUSH Buffalo

**2-34:** Photograph by Larry Beasley

**2-35:** Photograph by the City of Portland, Environmental Services

**2-36:** Photograph by the State of Oregon, Department of Environmental Quality

**2-37:** Site plan by the City of Stockholm, Planning Administration

**2-38:** Photograph by Arikogan, used under Creative Commons 3.0 generic license

**2-39:** Drawing from *The Hidden Potential of Sustainable Neighborhoods* by Harrison Fraker, published by Island Press and used by permission

**2-40:** Site plan courtesy of PWL Partnership Landscape Architects Inc.

**2-41:** Photograph by Country Wind, released into the public domain via Wikimedia Commons

**2-42:** Photograph by Larry Beasley

**2-43:** Image courtesy of City of Vancouver

## Chapter 3

**3-1, 3-2:** Chart courtesy of Metrolinx

**3-3:** Photograph by Mario Roberto Duran Ortiz, Mariordo, used under Creative Commons 3.0 generic license

**3-4:** Photograph by Myrat, used under Creative Commons 3.0 generic license

**3-5:** Photograph by Schwede 66, used under Creative Commons 3.0 generic license

**3-6:** Photorendering courtesy of VIVA, Metrolinx York Region

**3-7:** Photograph by flip 619 at used under Creative Commons 3.0 generic license

**3-8:** Photograph courtesy of Concert Properties

**3-9:** Photograph by GTD Aquitaine, who has released it into the public domain through Wikimedia Commons

**3-10:** Photograph by Larry Beasley

**3-11:** Photograph courtesy of Fountains Southend Apartments

**3-12, 3-13:** Aerial photograph and map courtesy of Fairfax County

**3-14:** Photorendering courtesy of the City of New York, Department of Transportation

**3-15:** Map courtesy of Omaha by Design

**3-16, 3-17:** Maps by Federal Highway Administration, 2012

**3-18:** Map courtesy of Georgia Institute of Technology, Center for Quality Growth and Regional Development

**3-19:** Map from Whitehouse.gov

**3-20:** Photograph by Heidas, used under Creative Commons 3.0 generic license

## Chapter 4

**4-1, 4-2:** Photographs by Larry Beasley

**4-3:** Photograph courtesy of the City of Airdrie, Alberta

**4-4:** Photograph by Larry Beasley

**4-5:** Photography by David Shankbone, used under Creative Commons 3.0 generic license

**4-6:** Photograph courtesy of the City of Airdrie, Alberta

**4-7:** Photograph by Larry Beasley

**4-8:** Photograph courtesy of Kobus Mentz

**4-9, 4-10:** Photographs by Larry Beasley

**4-11:** Zoning map courtesy of Penn Township

**4-12:** Aerial photograph courtesy of the Lancaster County Planning Department

**4-13:** Photograph by Larry Beasley

**4-14:** Zoning map courtesy of the City of Cherry Hill

**4-15:** Photograph by AgnosticPreschersKid, used under Creative Commons 3.0 generic license

**4-16:** Photograph from Wikimedia Commons used under Creative Commons 3.0 generic license

**4-17:** Photograph by Larry Beasley

**4-18:** Photography courtesy of Brent Brown

4-19: Photograph courtesy of NM

4-20, 4-21, 4-22, 4-23, 4-24, 4-25, 4-26, 4-27, 4-28, 4-29, 4-30, 4-31, 4-32, 4-33, 4-34, 4-35, 4-36: Photographs by Larry Beasley

4-37: Drawing courtesy of the New York Regional Plan Association

4-38: Photograph by *Complicated*, used in accordance with Wikimedia License 2.0

4-39: Photograph by Andrew Bossi, used under Creative Commons 2.5 generic license

4-40: Photography by Larry Beasley

4-41: Photograph courtesy of Paul Bedford

4-42: Photograph by Larry Beasley

4-43: Photograph courtesy of City of Vancouver

4-44, 4-45: Diagram and map courtesy of Wallace Roberts & Todd, LLC

4-46, 4-47, 4-48, 4-49: Photographs by Larry Beasley

## Chapter 5

5-1: Photograph by Larry Beasley

5-2: Photograph by Aleksande Zykov/Paris 17, used under Creative Commons 2.0 generic license

5-3: Photograph by Elizabeth Lloyd, used under Creative Commons 2.0 generic license

5-4: Photograph courtesy of George Stoltz

5-5: Photograph by Larry Beasley

5-6: Photograph by Hellogreenway, used under Creative Commons 3.0 generic license

5-7: Photograph by Billy Hathorn, used under Creative Commons 3.0 generic license

5-8, 5-9: Photographs by Larry Beasley

5-10: Drawing courtesy of the Seoul Metropolitan Government

5-11: Photograph by Sydmolen, used under Creative Commons 3.0 generic license

5-12: Photograph by Tamorian, used under Creative Commons 3.0 generic license

5-13: Photograph by Desopha, used under Creative Commons 2.0 generic license

5-14: Photograph by La Cita Vita, used under Creative Commons 2.0 generic license

5-15: Photograph by Beyond My Ken, used under Creative Commons 3.0 generic license

5-16: Photograph by Jim Henderson, dedicated to the public domain under Creative Commons Universal Declaration 1.0

5-17: Composite photograph by Gryffindor IIVaaa, used under Creative Commons 3.0 generic license

5-18: Photograph by Larry Beasley

5-19: Drawing and rendered site plan courtesy of Cooper Robertson + Partners; drawing by Brian Shea

5-20: Rendered site plan courtesy of the City of Vancouver

5-21: Photograph by Gryffindor, used under Creative Commons 3.0 generic license

5-22, 5-23, 5-24, 5-25: Photographs by Larry Beasley

5-26: Drawing courtesy of James K. M. Cheng Architects, Inc.

5-27: Photograph by Gryffindor, used under Creative Commons 3.0 generic license

5-28, 5-29: Photographs by Larry Beasley

5-30: Photograph by Gryffindor, used under Creative Commons 3.0 generic license

5-31: Photograph by Larry Beasley

5-32: Photograph by Sterilgutassitextin, used under Creative Commons 3.0 generic license

5-33: Photograph by David Moran, used under Creative Commons 3.0 generic license

5-34, 5-35, 5-36: Photographs by Larry Beasley

5-37, 5-38, 5-39, 5-40: Photographs courtesy of the New York City Department of Transportation

5-41, 5-42: Photographs by Larry Beasley

5-43: Photograph by Jean-Christope BENOIST, used under Creative Commons 3.0 generic license

5-44, 5-45, 5-46, 5-47, 5-48, 5-49: Photographs by Larry Beasley

5-50: Photograph courtesy of the ROMA Design Group

5-51: Photograph by Larry Beasley

5-52: Rendering courtesy of the City of Dallas and the Trinity Trust; rendering by Wallace Roberts & Todd, LLC

**5-53:** Photograph by Larry Beasley

**5-54:** Photograph courtesy of Peter Ladner, www.urbanfoodrevolution.com

**5-55:** Photograph by Larry Beasley

## Chapter 6

**6-1:** Photograph courtesy of the City of Dallas, CityDesign Studio

**6-2, 6-3, 6-4:** Photographs by Larry Beasley

# Notes

## Chapter 1

1. See Ian McHarg, *Design with Nature* (Garden City, NY: Published for the Museum of Natural History by the Natural History Press, 1969; repr., New York: Wiley, 1995); see also Philip H. Lewis, *Tomorrow by Design* (New York: Wiley, 1995).

2. Ken Yeang, *Ecodesign: A Manual for Ecological Design* (London: Wiley Academy, 2006).

3. For a more complete description of the alternatives open to city designers today, see Jonathan Barnett, *City Design: Modernist, Traditional, Green and Systems Perspectives* (London: Routledge, 2011).

4. Jaime Lerner, *Urban Acupuncture* (Washington, DC: Island Press, 2014).

5. 2012 U.S. Census Bureau *American Community Survey* data, released November 2013.

## Chapter 2

1. Paul J. Crutzen, "The Geology of Mankind," *Nature*, 415 (January 3, 2002).

2. For a current summary of the scientific case for climate change and its dangers, see *What We Know*, a report by the Climate Change Panel of the American Association for the Advancement of Science, March 2014.

3. National Climatic Data Center of the National Oceanographic and Atmospheric Administration.

4. Rebuild by Design was a project of the President's Hurricane Sandy Rebuilding Task Force; it involved New York University's Institute for Public Knowledge, the Municipal Art Society, the Regional Plan Association, and the Van Alen Institute. Funding to supplement federal government money came from the Rockefeller Foundation, plus the Deutsche Bank Americas Foundation, the Hearst Foundation, the Surdna Foundation, the JPB Foundation, and the New Jersey Recovery Fund. There were ten teams:

   - Interboro Partners with the New Jersey Institute of Technology Infrastructure Planning Program; TU Delft; Project Projects; RFA Investments; IMG Rebel; Center for Urban Pedagogy; David Rusk; Apex; Deltares; Bosch Slabbers; H+N+S; and Palmbout Urban Landscapes.

   - PennDesign/OLIN with PennPraxis, Buro Happold, HR&A Advisors, and E-Design Dynamics.

   - WXY architecture + urban design / West 8 Urban Design and Landscape Architecture with ARCADIS Engineering and the Stevens Institute of Technology, Rutgers University; Maxine Griffith; Parsons the New School for Design; Duke University; BJH Advisors; and Mary Edna Fraser.

   - Office of Metropolitan Architecture with Royal Haskoning DHV; Balmori Associates; R/GA; and HR&A Advisors.

- HR&A Advisors with Cooper, Robertson, & Partners; Grimshaw; Langan Engineering; W Architecture; Hargreaves Associates; Alamo Architects; Urban Green Council; Ironstate Development; Brooklyn Navy Yard Development Corporation; and New City America.

- SCAPE with Parsons Brinckerhoff; SeARC Ecological Consulting; Ocean and Coastal Consultants; the New York Harbor School; Phil Orton/Stevens Institute; Paul Greenberg; LOT-EK; and MTWTF.

- MIT Center for Advanced Urbanism and the Dutch Delta Collective by ZUS; with De Urbanisten; Deltares; 75B; and Volker Infra Design.

- Sasaki Associates with Rutgers University and ARUP.

- Bjarke Ingalls Group with One Architecture; Starr Whitehouse; James Lima Planning & Development; Green Shield Ecology; Buro Happold; AEA Consulting; and Project Projects.

- Unabridged Architecture with Mississippi State University; Waggonner and Ball Architects; Gulf Coast Community Design; and the Center for Urban Pedagogy.

5. National Research Council, *Water Reuse: Potential for Expanding the Nation's Water Supply through Reuse of Municipal Wastewater* (Washington, DC: National Academies Press, 2012).

6. *World Population Prospects: The 2012 Revision*, United Nations, New York, 2013.

7. Dickson Despommier, *The Vertical Farm: Feeding the World in the 21st Century* (New York: St. Martin's Press, 2010).

8. Thomas Tidwell, testimony before the Senate Committee on Energy and Natural Resources, June 4, 2013.

9. James Hansen, lecture at Columbia University, New York, September 22, 2012.

10. *The Future of Geothermal Energy Impact of Enhanced Geothermal Systems (EGS) on the United States in the 21st Century, An Assessment by an MIT-Led Interdisciplinary Panel* (Idaho Falls: Idaho National Laboratory, 2006).

## Chapter 3

1. The statistics are from the International Council on Clean Transportation's *European Vehicle Market Statistics 2013*. The current numbers and 2030 predictions for light and heavy vehicles are from this source. The population statistics in this paragraph are compiled from multiple sources that have variations in methodology, time frame, and so on. The resulting ratios of vehicles to people should be understood as approximations. Explanation of the ratios not spelled out in the text: for Canada, there were about 22 million cars and trucks on the road for a population of about 35 million, or 0.62 vehicle per person; for Australia, 15 million vehicles for 23 million people (0.652 vehicle per person); for Japan, 75 million vehicles for 128 million people (0.59 vehicle per person); and for the European Union, 274 vehicles for about 500 million people, or 0.55 vehicle per person.

2. Vehicle Projections for European Union countries are from a 2006 paper, *Vehicle Ownership and Income Growth, Worldwide: 1960—2030*, by Joyce Dargay of the University of Leeds,

Dermot Gately of New York University, and Martin Sommer of the International Monetary Fund, accessed from the website of Dr. Thomas W. O'Donnell of the New School. The population predictions are from the United Nations.

3. See, for example, *Capturing the Value of Transit,* a report for the U.S. Department of Transportation, Federal Transit Administration, prepared by the Center for Transit Oriented Development, November 2008.

4. BART Property Development, BART Transit-Oriented Development Program, November 2010.

5. Joel Garreau, *Edge City, Life on the New Frontier* (New York: Doubleday, 1991).

6. The Tysons Corner Comprehensive Plan is accessible online at http://www.fairfaxcounty.gov/tysons/comprehensiveplan/.

7. Matthew Braughton, Matthew Brill, Stephen Lee, Gary Binger, and Robert Cervero, *Advancing Bus Rapid Transit and Transit Oriented Corridors in California's Central Valley*, Institute of Transportation Studies at the University of California, Berkeley working paper UCB-ITS-VWP-2011-3, June 2011.

8. The partnership has been formed by the Urban Land Institute Seattle chapter, King County Metro Transit, the City of Seattle, the City of Shoreline, and the ULI/Curtis Regional Infrastructure Project.

9. *Road Traffic Deaths Data by Country*, Global Health Observatory Data Repository of the World Health Organization, accessible online at http://www.who.int/gho/road_safety/mortality/en/.

10. *2013 Report Card for America's Infrastructure*, American Society of Civil Engineers, accessible online at http://www.infrastructurereportcard.org/a/#p/home.

11. *Capacity Needs in the National Airspace System 2007–2025*, prepared by the MITRE Corporation for the Federal Aviation Administration, May 2007.

12. *Beyond the Tracks: The Potential of High-Speed Rail to Reshape California's Growth*, SPUR report, January 2011.

## Chapter 4

1. Lane Kendig with Susan Connor, Cranston Byrd, and Judy Heyman, *Performance Zoning* (Chicago: Planners Press, American Planning Association, 1980).

2. Mortgage interest is not tax deductible in Canada, but it is in the United States. Government support for extending roads and utilities to developing areas is also a form of subsidy.

3. See Jane Jacobs, *The Death and Life of Great American Cities* (New York: Random House, 1961).

4. A floor-area ratio of 10 permits the square footage of a building to be ten times the site area.

5. Clarence Perry, "The Neighborhood Unit," in *The Regional Survey of New York and Its Environs*, vol. 7, *Neighborhood and Community Planning* (New York: Regional Plan of New York and Its Environs, 1929).

6. The other founders were Peter Calthorpe, Daniel Solomon, Stephanos Polyzoides, and Elizabeth Moule.

## Chapter 5

1. Some historians have written that the great extension of Parisian boulevards under Napoleon III was planned to help the authorities keep control of the city. It is unlikely that anyone could have believed this would work, as shown by how easily the boulevards were blocked by barricades during the rising of the Paris Commune in 1870.

2. Much of the statistical information about the Cheonggyecheon comes from a presentation by Kie-Wook Kwon, director of the Water Quality Management Division of the Seoul metropolitan government.

3. Concept architects: The Hulbert Group, VIA Architecture, Downs/Archambault, James K. M. Cheng, Davidson, Yuen Simpson; landscape architects: Don Vaughn Associates (concept) and Philips Wuori Long (detailed design); principal city staff: Larry Beasley (manager, senior planner, and urban designer), Pat Wotherspoon and Ian Smith (project managers and area planners), Ralph Segal and Jonathan Barrett (urban design and development planners), Jim Lowden (parks planner), Elain Duvall (housing planner), and Susan Clift and Michelle Blake (engineers).

4. See Allan Jacobs, *Great Streets* (Cambridge, MA: MIT Press, 1995); and Allan Jacobs, Elizabeth MacDonald, and Yodan Rofe, *The Boulevard Book* (Cambridge, MA: MIT Press, 2003). Both books present clearly dimensioned plans of successful streets in many different cities, accompanied by Allan Jacobs's excellent sketches. Also see National Association of City Transportation Officials, *Urban Street Design Guide* (New York: NACTO, 2013); Barbara McCann and Suzanne Rynne, *Complete Streets: Best Policy and Implementation Practices* (New York: American Planning Association, Planning Advisory Service, 2010); and Victor Dover and John Messengale, *Street Design: The Secret to Great Cities and Towns* (New York: Wiley, 2014).

5. For a complete exposition of Gehl's philosophy and methods, see Jan Gehl, *Cities for People* (Washington, DC: Island Press, 2014).

6. See Lawrence Frank, Peter Engelke, and Thomas Schmid, *Health and Community Design: The Impact of the Built Environment on Physical Activity* (Washington, DC: Island Press, 2003); and Howard Frumkin, Lawrence Frank, and Richard J. Jackson, *Urban Sprawl and Public Health: Designing, Planning, and Building for Healthy Communities* (Washington, DC: Island Press, 2004).

7. Jan Gehl, in conversation with Jonathan Barnett, Copenhagen, July 2013.

8. As quoted in Maria Stambler, "Urban Planner Jan Gehl Wraps Moscow Project with Advice," *Moscow News* online, July 19, 2013.

9. See Ray Oldenburg, *The Great Good Place: Cafes, Coffee Shops, Bookstores, Bars, Hair Salons, and Other Hangouts at the Heart of a Community* (New York: Marlowe House, 1989).

10. See William H. Whyte, *City: Rediscovering the Center* (Garden City, NY: Doubleday,

1988); and also the earlier William H. Whyte, *The Social Life of Small Urban Spaces* (Washington, DC: The Conservation Foundation, 1980; repr., New York: Project for Public Spaces, 2001).

11. See Anne Whiston Spirn, *The Granite Garden: Urban Nature and Human Design* (New York: Basic Books, 1984).

12. See Herbert Dreiseitl and Grau Ludwig Dreiseitel, *Waterscapes: Planning, Building and Designing with Water* (New York: Princeton Architectural Press, 2001); Herbert Dreiseitl, *New Waterscapes* (New York: Princeton Architectural Press, 2005); and Herbert Dreiseitl and Dieter Grau, *New Waterscapes: Planning, Building and Designing with Water* (Basel: Birkhauser, 2009).

## Chapter 6

1. Miami 21 is an apparent exception: Transect-based nomenclature applied to the regulations for an entire city. Closer inspection of the ordinance, however, reveals many subcategories within the six transect zones and many additional districts, so the number of zoning categories is comparable to a conventional ordinance. There are also significant land use restrictions within the zones and districts. Regulations for many areas remain essentially the same except that the name of the district has been changed. The big innovations in this ordinance concern concentrating new development in corridors along major streets.

# Index

Note: Figures are indicated by the letter "f" following the page number.